AF538837

PARTICIPATIVE MANAGEMENT AND INDUSTRIAL PERFORMANCE

Participative Management and Industrial Performance

Jayashree Kulkarni
S.L. Hiremath

ANMOL PUBLICATIONS PVT. LTD.
NEW DELHI - 110 002 (INDIA)

ANMOL PUBLICATIONS PVT. LTD.
4374/4B, Ansari Road, Daryaganj
New Delhi - 110 002
Ph.: 23261597, 23278000
Visit us at: www.anmolpublications.com

Participative Management and Industrial Performance

First Published, 2005

ISBN 81-261-2211-0

PRINTED IN INDIA

Published by J.L. Kumar for Anmol Publications Pvt. Ltd., New Delhi - 110 002 and Printed at Mehra Offset Press, Delhi.

Contents

Preface

The contemporary Indian society, which is caught in the crossfire of forces of economic and social transformation, finds itself at the crossroads of progress in every sphere of existence. Further, it is the process of industrialization that has exerted the most profound influence on an otherwise traditional Indian social fabric requiring an in-depth study of social implications of industrial development particularly from Sociological perspective. The basic question that occupies the place of priority in research on interface between society and industry in India is that, how far and how well the people of a predominantly agrarian society have adapted themselves to industrial way of life, and what are the indices and measures of such adaptation. One such measure is, how much at ease are the Indian workers in managing their own affairs and how effectively they do so.

Another major assumption that emanates from the human relations approach is that, participation in the management or involvement in the affairs of the organization breeds commitment, boosts morale and enhances productivity. This has given rise Participative Management (PM) or to "Workers' Participation in Management" (WPM) as positive practice and intervention at place of work as well as a major area of study and research in academics. It is at this academic juncture we thought of undertaking an empirical study of the extent, determinants and implications of workplace democracy in Indian industrial setting. Further, we noticed that though Workers' Participation as an instrument of Industrial Democracy and as an area of Sociological specialization has been a widely debated topic for a number of years throughout the industrial world, it is still in the nascent form in India and efforts need to be put to render it more effective instrument and a more definite area of research as it is of great relevance and practical value in the context of the changing socio-economic milieu of contemporary Indian society. We could realize that, this is an area where empirical research is needed not only to understand empirically the social realities pertaining to workers' participation, but also to make certain suggestions based on findings which could be of significant applied implications for the industrial and economic development by way of rendering the process and mechanisms of PM better tuned to the socio-cultural milieu in which the Indian industries operate. Though there are numerous studies on PM in the context of Indian work organizations, the empirical studies on dispositions and experiences of actors, extent, determinants, effectiveness and the implications of WPM particularly from Sociological perspective are lacking warranting a study such as this. This gap in empirical literature and the importance of its being bridged, motivated us to take up the present study on WPM and the social realities pertaining to it with Sociological perspective.

An academic endevavour such as this, cannot be accomplished without help and assistance from several organizations and individuals, whose efforts have gone into the making of this book. We wish to place on record the assistance we received from the Gulbarga University, Gulbarga in carrying out this study. We place on record with pleasure our deep sense of gratitude toward the management of firms and the respondents who extended their wholehearted cooperation during our field work. We are grateful to Dr. Ravi Gaddgimath, Chief Librarian, Gulbarga University, Gulbarga and Dr. C. Somshekhar, Reader, Dept. of Sociology, Bangalore University, Bangalore for their invaluable help. We gratefully acknowledge the encouragement, support and help we received from all our near and dear ones. We thank Shri J.L. Kumar, Managing Director, Anmol Publications Pvt. Ltd. for agreeing to bring our study out in the form of a book.

Dr. Jayashree Kulkarni
Prof. S.L. Hiremath

List of Tables

1

Introduction

Perhaps the most important and universal change that has occurred throughout the industrial world is the shift in values and attitudes toward authority. It has now come to be universally recognized in the disciplines dealing with organizations, organizational behaviour, organizational development, industrial relations and business administration that if the organizations have to be effective, viable, accountable and competitive, they are obliged to provide some means and mechanisms of participation to the members in the process of decision making known as Participative Management (PM) Workers' Participation in Management (WPM) Industrial Democracy (ID), Workplace Democracy (WD), Co-determination, syndicatism and the like at different geographical settings, that are likely to affect their work and even non-working lives. As such, different forms, fora, mechanisms and machineries of PM or WPM have been envisaged and evolved in both Capitalist and Socialist systems world over. PM, WPM, ID, WD, Co-determination, Syndicalism and so forth all meaning the same have come to be the catchwords in progressive and professional management circles, which is a significant deviation from the ideology which held that decision making, exercising or delegation of authority as the privileges and prerogatives of the management, in more rigid milieu, the employers alone.

SIGNIFICANCE

There is hardly a study in the entire literature which fails to testify to the fact that genuine increase in the workers' decision making power enhances the productivity, satisfaction from work, identification with and commitment to the firm and such other positive implications for the process of production and people involved in it (Blumberg, 1968). There are three main sources of pressure for providing workers with scope for greater say in decisions. Firstly, it is the increasing acceptance of simple, commonsense proposition by the managements that people are more committed to aims or goals that they themselves have played a part in setting than they are to those that are imposed upon them from above. The second source of pressure has its roots in the social values rather than in the practical need to increase productivity by making the process of production, distribution and exchange more efficient. The third chief source of pressure for accepting increased employee involvement is the realization by the management that they will increasingly be able to retain or recover control or power only by sharing it. Apart from considerations of social justice, human rights and human dignity, which are more ideological in nature, the WPM has been found to be of material and practical utility in terms of productivity, commitment, job satisfaction, morale, climate of industrial relations and human development indicators. Irrespective of different meanings and machineries that WPM comes to be associated with, there has been a universal consensus among the social and management scientists, practitioners of the managerial profession as well as among the policy makers, in the nations with every political and economic ideologies about the positive consequences and hence the desirability of PM. It has been found to be an effective means of optimizing production (Tannenbaum, 1968) through co-operation between labour and management, which is essential for the growth of organization in general and improvement of productivity in particular (Hebden and Shaw,

1977). The production management has come to stress the need for efficient use of capital, machinery and particularly, the human labour, which is possible through involvement of employees in the decision making process (Drucker, 1964; Branen, et al. 1976; Davis, 1967). Production and its efficiency includes factors such as increase in output, elimination of wastage, reduction in cost of production, optimum utilization of tools, machineries, raw materials and man power, as well as improvement in the quality of output which is attained by participation through tapping the abilities of all the people in the organization (Anthony, 1978; Saxena, 1979; Vishwa Nath, 1992). Participation is found to be increasing productivity by fulfilling the social and psychological needs of the members in work organizations (Seasore and Bowers, 1963; Vaidya, 1974; Pylee, 1975; Talpule, 1984; Kumar, 1992). The results of the Hawthorne experiments at the Western Electric Company indicate that group cohesion and involvement of workers determine productivity to a considerable extent (Mayo, 1941).

WPM, further, has come to be identified as one of the modern and scientific approaches for maintaining cordial industrial relations (Derber, 1970; Vakil, 1974; Sahu, 1985). WPM has been found to be an effective stimulus to overcome the problem of breakdown in industrial relations (Thakur, 1973; Hebden and Shaw, 1977; Subbarao, 1990; Kumar, 1992) by promoting goodwill and understanding among the employees and employers on the one hand and by providing an effective means of communication for resolving industrial conflicts (Pylee, 1975; Alexander, 1972; Talpule, 1984; Sarikwal, 1990; Vishwa Nath 1992) and reducing number of grievances on the other.

Similarly democratization and humanization of workplace have been viewed as the sure outcome of PM (Strauss, 1963; Argyris, 1967; Hameed, 1973; Vishnu Gopal, 1984; Sherlekar, et al. 1986). WPM is found to be democratizing industrial milieu, ensuring egalitarianism and facilitating the humanization of workplace (Verma, 1972; Hebden and Shaw, 1977; Sarma, 1990). Such a situation, in turn is found to be promoting and reinforcing higher levels of morale (Strauss and Rosenstein, 1970; Davis, 1976; Chhabra et al. 1977; Anthony, 1978), job satisfaction (Morse and Reimer, 1956; Vroom, 1960; Blumberg, 1968; Strauss and Silverman, 1977; Goodman, 1979; Singh and Pestonjee, 1990), commitment (Coch and French, 1948; Siegel and Ruh, 1973; Davis, 1976; Francis and Milbourn Jr, 1980; Anderson, 1984; Kumar, 1992; Vishwa Nath, 1992) and identification with the firm (Huneryager and Heckman, 1967; Macy et al. 1989).

Thus, due largely to an increasing awareness of the need to make people feel a part of their social and vocational environment, PM has been a widely debated and contemplated topic for quite sometime now (Guest and Fatchett, 1974). In view of these positive consequences of WPM and in view of WPM in itself being viewed as a positive organizational intervention, efforts have been made by management experts and behavioural scientists to evolve a system of industrial management which fosters a climate conducive for constructive and creative cooperation and mutual trust and respect between labour and management leading to the replacement of industrial autocracy by industrial democracy which has been an accepted doctrine of progressive management world over.

India could be taken as a nation with a perfect backdrop for this kind of a positive intervention at place of work, particularly as the world's largest democracy established on the Socialist edifice, having wedded itself not only to the ideal and goal of Welfare State but also to the policy of rapid industrialization and as a nation which finds itself at the industrial cross-roads of the world, tipped to be industrial superpower in the 21st century. Having resolved to realize the goal of democratizing and humanizing the work place, the Government acted as early as 1956, pursuant to the Industrial Policy Resolution, leading to the birth of Joint

Management Councils (JMCs) in 1958, which did not meet with the desired level of success. A new experiment was, therefore, attempted during October 1975, leading to the establishment of Shop Councils at shop level and Joint Councils at plant level in all the industries employing 500 or more workers. Almost quarter of a Century has passed since the inception of these statutory provisions but the situation appears to be still wanting in terms of the nature, extent, effectiveness and consequences of WPM in Indian industries (Alexander, 1972) warranting empirical inquiries into the structure, composition and functioning of the various machineries of WPM and the contextual, environmental and more significantly, the socio-cultural variables influencing the actual process of WPM, particularly from an integrated Sociological perspective.

There has been consensus among those concerned with this area of industrial relations that, although the notion and practice of WPM is in vogue in Indian system of industrial relations for nearly half a century and has been a focus of Indian industrial relations policy, and although several scientific and academic attempts have been made to evaluate the functioning of WPM and ascertain as well as attribute the poor track record of WPM in Indian industries, none, however employs the much needed Sociological and Socio-analytical approach in the study of this phenomenon (Vishnu Gopal, 1984). This approach becomes singularly pertinent as industries are no longer viewed as only productive structures but as a socio-technical system by the contemporary management theory and practice (Alexander, 1972). An area of such an academic and applied significance is, unfortunately, not focused upon from the perspective and approach it warrants and as such several inconsistencies and gaps do exist in the empirical literature on this subject (Kumar, 1992). Thus, any study on WPM in Indian context is a worth while academic and applied effort, particularly, in view of the fact that, though WPM is in operation for quite sometime, it has not yet attained the shape of a streamlined scheme and the models developed and experiences observed elsewhere are far from being applicable to Indian scene. The conceptual and procedural comprehensions are inconsistent and reactions to the scheme itself are mixed, ranging from looking at it as political overtone devoid of practical utility by some, with others visualizing the scheme as an instrument for correcting various industrial ills and contributing to the economic development (Varandhani, 1989). Further, most of the studies undertaken hitherto have failed, according to Aziz (1980), to focus on the basic perspective of the scheme and a Sociological perspective is grossly missing in the studies so far (Vishnu Gopal, 1984). It may also be noted here that studies have not taken into account the dispositions and experiences of the actors concerned (Sahu, 1985) as attempted in the present study, leading to the institutionalization of the scheme in Indian enterprises (Alexander, 1972) and such an empirical analysis of WPM could prove to be of immense practical help to an average Indian manager, who has begun to experiment with WPM (Foreword by Joshi in Alexander, 1972).

Highlighting the need for such academic and empirical endeavors, Kumar (1992) states that notwithstanding the numerous studies on WPM in the context of Indian work organizations, several gaps still exist in the empirical literature pertaining to textual and contextual aspects of WPM and the abundant material available is still plagued with inconsistencies and incongruities. This field of academic specialization thus, is still wide open for more empirical investigations and verification of findings reported by the earlier investigations. Other conditions that warrant more structured empirical studies on WPM are the diversity of composition and ideologies among workers and management, diversity of industrial undertakings in terms of sector, size and technology and regional differences in social, cultural, economic and contextual variables associated with different undertakings. These variables are of critical importance in undertaking empirical inquiries into the nature, functioning and effectiveness of the WPM machineries in Indian industries, and a study which keeps this perspective and approach as guiding principles could prove to be of applied significance, in so far as it seeks to develop a theory and evolve a model that could explain scientifically the nature, extent, effectiveness and the determinants of WPM in Indian work organizations.

Hence, the present study which seeks to focus on the phenomenon of WPM in Indian work organizations from the perspective and approach mentioned above, keeping in view the variables thrashed out therein, could be considered as an empirical effort and attempt in the direction recommended and endorsed in the academic circles and literature relating to WPM. As such, the need as well as the academic and applied significance of the present study being so testified need no emphasis.

ABOUT THE STUDY

In consonance with the justification established in the foregoing discussion, the present study seeks to probe empirically into the socio-cultural realities pertaining to the WPM from a Sociological perspective in general and structural functional perspective in particular. In doing so, it seeks to focus empirically upon the nature, extent, determinants, effectiveness and the consequences of WPM in Indian work organizations. It purports to explain the machineries, their constitution, functions and functioning on the one hand and the structural, environmental and socio-cultural determinants of their function on the other, seeking to establish causal relationships and identify recurrent patterns with a view to develop empirical model and a theoretical framework for the scientific understanding of PM in Indian context. Further, the study having focused on the extent, effectiveness of WPM and its determinants, seeks to come out with applied suggestions and recommendations based on the findings, to enhance the effectiveness and thereby the positive consequences of WPM in Indian work organizations. Thus, the study while seeking to fulfill an academic need for the systematic study of WPM, is also of applied significance by virtue of its findings, which in the final analysis and application could be of positive implications for the machineries of WPM in operation in Indian work organizations.

Academic Antecedents of PM

The WPM, of late, has caught the scientific attention of Sociologists, particularly since the establishment of Human Relations School pioneered by Elton Mayo in the twenties of this Century. The Human Relations School laid emphasis upon social process in the work environment and argued that management, in order to operate effectively, has to take social system into consideration. To put it in other words, management should provide an area of freedom within which the social processes could find expression. It was hoped that such an attempt or approach would obtain the involvement and commitment of the workforce, satisfy the needs of the workers for social control and would also further managerial goals (Guest and Fatchett, 1974). Thus, Elton Mayo and his colleagues, John Dewey and Kurt Lewin in their famous Hawthorne Experiments made it clear that workers should be entrusted with a substantial voice in the determination of their conditions of work in order to secure their cooperation and in order to make them work hard and enthusiastically (Blumberg, 1968). It has come to be realized in Sociological circles that participation is a growing phenomenon. There is pressure for participation in so many areas and pressure for participation at work is particularly strong. Throughout the development of industrial society workers have struggled to assert a key voice in the determination of their work situation. Interest in participation and industrial democracy, thus, is not a recent phenomenon (Broad and Beishon, 1977). Although the concept of industrial democracy was in vogue in the Western European countries as evidenced by master pieces like 'Industrial Democracy' by Webbs (1897), way back in later part of nineteenth century, the machineries for putting the concept of industrial democracy into practice came to be evolved during the World War period as a result of the emphasis that came to be placed on the significance of participatory management in the managerial circles world over.

With the art of management evolving into a rational science and with management coming to be identified as a streamlined profession, the scientific study of human behaviour at work came to prominence in social sciences eventually leading to the establishment of management science as an independent branch of knowledge and ever since then several experiments have been conducted to identify the positive interventions at work place and in work process which could yield better results in terms of productivity, climate of industrial relations, development of a democratic sub-culture at work place, increased levels of commitment, identification, morale and job satisfaction leading to the overall industrial and economic development. Accordingly the much debated and widely acclaimed practice of PM is one of the prominent positive interventions in the management of work organizations. A number of social science perspectives and scientific studies have concluded that progress and prosperity of an enterprise depend on workers' devotion and commitment to the firm which ultimately depend on democratization of industrial management through recognition of workers' right to participate in it (Foreword by Srivastava in Vishnu Gopal, 1984).

As a result of the growing awareness of employers and employees that human resource management is a key factor in the growth and effectiveness of organizations coupled with the increasing professionalization of management in India, the stage is now set for increased efforts towards employer-employee collaboration through participatory systems of management (Mankidy, 1995). Managers accomplish results through subordinates and hence latter are always directly and intimately affected by managerial decisions, as such, they may have a considerable interest and a strong desire for participation in the decision process affecting their lives, particularly in a nation with deep and strong democratic roots (Tannenbaum and Massarik, 1970).

Thus, in view of its significance, WPM has been included in the curriculum of invariably every course on management and branches of social and behavioural sciences dealing with industry in addition to being identified as a major field of empirical enquiry in all the above disciplines. This concerted interest in the study and research on PM has given rise to an unprecedented growth in the empirical literature with these disciplines contributing their mite from their own respective perspectives. However, in spite of considerable research activity focusing on WPM, stretching back to several decades, the empirical studies on the extent, determinants, effectiveness and the positive implications of the WPM from Sociological perspective and approach are lacking warranting a study such as this. Further it goes without saying that the findings of such a study would be of significant applied implications for the industrial and economic development by way of rendering the process and mechanisms or machineries of WPM better tuned to the socio-cultural milieu in which the industries operate as well as to the capabilities and limitations of workforce operating in Indian work organizations.

History of PM

The roots of the modern demand for participation are deep in history (Balfour, 1973). It emerged as an ideological concept and afterwards took the shape of concrete social reality. Social thinkers were concerned with the problem of the status of workers in the factory organization and society since the very beginning of modern industrial era. They wanted protection of workers against the exploitation by capitalists and managers and they pleaded that workers should have equal power with the managers. Thinkers like Comte and Owen advocated the participation of workers in management in order to achieve distributive social justice. The radicals were opposed to private ownership of the means of production, concentration of wealth in a few hands and the Capitalist controlled machinery of the State, advocating drastic changes (Mamoria and Mamoria, 1988). Karl Marx as well as the Syndicalists advocated strongly for socialization of means of production and complete control of the enterprise by workers. "As time went on, however, it was found that complete control of industry by workers was neither feasible nor desirable at least in political democracies where the representatives of the people freely elected, had the power to curb the evils of capitalism, statism and bureaucratism" (Das, 1964: 6). Therefore, thinkers like Webb and Cole thought that participation of workers in management would be sufficient to meet the needs of social justice (Cole, 1957).

Besides the ideological attack from the radicals and the need for reforms in the Capitalist system, the trend towards bringing about changes in the style of industrial management was also influenced by two other factors. During the two World Wars there was a demand for continuous production. This prompted managers to introduce new strategies which could ensure uninterrupted industrial activity. Along with this, the differentiation between management and entrepreneurs accelerated the pace of professionalization in industrial management. These two elements set the tone for a series of experimentation in management rendering it more participative and responsive (Thakur and Sethi, 1973). The most important experiment among these was the one initiated by Elton Mayo and his colleagues who belong to the Human Relations School. They stressed that social capacity determines the amount of work done by a worker and not his physical capacity; non-financial rewards play an important role in determining the motivation and satisfaction of the worker. They emphasized the role of communication, participation and leadership in the management of enterprise. Several management scientists have also emphasized the importance of human side of an enterprise. It is stated that, an organization which associates members in the managerial process and takes into account human feelings and aspirations is likely to be more efficient and healthier as compared to an organization which uses the authoritarian way of dealing or managing the people (Chhabra et al, 1977).

The development of the concept of WPM can also be traced which finds its expression in the generally held opinions and recently developed notions such as-worker is not a marketable commodity or an article of commerce, he is a self-respecting human being. The Clayton Act of 1914 gave due recognition to this fact. The seed of WPM was sown immediately after the cessation of the World War as a result of the setting up of the International Labour Organization in 1919. The International Labour Organization was founded under the influence of workers' right to organize. Next crucial step was the appointment of the Royal Commission on Labour in the year 1929, which recommended workers' participation. Another milestone which helped the growth of Participative Management was the Declaration of Philadelphia of 26th May, 1944 which upheld personality and dignity of the individual (Varandhani, 1989). As a result of this world-wide trend, as of now, about 50 countries, nearly one-fourth of the world have experimented WPM in various forms (Sarikwal, 1990).

History of PM in India

Participative spirit is not alien to the Indian tradition. As a matter of fact Gandhiji's concept of trusteeship embodied labour management collaboration (Nadkarni, 1990). Gandhiji stressed the importance of equal partnership. He advised the Capitalists to consider themselves as trustees of the labour they employ and advised labourers to consider themselves as trustees of capital. Thus, both labour and capital should consider themselves as co-trustees for the welfare of the community (Mongia, 1980).

Democratization of workplace through Participative Management has been an integral part of Indian Labour Policy right since Independence and has come to guide the legislation pertaining to industrial relations. This could be attributed partly to the strong democratic traditions of post-independent India and partly to the realization that, democratization of workplace could have positive implications for the functioning of the enterprises. Further, Participative Management could provide an institutionalized structure in which conflict of interests could be made less damaging to the industry in general.

Thus, India has a long history of WPM. History of Participative Management in India is traced back to 1919, when Tata Iron and Steel Company (TISCO) constituted a Works Committee (WC) comprising representatives of union and management. But this Committee could not work for long. In the year 1920, a Textile industry in Ahmedabad tried to settle disputes by mutual discussion. This can be considered as a milestone in the history of joint consultation in India. In 1921, number of WCs were set up on the recommendations of the Committee appointed by Government of Bengal to study the causes and remedies for industrial unrest (Mamoria, 1971). In 1931, the Royal Commission on Labour advocated the setting up of Joint Consultative Bodies along the lines of Whitley Councils (Mongia, 1980). The years between 1934 and 1937, a period of industrial unrest, forced the employers to go for conciliation, mediation and joint consultation measures. In the year 1942, a tripartite machinery, an advisory body, based on I.L.O. model was set up to consider all current proposals for labour legislation and the promotion of labour welfare including ways and means for increasing production (Mamoria, 1971).

Although the history of PM in India could be traced back to 1919, when the Tata Iron and Steel Company (TISCO) set up a Joint Works Committee, it was the Industrial Disputes

Act of 1947 that initiated Participative Management in India by making WC a statutory requirement. Industrial Disputes Act of 1947 (Section 11[3]), stipulates that all industrial units with more than 100 employees must establish WCs with an equal number of representatives from employers and employees. When it was observed that WCs are not effective, attempts were made to find out alternative models of participation. As a result of this, Joint Management Councils (JMCs) came into being in the year 1958. JMCs were also joint bodies consisting of employers and labour representatives. When these two forms of participation did not work up to expectations, Government thought of introducing Participative Management at the policy making level of enterprises. Accordingly, Worker Directors were appointed to the Boards of organizations. This was reflected in a piece of legislation enacted in the year 1970. In 1975, Government came out with another scheme called Shop and Joint Councils Scheme which intended to provide institutionalized forms for communication between employers and employees at Shop-floor and Plant levels. WPM also found a mention in the Government's prestigious 20 Point Programme in the year 1975 and in the Directive Principle of State Policy (Article 43 A) in the year 1976. 1980s saw another form of WPM, popularly known as Quality Circles (QCs) whereby management create opportunities for voluntary participation at the Shop-floor level or at the grass roots level (Mankidy, 1995).

The Concept of WPM

The concept of participation allows variety of interpretations as it does not have a universally accepted meaning. Industrial Democracy, Workers' Participation, Participative Management, Co-partnership, Co-determination, Co-management, Syndicalism, Participation of Workers in Decision Making Within Undertakings are all variants of the concept of WPM. For the purpose of scientific understanding the concept of WPM has been conceptualized as the upward exertion of control by employees over various forms of organizational activity, wherein, control may be exercised either directly by the worker himself or through some means of representation (Guest and Fatchett, 1974).

Workers' participation takes place when workers contribute to the managerial functions of the organization such as planning, organizing and the like (Bhatnagar, 1991). Participative Management differs from the hierarchical structure. It puts all emphasis on individual responsibility and group action instead of delegating the authority from the top to bottom (Huss, 1973). WPM uses the expertise and creativity of subordinates in solving important managerial problems by involving them actively in decision making process. It rests on the concept of shared authority whereby a manager shares his managerial authority with his subordinates in order to use the creative energy of subordinates to further managerial goals (Anthony, 1978). In other words, participation is a managerial technique of involving subordinates in decision making process. It is an interaction in which communication occurs among participants resulting in positive outcome for the organization (Singh and Pestonjee, 1990). In participation subordinates have a say in the selection of an alternative and provide inputs to the decision. Thus, employees are involved in decisions which are the responsibilities of the manager (Anderson, 1984). For workers it is a codetermination, for managers it is a joint consultation prior to decision-making and for Government it is an association of labour with management in the decision making process. Participation is generally conceived of as a way of reducing power inequality between employees and employers (Monappa and Saiyadain, 1996).

The WPM has been conceived by different disciplines in different ways. Sociologists view workers' participation as an instrument of varying potentialities which improves industrial relations and promotes industrial peace. Psychologists view it as an emotional involvement of a person in a group where he shares managerial responsibility or it is a psychological process in which workers or subordinates become self-involved in an establishment. Higher productivity of labour is the real objective of workers' participation according to economists. Lawyers view workers' participation as a legal obligation upon the management to permit involvement of workers by providing proper representation to them at all levels of management in the entire range of managerial action (Varandhani, 1989).

Further, WPM has been variously defined in diverse terms. Chaudhuri define workers' participation as, "an act of taking part in managerial functions like planning, organizing, directing and controlling either directly by the workers or indirectly by their representatives" (1990: 258). Athreya observes, "at the enterprise level, it could refer to the involvement of worker in the conduct of enterprise affairs" (1973:67). According to Alexander a management is participative, "if it gives scope to the workers to influence its decision making process on any level or sphere, or if it shares with them some of its managerial prerogatives" (1972:8). Davis defines it as, "an individual's mental and emotional involvement in a group situation that encourages him to contribute to group goals and to share responsibility for them" (1967:617). In the words of Mamoria and Mamoria it is, "a system of communication and consultation either formal or informal by which employees of an organization are kept informed about the affairs of the undertaking and through which they express their opinion and contribute to management decisions" (1988: 479). According to Beach, "participation is the process by which people contribute ideas towards the solution of problems affecting the organization and their jobs. It includes not only the physical participation of a person but also his intellectual and emotional involvement in the affairs of an organization" (1965:510). Mehtras describes it as, "sharing the decision making power by the rank and file of an industrial organization through their proper representatives" (1966:11).

In most of the definitions, there is a frequent reference to lower members of an organizational hierarchy having some 'say' or 'influence' over decision making (Guest and Fatchett, 1974). On the whole we can say that influencing managerial decisions, not by confrontation but by persuasion is the crux of participation. Their involvement in decision making process may be in limited or in the entire range. In participation workers avail the opportunity to place a point of view as equals (Saxena, 1979).

Thus, the concept of WPM has variously been conceptualized, defined, understood and employed warranting a consensus among the academicians and researchers focusing on the phenomenon. However, spirit and ideals behind and goals and objectives of WPM, at least, have come to be subscribed to by the academicians and managerial sections alike universally. An attempt, as such, is made in the Chapter on Review of Literature to bring forth the theoretical and empirical endeavours focusing on the forms, machineries and the operation of WPM in different cultural contexts in general and in Indian context in particular.

As could be understood and ascertained from the foregoing discussion, the PM as an innovative and positive intervention in the management of work organizations has come to stay, however intricate and complex may be issues relating to the actual process. Further, as a recent phenomenon having important implications for the management of firms in particular and the economic development in general, more than deserves and justifies the systematic and scientific attention of the social and behavioural scientists. The present study, hence, could be viewed as an academic and scientific necessity in so far as it seeks to focus empirically on the nature, forms, machineries, extent and the determinants of effectiveness of WPM in Indian work organizations from much needed Sociological perspective.

OBJECTIVES

In view of the applied positive implications of PM amply testified by the findings of empirical studies perused herein before, the present study seeks to address itself to several issues and questions pertaining to PM in the Indian industrial context, so widely debated and speculated in academic circles. In doing so, due consideration is given to the gaps in empirical literature, areas that seem to be lacking in empirical coherence and consistencies as evidenced by the existing literature as well as those aspects that could be of immediate applied significance and could lead to systematic theorizing through casual analysis and identification of recurrent patterns. In pursuance of this logic and rationale the following objectives are identified to be researched upon.

One of the prime objectives of the study is to probe empirically into the nature and extent of WPM in Indian work organizations. In realizing this objective an attempt is made to ascertain and attribute the mode and methods of WPM practiced on the one hand and the extent of which such participation of workers or their representatives is realized on the other. Further, WPM can be thought of as taking place at different levels in the work organizations. It could be at Shop-floor or Middle management level or at the Board level through Worker Directors. As such, the study seeks to ascertain empirically at what level participation takes place in the management of Indian work organizations and a causal explanation is attempted by attributing the level of participation to the contextual and socio-cultural variables.

There are several functional areas of management wherein WPM is contemplated. It could be production, personnel, planning and so forth. However, the actual area of participation is assumed to be the function of several organizational, socio-technical and contextual variables. An attempt as such, is made in the present study to identify the areas of participation and their determinants.

The study further seeks to ascertain and measure effectiveness of WPM and identify the factors that have bearing on the extent, nature and effectiveness of participation and render a particular form and area of participation rather imperative. The factors that facilitate or retard WPM and its effectiveness could be varying from one socio-cultural and industrial context to another as functions of varying socio-cultural milieu, varying degrees of economic development, differential composition of workforce as well as differential stages of evolution in the organizational patterns that come to be adopted for the purposes of managing industrial activities.

However, the major applied thrust of the present study is to ascertain empirically the implications of WPM for the industry, workers and thereby for the economy as manifested in the levels of production, climate of industrial relations, the development of democratic milieu at work plant and evolution of a positive work-culture at place of work. Hence, having ascertained the nature, extent, level, areas and effectiveness of WPM, the study seeks to ascertain the implications of PM for the industrial performance.

Based on these findings of the study, which could be in the form of generalizations with predictive and theoretical value, as well as based on the major conclusions drawn based thereon, the study seeks to come out with recommendations and suggestions which could, if employed and implemented, improve the nature and extent of WPM and enhance the effectiveness of the machineries of WPM in Indian work organizations, which are lamented to be far below the desired levels and not yielding the intended results. Hence, the following objectives of the study, deduced from the foregoing statement could be viewed as of applied and academic significance.

1. To ascertain empirically the nature and extent of WPM in Indian work organizations.

2. To identify the forms and levels of WPM therein.
3. To provide a social profile of actors or parties to the process of WPM.
4. To study the machineries of WPM, their composition, powers and functions.
5. To ascertain and measure the effectiveness of WPM in Indian industries and attempt a causal explanation of the same in terms of socio-technical, contextual and organizational variables.
6. To probe empirically into the applied implications of PM for industrial performance, climate of industrial relations and such other traits of industrial milieu.

HYPOTHESES

Based on the objectives outlined and explained above, a few tentative statements are proposed to be tested in the study. These statements are also drawn from the opinions, assumptions and speculations widely held in the academic circles and also on the findings of other studies undertaken in different socio-cultural setting elsewhere.

The hypotheses, the validity of which the present study seeks to test are:

1. The extent of WPM is the function of the sector of industry.
2. Organizational variables such as size and type of technology determine the areas and levels of WPM.
3. The effectiveness of WPM is independent of socio-technical and organizational milieu.
4. WPM has positive implications for productivity.
5. The industrial performance varies in proportion to the effectiveness of WPM.

2
Methods and Field

An attempt is made in this chapter to explain and justify the methods, tools and techniques employed in the present study as well as to provide a bird's eye view of the field where the study was undertaken. This is followed by an attempt to depict a socio-ecological and economic portrait of the study setting and the study group. In doing so the chapter purports to explain the methods and tools of data collection employed, the techniques of sampling adopted and the methods of analysis subscribed to in addressing empirically the objectives of the present study. An attempt is also made to explain the scheme of conceptualization and operationalization of the concepts employed in the study as well as the framework of analysis which could lend verifiable validity to the findings of the present study.

Under the section on Field, an attempt is made to present the industrial profile of the State of Karnataka in general and the Bangalore region, which represents the hub of industrial, commercial labour and business activities of Karnataka, in particular. This section also focuses on the industrial relations scene and unionism in Karnataka which could provide a necessary contextual backdrop for the analysis of the findings of the present study. Lastly, an attempt is made to present a close and intense profile of the setting of the study and the study group who represent the main source of empirical data on which the present work is based. In short, the chapter deals with "how" and "where at" dimensions of the present empirical study.

THE METHODS

Of late, the methods, tools and techniques of social research have come to attain ever increasing levels of sophistication and refinement elevating social sciences to a level of systematism and validity almost that of natural sciences. Application of fundamentals of science to the field of Sociology represents method and specific procedures by which the Sociologists gather and order their data and subjects them to logical or statistical analysis are known as techniques (Goode and Hatt, 1952). For the purpose of achieving objectives of research and in this process to collect and analyze the data several methods, tools, techniques and scales are employed. An attempt is made in this section to identify and explain the methods, tools and techniques that have been employed which were viewed as those that suit the purpose of the present study best.

Methods of Sampling

For the purpose of present study the method of sampling adopted was purposive random sampling based on size and sector, which were the two main explanatory variables employed in the analysis of the findings. Many similar studies in the past have employed random sampling as the reliable technique. Arya (1983) in his study 'Labour Management Relations in Public Sector' adopted systematic stratified random sampling method. Dhingra (1973) in his 'Participative Predisposition of Managers in the Indian Public Sector Industry' administered a personal value questionnaire to a randomly selected sample of 265 managers. Michael (1979) also made use of random sampling method in his study on 'Industrial Relations in India and Workers' Involvement'. Vishwa Nath (1992) in his study, 'Workers' Participation In Management' and Bhabatosh Sahu (1985) in his study,

'Dynamics of Participative Management: Indian Experiences' adopted stratified random sampling method.

In commensuration with the objectives of the study and keeping in view its logical requirements, it was decided to confine the study to the industrial units with a minimum size of 400 operatives. It was logically assumed that for machineries of WPM to be meaningfully in operation, the firm needs to be of a minimum size with a coherent and definite organizational structure. This is the reason why statutory requirement for the establishment of machineries of WPM is applicable to the firms of some minimum size. There were in all 67 such units in Bangalore Labour Division I and II and eight units, based on size and sector were randomly selected for the purpose of the present study. The sampling is purposive to the extent, that it was so ascertained as to have a sample that best represents the major variables assumed to be significantly associated with the extent and determinants of WPM as identified and explained in the main hypotheses. Size, sector, type of industry, industrial performance and climate of industrial relations were a few traits that were kept in view as purposes to be met with in selecting the sample of industries. Coming to the selection of sample of respondents from managerial, unionist and worker categories, care was taken to see to it that, the sample is as random as possible. Seven representatives each from managerial and unionist categories and sixteen representing workers were drawn from each industry, constituting the total sample of 240 respondents.

Methods of Data Collection

The primary data relevant for the purpose of identification of indices, extent and measurement of WPM have been obtained through the introduction of an organizational information schedule and three independent interview schedules, one each for managerial personnel, union leaders and the operatives were introduced to gather data pertaining to opinions, experiences and determinants. The findings of the present study are based principally on the data collected through these four instruments.

Interview schedules are one of the most commonly employed tools of field research. The main function of the interviews in the overall research design is to gather information directly which will put the assumptions involved in the hypotheses to test (Melling et al, 1976). Owing to its applied significance this method of data collection has been adopted by several researchers in their study. Arya (1983) devised three structured interview schedules, one each meant for managerial personnel, trade union leaders and workers. Similarly three sets of interview schedules were drawn one each for management representatives, union members and workers by Varandhani (1989) in his study on WPM. Aziz (1980) in his study on 'WPM' has used the interview canvassing technique for workers and management representatives in the councils, top management personnel and trade union leaders. Sahai and Mishra (1990) in their study on WPM constructed interview schedules for managers and workers in order to know the existing trends and patterns of WPM. A structured interview schedule was also used by Brannen and his associates (1976) in their study, 'The Workers' Directors: A Sociology of Participation'.

In the present study, three interview schedules were specially devised to be introduced to the three significant actors in the process of PM, incorporating several scales for identification of the indices of participation, its extent, determinants and its effectiveness. These interview schedules also incorporated a section eliciting data on the social, economic and professional background based on which the social origin and other background variables pertaining to the respondents could be formulated which in turn also are employed as explanatory variables. Care was taken while selecting and employing suitable coding and scoring techniques to see to it that, the data generated and the variables identified through the introduction of three interview schedules to three different categories of respondents would enable, and become amenable for, a comparative study of attitudes, dispositions, patterns and effectiveness of WPM in the context of industrial milieu chosen for the study at large.

The organizational information schedule referred to earlier, seeks to ascertain details pertaining to the organizational features such as size, sector, installed capacity, capacity utilization, type of technology employed, machineries of WPM in operation, the climate of industrial relations, levels of productivity and so forth which could serve as the explanatory variables in the analysis of nature, extent, effectiveness and implications of WPM and also provide a necessary and meaningful backdrop against which the findings of the study could be meaningfully discussed and interpreted.

Further, based on the data generated through these instruments, composite variables such as the extent of participation, nature of participation, effectiveness of participation, industrial performance, social origin and the like have been developed and operationalized which would be explained in the section on conceptualization. These variables represent the prime focus and major thrust of the study.

The data were also gathered from the office of the industries and unions to cross verify and authenticate the information obtained from the field. A field diary was also maintained to record the significant observations made during the field work which could be brought to bear upon the data gathered through the instruments and to supplement the inadequacies whenever faced and also to document the information which was not sought through the instruments, nevertheless was of help and relevance in the explanation of the findings.

Methods of Analysis

The data so gathered through the instruments described above were primarily qualitative in nature. The same were transformed into quantitative data by employing suitable coding and scoring techniques rendering the data amenable for statistical analysis. The data are analyzed through computation applying SPSS software. The computerized tabulation of data yielding the linear, bivariate and multivariate tables required to address and analyze the objectives of the study was undertaken at Indian Institute of Social and Economic Change (ISEC), Bangalore. The statistical measures of central tendency such as mean and median, and measures of association like correlation, chi-square, the measures of the strength of association such as 'C' test and 'T' test have been employed in the study wherever required so as to arrive at valid and verifiable generalizations as well as to test the hypotheses formulated.

Conceptualization

For the purpose of analysis and interpretation of factual findings of the study, several concepts have been evolved and operationalized in the present study. Under this section, various concepts that have been employed in the analysis of data are defined so as to ward-off ambiguities in the interpretation of findings and enable the reader to comprehend the generalizations in a particular framework of analysis. It is a common practice in social science research to develop and define all the concepts employed in the study, particularly those concepts that have specifically been devised for the purpose of the study and those concepts about which there is lack of unanimity of meaning. Keeping in view the objectives of this study, and their analytical requirements, several concepts have been devised combining several variables and employing suitable scaling techniques. These concepts, also referred to as composite variables, have been defined and explained under this section on conceptualization.

Social Origin

In Sociological research, of late, social origin has come to be employed as a more realistic measure or index of socio-economic background of the subjects or respondents being studied. Earlier, caste, income, occupation, and education were employed as independent and discrete background variables. But, the increasing structural complexity of Indian society and forces of social transformation operating therein have rendered these variables redundant in providing a realistic background of an individual. For instance, caste alone, these days, can not present the realistic and rational estimate of an individual's social status in society - it is rather an inadequate basis for the estimation owing to the dilution of caste hierarchy, hereditary occupations and inter-caste relations. Thus, in order to provide a more realistic and rational social profile of the respondents, the composite variable of 'social origin' is devised and employed, which is developed combining the caste, income, occupation and educational status of the family. Caste was divided into 'high', 'intermediate' and 'low', income was divided into 'high', 'moderate' and 'low', family occupations were divided into 'high', 'medium' and 'low' and father's education was divided into 'high', 'moderate' and 'low'. These categories were suitably scored which provided the range of variation between 'four' and 'twelve'. The respondents with a score of 4 to 8 were classified as those with 'low' social origin and those with a score of 9 to 12 were classified as those with 'high' social origin.

'Caste'- Caste as a component of social origin was classified into three categories as 'high', 'intermediate' and 'low' based on ritual status, caste occupation and food habits. Here, the ritual status of the caste pertains to its being known as 'once born' or 'twice born' vis-a-vis other castes, the rituals observed by the caste and the seriousness attached to this observation. Caste occupations were graded based on their being manual, non-manual but materialistic, and non-manual-intellectual and ranked in the same order from 'low' to 'high'.

Vegetarianism and non-vegetarianism were the type of food habits classified and graded. Based on the score of respondents on each of these components, their caste was classified as 'high', 'intermediate' and 'low'.

'Occupational Level'- Occupational level of the respondents was classified as 'high', 'medium' and 'low' depending on their being professional, non-professional, non-manual and manual, as well as the requirement of training, education and experience for pursuing these occupations.

'Educational Level'- The educational level of the respondents was classified as 'high', 'moderate' and 'low'', keeping in view the general level of educational attainments of the people in society at large. Accordingly those with no schooling (illiterates) or primary education or those with some secondary education were classified as those with 'low' level of education and those with secondary education (SSLC) or some college education were classified as 'moderately' educated and lastly, those with first degree and post-graduate or professional qualifications were classified as those with 'high' level of educational attainments.

Span of Career

Total length of experience on work or profession is taken as span of career. The span of career is divided into three categories, that is, 'short', 'moderate' and 'long'. Less than 10 years of professional or work experience is considered as 'short' span of career, 10 to 19 years of professional standing is considered as 'moderate' span of career, and an experience of 20 years or more in the profession or work is considered as 'long' span of career.

PM is concerned in this study as any practice through any reason of medraism that facilitates participation workers in the process of taking decisions that affect their work and non-work lives. It is used of synonymous to other terms in currency such as, Workers' Participation in Management,

Industrial Democracy, Workplace Democracy, Co-determination Syndicalism and so shall that are used in this study interchangeably.

Disposition Toward WPM

In a study of WPM, measures indicating the experience and disposition of workers, trade union leaders and managerial representatives are indispensable as they provide a necessary backdrop against which the findings of the study could more rationally be interpreted and attributed. Thus, these two composite variables have been developed and operationalized in the study.

Accordingly, the 'disposition' of management representatives, trade union leaders and workers toward WPM was ascertained by eliciting their responses to the statements and questions focusing on need for workers say in the management of the firm, need for WPM in the current context, ideal level at which WPM should be realized, opinion regarding the impact of WPM on industrial relations, organizational climate and productivity, ideal form of participation, their opinion regarding the need for more areas and wider scope for participation and so forth. The responses of the respondents were suitably coded and scored and by employing a rational scale, the respondents were classified as those with 'favourable' or 'unfavourable' disposition toward WPM.

Experience of WPM

Just as in case of 'disposition', the 'experience' of management representatives, trade union leaders and workers was ascertained based on their exposure to and participation in the machineries and the actual process of WPM. Contextual and personal variables such as the frequency, nature, seriousness and regularity of their participation, extent of participation, response of their counterparts in the process, assumed impact of WPM, relevance of issues involved, the extent of implementation of the decisions taken through WPM and so forth were taken together to develop the composite variable of 'experience on WPM'. Using suitable coding and scoring techniques, the respondents were classified as those with 'positive' and 'negative' experience of WPM.

Climate of Industrial Relations

The climate of industrial relations is another important concept used in the study and is viewed as being a positive implication of WPM on the one hand and a necessary pre-condition for WPM on the other. The criteria or indices used to ascertain the climate of industrial relations are the frequency and duration of strikes and lockouts during the last five years, number of man days lost, nature of strike in terms of intensity and violence, nature of interaction between union and management, number of disputes pending before mediation machineries, management attitude toward union and vice-versa and so forth. Based on these criteria, the plants are classified as those with 'peaceful', 'turbulent' and 'mixed' type of climate of industrial relations and are coded for analysis accordingly.

Extent of WPM

The extent of WPM is an important variable and represents an important objective of the study. It is employed in the analysis as both dependent and independent variable, depending on the context. The extent of WPM was ascertained on the basis of the scope, areas and level of WPM, number of machineries in operation, frequency of meetings, and number of decisions taken through WPM. The data pertaining to these were coded and scored based on which the extent of participation was classified as 'high', 'moderate' and 'low'.

Effectiveness of WPM

The effectiveness of WPM represents one of the core objectives of the present work, which, as in case of extent, is viewed as both dependent and independent or explanatory variable. The composite variable of effectiveness of WPM was ascertained only as an index of the effectiveness of the functioning of the machineries of WPM and was de-linked from its implications or the total impact on productivity or profitability which is considered separately as the implications of WPM. The effectiveness as a concept was developed by combining several indices or criteria such as extent of workers' say in JMCs, SFCs, QCs and WCs, number of grievances that could be resolved through participation, the influence of these machineries on the process of decision making and general administration of the firm, the number of decisions taken in these machineries and the extent of their implementation, the ease with which the machineries of WPM function in the plant without friction, bottlenecks, apprehensions or reservations and the like. Based on these criteria, the effectiveness of WPM was classified as 'high', 'moderate' and 'low'.

Industrial Performance

Industrial performance was one such variable developed in the study which could be viewed as the function of WPM. Although, WPM may not be the only factor determining the performance, a causal relation can be attempted by keeping other possible variables constant. Thus, industrial performance was ascertained on the basis of criteria, such as the percentage of capacity utilization, extent of productivity, operating status (profit-loss) and extent of commitment and job satisfaction among the workforce. Based on these criteria, the plants were classified as those with 'high' or 'low' performance.

Thus, several such concepts were evolved specifically for the purpose of the present study and were operationalized to realize the objectives of the study. A few of the concepts developed, in themselves could be seen as innovative approaches to the subject of WPM and could serve as sources of gratification and credit to the authors. A few other concepts developed, which do not find a place in this section on conceptualization are defined and explained elsewhere in this book.

THE FIELD

The State of Karnataka - The Industrial Scene

The present research is based on the study of WPM in both public and private work organizations in Karnataka, which is one of the highly industrialized States in the Union of India. Karnataka has figured prominently on the industrial map of India as a leading State in the field of industrial development and the State's industrial history is remarkable in many ways. There is no other State in India with as diverse industrial units as found in the State of Karnataka. There are more than 9,000 public and private sector industries in diverse fields of manufacturing and services. Major public sector enterprises such as HAL, HMT, BEL, BHEL, BGML, ITI, NIC, BEML, IDPL, CCI, SAIL, have their plants located in Karnataka. In addition, there are State units such as NGEF, VISL, KSDC, KPCL and so forth. Further, giant private sector corporates such as Voltas, Tatas, Birlas, Larsen & Toubro, ACC, ITC, RIL, MICO, Ideal Jawa, Garware, Kirloskar, Binny and others have their prime plants located in Karnataka. Diverse manufacturing units representing sectors such as Aeronautical, Automobile, Heavy Electrical, Electrical, Electronics, Tele-Communication Equipments, Textile, Machine Tools, Chemical, Pharmaceutical, Fertilizer, Mining, Cement, Ceramics, Tobacco, Synthetics, Leather, Paper, Sugar, Liquor, Steel, Food and Beverages are located in the State. Besides these manufacturing units, there are large service establishments catering to the needs of transportation, power generation, power supply, water supply and sewage, communication, education and the like. There are also varieties of business, trading and commercial establishments, which could be, classified as white-collar units. As such, the setting of the present study represents one of the highly industrialized regions in the nation with Bangalore as its capital which is known as the fastest growing industrial city in Asia.

As a consequence of this diverse and large-scale industrial activity, the State of Karnataka represents a seat of intense labour activity as manifested in large number of trade unions of varied types, sizes, affiliations and ideologies. But all these industries did not appear all of a sudden like a bolt from the blue. The State of Karnataka has a rich and varied tradition supported by an efficient economic system incorporating diverse village and cottage industries and much cherished and preserved handicrafts that are famous world over. However, there are many ups and downs in the industrial history of Karnataka, a brief account of which is given below to provide a necessary profile of the setting of the study.

Karnataka is one among the States that flagged-off industrial revolution in India. The industrial history of Karnataka is in many ways unique, illustrious and remarkable. In fact, the State had sugar mills as early as 1800. However, industrialization in true sense of the word may be said to have got off to a start only in the year 1884, when the first Textile Mill of the State was established. Another Textile Mill was set up in the year 1887. These mills had to suffer serious constraints right since their inception and as such, the Government had to rush to rescue the units by assisting and supporting them in various ways including subscription to the share capital of these industries. This event marked an important landmark and started a new era in the industrial development of the region as it was the first instance of the State participation in industry. Hence, it could be stated that Karnataka set an example to the rest of the country by its capital participation, which later came to be labeled as public sector (Madaiah and Ramapriya, 1989).

Karnataka is endowed with rich and varied natural and mineral resources so indispensable for industrial development.

Much of the State's plan resources are utilized to create required industrial infrastructure by way of development of industrial estates with requisite facilities and providing financial, technical and consultancy services to the entrepreneurs of the State.

First two decades of the present century were marked by a phenomenal increase in the large-scale industrial activities contributing to rapid industrial growth. The industrial map of the State came to be spotted with Rice mills, Oil mills, Saw mills, Steel and Brass foundries, Tobacco industries, Tile factories, Distilleries and so forth. The real breakout of industrial revolution, in true sense of the term, can be stated to have occurred between the outbreak of Ist World War and Indian independence. It could represent an age which shaped the things to come and as such, could be considered as a formative period of highly developed modern industrial economy, as much for the State of Karnataka as for India at large. The War gave an unprecedented impetus for the industrial activity. Every sphere of industrial activity was geared to War effort and was producing well beyond its installed capacity, to meet demands placed by the War. War also provided protection from foreign competition to Indian industries both due to greater demands for the goods and blockade of sea routes. This protection was crucial for industries in their nascent stages. Further fillip to industrial growth was experienced due to State taking up the entrepreneurial role to supplement and stimulate private enterprise. Several large-scale industrial units, such as Mysore Iron and Steel Works, Government Central Industrial Workshop, Government Soap Factory and Government Sandal Oil Factory were established in the public sector between 1914 and 1924. On the other hand, in private sector, Krishnarajendra, Minerva and the Mahalakshmi Woolen and Silk Textile Mills, the Standard Tile and Clay Works Limited, Mysore Abestos, Mysore Premier Metal Factory, Sindhurath

Chromite and number of other concerns were started in the same period.

Two decades following 1924 were characterized by even more intense industrial activity and laid the foundation for strong industrial empire in the State. This was manifested in the variety and number of industrial concerns that came up during this period. This period witnessed the rise of quite a few industries of national importance due to which, Karnataka came to have more than a fair share in the industrial development of the country, and emerged as a leading industrial State.

Industrialization has come to be accepted as an inevitable and the most potent source of social change in the twentieth century. Though late to catch up with large scale industrialization, Karnataka has taken big strides in economic development through its emphasis on heavy industrialization. The decade of 1931-41 represents the highest mark of the industrial activities in the State. The most striking feature of this decade was the setting up of the first Aircraft Factory of the nation in Bangalore in the year 1940. This gave a strong impetus to the core industrial activities conducive for the industrial development of the State. Industries, as diverse as Cement, Sugar, Chemicals and Fertilizers, Paper, Agricultural Implements, Electrical goods like Lamps, Transformers, Batteries and Insulators, Bakelite Products, Machine Tools, Glass, Enamel Paints, Porcelain, Matches, Spun Pipes, Potteries, Chrome and Leather Goods, Vegetable Oil, Tobacco and Coffee, Alcohol, Silk and Engineering were a few of the units established between Wars. The credit of fostering such a spectacular industrial growth goes mainly to the pioneering work done by Sir. M. Vishweshwarayya, who was responsible for designing and executing a number of important projects which paved the way for the industrial development of the State. A good number of industries were established in public sector through the policy of State Government, much before the initiation of Industrial Policy Resolution at the Centre. As a result of this commitment, the Government had to utilize most of its plan resources for industrial development. In the meanwhile, Government of India and Karnataka set up a number of giant industries in the core sector which were of national significance such as HAL, BEL, ITI, BEML, HMT, MISL, BGM, HGM and so forth.

The reorganization of the States saw unprecedented industrial activity in the State due to which it rightly came to be known as a model industrial State. The progress made by the State, at least during 1950s and 1960s, has no parallel elsewhere in the country. If we scan post-reorganization era, it becomes evident that there has been an enormous growth of industry in the State.

By the end of 1984, Karnataka had 357 large and medium scale industries, with a total investment of Rs. 1,496 crores employing about 3.2 lakh people. More than half of the large and medium scale industries are located in and around Bangalore district leading to the exponential growth of the metropolitan city.

TABLE 2.1

Number of Registered Factories and Employment in Karnataka

Year	*No. of Registered Factories*	*Employment (in Lakhs)*
1977-78	8448	5.16
1978-79	9442	5.20
1979-80	10142	5.31
1980-81	10911	5.50
1981-82	10379	6.08
1982-83	10710	6.95
1983-84	11073	7.19
1984-85	11348	7.40
1985-86	11846	7.61
1986-87	12095	7.83

Source: Directorate of Economics and Statistics, Bangalore.

Coming to the Joint Stock Companies, the State has showed a steady progress, as can be observed from the following table.

The data from the table 2.2 reveal that the total number of Joint Stock Companies has almost doubled within a span of five years, from 1985 to 1990. It increased from 5,341 in the year 1985-86 to 9,624 in the year 1992. Similar trend could also be observed with respect to both public and private companies separately too. However, it is significant to note that about 90 percent of the total Joint Stock Companies operating in the State during September 1992, are in the private sector and public sector companies constitute only about 10 percent. This might be attributed to the liberal industrial policy and incentives offered by the State to industrial activity. Even in terms of total number of industrial units, the State ranks 5th in the country, representing one of the leading industrial States in the Union.

TABLE 2.2

Growth of Joint Stock Companies in Karnataka

Year	*Public*	*Private*	*Total*
1985-86	557	4784	5341
1986-87	628	5424	6052
1987-88	677	6093	6770
1988-89	737	6747	7484
1989-90	817	7643	8460
1990-91	872	8354	9226
September 1992	904	8720	9624

Source: Directorate of Economics and Statistics, Bangalore.

Successive Five Year Plans have accentuated the industrial sub-culture. In the Five Year Plans, the Government has assisted financially both the public and the private entrepreneurs to expand and modernize the undertakings.

Five Year Plans have emphasized the development of large and medium industries and have encouraged private entrepreneurs to start large and medium scale industries. Industries such as MICO, Kirloskar, Karnataka Scooters and the like have been set up. As on 31-3-1995 there were in all 7,765 factories in Karnataka. Among them 401 are Chemical factories, 1,761 Engineering and 1,266 are Textile factories. These industries together provided direct employment to 8,18,032 workers.

The State has currently 998 large and medium industries employing 4.47 lakh workers with an investment of Rs. 18,675.41 crores. The State also has 2,23,311 small scale industries employing 13.48 lakh workers with an investment of over Rs.3290.39 crores. Since 1966, that is since its inception, and up to September, 1999, the Karnataka Industrial Area Development Board (KIADB) has developed 70 industrial estates with 25,143 crores of developed plots and has acquired and provided 27,782 acres for single unit complexes and Government organizations (The Hindu, November 1, 1999).

Karnataka has traditionally been in the forefront of Electronic and Information Technology industry with more than 20 percent of national production originating from the State. So far as the IT hardware industry is concerned, Karnataka again ranks number one in the country, contributing 32.2 percent of the national IT hardware production priced over a billion US dollars during 1995-96. Major IT hardware manufacturers in Karnataka are ITI, BEL, IBM, HP, Wipro, BPL and the like. The Government of Karnataka has taken several steps to promote the hardware industry (The Hindu, November 1, 1999).

The Government is expanding the existing Electronic City at Bangalore by setting up phase II Electronic City on an area of 150 hectares. Infrastructure of international standards are being made available for the hardware industry in the $ 208 million "International Technology Park" set up jointly by the Government of Karnataka, Tatas and a Singapore Consortium (*The Hindu*, November 1, 1999), rendering the State in general and Bangalore in particular a most sought after IT destination in the world.

Industrial Relations

Coming to the industrial relations scene, the State can be said to represent an ideal place for industrial ventures. Compared to other leading industrial States in the nation, Karnataka stands out as a State known for industrial peace and harmony. Traditionally, the State has been an ideal setting for industrial ventures owing to a favourable industrial relations climate. Long drawn and violent industrial disputes are a rarity facilitating the peaceful and harmonious coexistence of labour and capital. In a State with as many as 12,000 registered factories, and another 50,000 small scale registered units, couple of industrial disputes a month may be taken as an index of high degree of industrial peace.

The reorganization of the State in 1956 changed the industrial relations scene in the State due to the change in the labour jurisdiction of the State. The year 1957-58 witnessed an abnormal increase in the number of strikes and the number of man days lost. This sudden increase was due, among other causes, to increase in the area and the number of industrial concerns coming under the jurisdiction of the reorganized State of Karnataka. The adoption of the code of discipline in 1958 and the ratification of the Industrial Truce Resolution in 1962, in the wake of Chinese aggression, at the Centre and in States led to a temporary reduction in the number of strikes and lockouts as well as man days lost. So far as the trend is concerned, the data reveal that on an average 83 strikes take place per year in the State and the number of strikes per year is still coming down (Nagaraju, 1981). Coming to the nineties, the data indicate that on an average only 24 strikes take place per year in the State, which could be considered as considerably low.

Unionism

In the State of Karnataka the trade union movement was lagging behind unionism at the national level. There was not even a single union, not to speak of a movement, before 1920. Only minor and feeble labour activity at plant level could be observed. Manifestations of labour discontent, though in a weak manner, could be observed in Mysore and Bangalore at Binny Mills around 1920. But what could be called as the first active, forceful, regular and well organized trade union of the State came into existence in the year 1929. Though the Trade Union Act at all India level was passed in the year 1926, the unions in the State did not have legal status till as late as 1942, when the Mysore Labour Act was passed. As such, the development of trade unionism in Karnataka was rather slow as compared to the overall situation in India.

This slow development of trade unionism in the State has been attributed to various factors such as absence of skilled workforce in the beginning of the process of industrialization in the State and resultant willingness on the part of employers to offer better terms and conditions of work and lack of solidarity among the heterogeneous labour force as a result of immigration of workers from neighbouring States of Andhra and Tamil Nadu. These migrant workers along with the local labourers formed heterogeneous workgroups dampening the solidarity. The slow growth was also due to the absence of favourable legislation promoting trade unions in the State. On the other hand, the Government was not interested in enacting labour laws, and on the other, there was no compelling urge among the workers to have such legislation promulgated. In addition to these factors, there were many other that led to the slow and tardy growth of unionism in the State.

In the meanwhile, a few important unions were established in the State. 'Hindustan Aeronautics Employees' Association' was formed in January 1947. The 'Imperial Tobacco Company Employees' Union' was established in the year 1949 and

'Indian Telephone Industries Employees' Union' was formed in the year 1950. It was only in the 1950s that the union movement in the State received the impetus it needed which was mainly due to the intense labour activities in the HAL and other such big industries and the large scale entry of white-collar workers into unionism. Seven unions of white collar workers were formed between 1956 and 1958. These unions were formed mainly by the Bank and Insurance employees. In addition to these, unions were also formed in HMT and BEL in the year 1956. Thus, by the end of 1950s, unionism was firmly entrenched in the State (Reindrop, 1971). And ever since, there has been a phenomenal increase in the number of unions and total union membership. The following table depicts decade-wise growth in the number of unions in the State as well as percentage increase in the number of unions at the end of every decade.

A brief report on unionism in the State, is attempted in tables 2.3. In all, the State has 3,901 registered trade unions as on 30th November, 1999 and these are distributed over nine labour divisions comprising twenty three districts. The division-wise distribution of the unions is given above in the table 2.4.

TABLE 2.3

Decade-wise Fresh Registration of Unions

Decade	*No. of New Unions Registered*	*Total No. of Unions at the End of Decade*	*Percentage Growth from the Pervious Decade*
Till 1950	—	22	—
1951-1960	83	105	377.3
1961-1970	238	343	226.7
1971-1980	1099	1442	320.4
1981-1990	1663	3205	115.3
1999 Nov.	696	3901	21.7

Source: Monthly Report of Registrations and Cancellations of Trade Unions in Karnataka, published by the Commissioner of Labour in Karnataka, 1999.

TABLE 2.4

Division-wise Distribution of Trade Unions in the State (as on Nov. 1999)

Division	*No. of Unions*	*Percent of Total*	*Total Membership*	*Percent of Total*	*Average Size*
Bangalore-I	1032	26.5	245585	36.6	238.0
Bangalore-II	786	20.1	106102	15.8	135.0
Mysore	351	9.0	56932	8.5	162.2
Mangalore	366	9.4	105576	15.7	288.5
Davanagere	308	7.9	41198	4.6	79.4
Hubli	211	5.4	16735	2.5	83.9
Gulbarga	370	9.5	31047	4.6	83.9
Chikkamangalur	111	2.9	27569	4.1	248.4
Belgaum	366	9.4	40370	6.0	110.3
Total	3901	100.0	671114	100.0	172.0

Source: List of Registered Trade Unions published by the Commissioner of Labour in Karnataka, 1999.

The table indicates the uneven distribution of unions over the State. It could be observed that, Bangalore Division-I and Bangalore Division-II together account for nearly 50 (46.6) percent of the total unions in the State. Even in the case of membership, this region accounts for 52 (52.4) percent of the total union membership in the State, whereas, Hubli with 2.5 percent of the total union membership stands as the division with minimum membership contribution. Chikkamangalur division with only 111 unions represents the division with least number of unions. The data reveal that the average size of the unions in the State stands at 172.0 members per union. However, variations do occur from this State average with regard to the average size of unions in each division. The range of variation being 79 (79.4 percent) to 288 (288.5 percent) members per union. The data also reveal that, only three divisions have the average size more than the State average, with Mangalore Division being the one with largest average size at 288 members per union. The average size of union gains significance in view of the fact that it can be an index of union proliferation and multiple unionism. In general, it could be stated that considerable regional variations are observed in the unionism in the State, with Bangalore Division-I and II together representing nearly half of the total number of unions and more than half of the total membership. Even in terms of average size of the unions, regional variations range from as small as 79 to as large as 288.

Setting of the Study

The State is divided into four regions for the purpose of industrial and labour administration namely, Bangalore, Hassan, Gulbarga and Belgaum. These four regions are further divided into nine divisions. The present book is based on a study into the nature, extent, effectiveness, determinants and consequences of WPM in the two Labour Divisions of the State, that is, Bangalore Division I and II. Bangalore Division-I has labour jurisdiction over the Bangalore City Corporation Divisions-1 to 16,17,19, 43 to 50, 52 to 60, Bangalore North Taluka excluding the area within the corporation limits, Doddaballapur, Devanhalli and Nelamangala talukas of Bangalore district and the district of Tumkur. The Bangalore Division-II covers the Bangalore City Corporation Divisions 18,20 to 42, 51,61 to 63, Bangalore South Taluka excluding the area within the corporation limits, Ramanagaram, Channapatna, Kanakapura, Magadi, Hosakote and Anekal Talukas of Bangalore district and the district of Kolar. In all, these two divisions together extend over the districts of Bangloare, Tumkur and Kolar.

The Bangalore Region* comprising Bangalore Division I

---

* Though the official jurisdiction of the Bangalore Region extends over five districts namely Bangalore, Tumkur, Kolar, Mysore and Mandya, the Bangalore region referred to here is taken to represent Bangalore Division-I and II, to which the present study is confined.

and Bangalore Division-II is characterized by heavy concentration of diverse industrial undertakings, both public and private. This region is recognized as one of the foremost industrial center in the nation with as many as eight large public sector industrial undertakings and numerous medium and small public and private industries. This region has diverse types of industries such as Aeronautical, Electronic, Electrical, Heavy Electrical, Automobile, Watch, Telephones, Textile, Soap, Chemicals, Plastic, Food, Brewery, Mining and Pharmaceutical. Due to heavy concentration of industrial labour, and also of trade unions of different sizes and shades of political affiliation, this region represents a seat of intense industrial activities.

The Bangalore Labour Division I and II were selected for the present study keeping in view the fact that this region represents one of the leading industrial regions in the nation. Bangalore, a part of this region, in particular is known as the fastest growing industrial region in Asia. Bangalore is about 350 Km West of Chennai on the Bay of Bengal, and about 350 Km East of Mangalore on the Arabian sea. The climate of the city is never unbearably hot, since it stands on the Deccan plateau, at an altitude of 900 meters. This congenial environment is one of the reasons for the presence of so many reputed research institutes and high-tech industries, which also attract highly qualified manpower and capital (Holmstrom, 1994).

Founded in the sixteenth century, the Bangalore city quickly became a rich weaving and trading center. India's first Aircraft factory, Hindustan Aircraft (now Hindustan Aeronautics) was founded in Bangalore during the Second World War. In the years after independence the Indian Government established some of the country's biggest public sector units (Holmstrom, 1994). The industrial scene of the city is dominated by such leviathans as ITI (Indian Telephone Industries), HMT (Hindustan Machine Tools), BEL (Bharat

Electronics Ltd.), BHEL (Bharat Heavy Electrical Ltd.), BEML (Bharat Earth Movers Ltd.), Wheel & Axle Plant, L & T, ITC and the like. A rough calculation, would place public sector employment at about two thirds of the total blue-collar force. Thus, Bangalore is the citadel of the giant public sector enterprises (Ramaswamy, 1998). Nehru on a visit to Bangalore said that Bangalore is very much a picture of India of the future, especially because of the concentration of science, technology and industries in the public sector here. The private sector followed, taking advantage of the large number of engineers, technicians and skilled workers trained in the vast public sector enterprises (Holmstrom, 1994). Private sector industries like Binny Ltd., Tata Tea Ltd., Triveni Engineering Works Ltd. and so forth are situated in the city.

Light and heavy engineering account for the bulk of the manufacturing activity of the city. Bangalore has basically a capital goods industrial base. Large industrial undertakings manufacture capital goods, serviced by a large number of medium and small scale, ancillary and sub-contract industries, for various components and services. Since 1975, there has been a rapid growth in the Electrical, Electronic and Metallurgical industries, Rubber and Plastics, Leather, Glass and Ceramics. By the 1980s Bangalore had become one of the country's major producers of electronic hardware. The State Government, in addition to the older industrial estates mostly for small scale industries, has established the 'Peenya Industrial Area' on the outskirts of the city with a mixture of large and medium sized firms, most of which are Engineering and Electronic industries. This 'Peenya Industrial Area' is claimed to be the 'biggest industrial estate in Asia'. The State Government has also established a new 'Electronic City' near Bangalore (Holmstrom, 1994).

In 1992, the 'organized sector' in Bangalore District Urban and Rural employed 4,68,819 persons, including 89,807 women (19 percent) (Government of Karnataka, 1992). Sixty three per cent of these 'organized sector' jobs were in the public sector. In the year 1991, Bangalore District Urban had 3,437 registered factories (including 1,113 engineering industries), employing 3,65,000 people (an average of 106 per factory) and 13 industrial estates. 20,400 small scale industrial units employed 1,94,800 workers (average 9.7 per unit). There are certainly many more unregistered units as well (Holmstrom, 1994).

In total, Bangalore has acquired the image of India's industrial success story. It remains India's major industrial centre, with industries of diverse types and sizes (Holmstrom, 1994). And as such, it could justifiably be assumed and taken as an ideal setting for an empirical study into the social realities pertaining to the WPM in an Indian context.

Study Group

To draw the sample of industries to be included in the study, the total list of industries in the State was collected from the office of the Chief Inspector of Factories and Boilers, Bangalore. It was decided to consider industries with a strength of 400 or more, as the practice of WPM could be more streamlined, definite and better understood in industries with a minimum organizational size. In all 67 such industries were identified in Bangalore Labour Division I and II for the purpose of present study and were communicated for the presence of machineries of WPM in operation. Out of 67 industries identified and communicated for the presence of machineries of WPM in operation in Bangalore Labour Division I and II, responses were received from 31 industries, out of which 8 industries were selected keeping in view the machineries in operation and other variables such as size and sector. These 8 industries were operating in diverse sectors such as Machine Tools, Heavy Electrical, Electronics, Engineering, Textile and Food and were also from both private and public sectors. Five industries were from public sector and three from private sector. With regard to size, industries were classified as large, medium and small. Industries with 2000 or more workers were classified as large, industries with 800-2000 workers were classified as medium and industries with less than 800 workers were classified as small. According to this classification, 4 were large, 2 were medium and 2 were small industries.

In all 56 managerial personnel, 56 union officials and 128 operatives were selected to constitute the study group of 240 respondents. Out of 56 managerial personnel, 35 were from public sector and 21 were from private sector. Similarly out of 56 trade union officials, 35 were from public sector and 21 were from private sector. Out of 128 operatives, 80 belonged to public sector and 48 to private sector. So far as size is concerned out of 56 managerial personnel, 28 were drawn from large industries, 14 from medium and another 14 were drawn from small units. Out of 56 trade union officials, again 28 were drawn from large industries and 14 each from medium and small industries. Out of 128 operatives, 64 were from large industries, 32 were from medium industries and 32 were from small industries. The respondents were contacted well in advance to take appointments and naturally it was rather difficult to contact the managerial personnel owing to their diverse pre-occupations and responsibilities. Whereas, trade union leaders and workers could be confacted and interviewed with greater ease. In general, the response of the respondents was quite positive and encouraging.

Plant Profile

As mentioned under the section on Study Group, 8 industries with machineries of WPM in operation have been chosen for the purpose of present study and these 8 industries represent the cross-section of Indian industrial and business world in terms of product, sector, size and technology. An attempt is made under this section to provide a profile of each of the plants chosen for the study.

1. BHEL (Electronics Division)

The Bharat Heavy Electricals Limited (BHEL), Electronics Division is one of the fourteen Manufacturing plants of the giant public sector unit BHEL. Established in the year 1977, the plant is known for its products' application in diverse areas of industry and business. With an employee strength of 2,198 and a capacity utilization of 90 percent, this plant is one of the few profit earning public sector units. A highly unionized plant with one union operating in it, the plant has a track record of intense labour activities, though of less negative consequences to the production process. The workforce is constituted of highly skilled personnel required to run and manage an electronics unit. The workforce appears to be moderately committed and satisfied with organization structure having minor bottlenecks for flow of communication, authority and information.

2. BHEL (EPD)

BHEL is a large public sector multi product enterprise having 14 manufacturing plants and 150 project sites countrywide. The Electro-porcelains Division of BHEL (EPD), which is chosen for the present study is a leading manufacturer of High Tension Electro-porcelain Insulators for the last 70 years. Apart from being a recipient of the ISO-9001 certificate for quality systems in design and manufacture, recognition has also come by way of awards for National Productivity, Safety and Quality. BHEL which has a product presence in core sectors like Power, Industry, Transportation, Oil & Gas, Telecommunication, Defence and Non-Conventional Energy sources is a leading public sector unit having exported its products to over 52 countries worldwide. The EPD produces disk insulators, cap & pin type post insulators, solid core insulators, hollow insulators, wear resistant materials and industrial ceramics. These products apart from being in use in India in major core sectors like Power, Steel, Cement and Coal have found markets in UK, Australia, Egypt, Middle East, USA, Iran and so forth.

The plant has a total workforce of 875 operatives, supervisors, clerks and managers. Inspite of being highly unionized with almost 100 percent unionization represented by one union, the union management relations are found to be cordial and the organizational climate appears to be conducive for high degree of job satisfaction and commitment.

3. *Bharat Electronics Limited*

Established in 1954 as a major public sector unit Bharat Electronics Limited has been identified as a pioneer Electronic industry. Bharat Electronics has developed a wide range of electronic products in the areas of defence communications, telecommunications, satellite communications, radars and sonars, sound and vision broadcasting, opto-electronics, medical electronics and electronic components. Of late, Bharat Electronics has embarked upon software development and has captured markets abroad through its Software Exports Division. It is an industry wedded to the policy of Total Quality Management and in recognition of its exceptionally high quality products, it has been India's first defence and professional electronics company to get the coveted ISO-9002 certification from National Quality Assurance of UK and all the nine units of Bharat Electronics across India, divided into 26 divisions are certified in the ISO-9000 series. It has a prestigious customer profile with Army, Navy, Air Force, Para Military, Space Department, All India Radio, Doordarshan, Ministry of Education, Department of Telecommunications, Videsh Sanchar Nigam, Civil Aviation, Meteorological Department, Power Sector, Oil Industry, Forest Departments, Medical and Health Care Department, Railways, Telephone Industry and Entertainment Industry as its main clients. It is an industry with capital layout of 800 crores with turnover of 8000 crores employing over 18,000 technically qualified manpower. It has prestigious collaborators in NEC of Japan, HSA of Holland, Thompson CSF of France, Motorola, Hewlett Packard and Rank Xerox of USA, Anritsu of Japan and so forth. In short, it could be taken as the flagship company of Government of India in the Electronics sector.

Further, though the plant is somewhat highly unionized with four unions operating in it, the climate of industrial relations appears to be quite cordial with no strike having taken place during the last five years and collective bargaining being the most preferred, employed and effective method of resolving industrial disputes. In commensuration with its diverse areas of production, the organizational structure is characterized by high degree of division of labour and specialization, but nevertheless, exhibits moderate degree of bureaucratization and higher degree of delegation of authority with communication process being quite free and open with not too much of formalism.

4. Binny Mills

Binny Mills is a well known private sector Textile unit established almost a century ago. The plant with about 1,300 workers was known to be one of the pioneers of Indian Textile industry manufacturing high quality cotton, synthetic and blended textiles quite popular in India and abroad. It was one of the leading suppliers of uniform clothing to the Indian armed forces and their products are equally popular as material for school uniforms. Although, at present, it is incurring losses, it was one of highly profit making Textile plants in the country. It has a history of violent and hostile unionism owing to which strikes and lockouts were quite common about a decade or two ago which made it one of the sick Textile units. However, it resumed production and is operating at 90 percent of capacity utilization. The plant is highly unionized with one union affiliated to INTUC operating within and at present the climate of industrial relations appears to be positive with levels of job satisfaction and commitment among the workforce being moderate.

5. Wheel & Axle Plant

Wheel & Axle Plant is another large industrial plant which is the production unit of Indian Railways. This prestigious production unit aimed at import substitution was sanctioned initially in the year 1973 with its reappraisal being finally cleared by Government of India in 1978. The plant established at an approximate cost of 146 crores supported by World Bank loan is situated at Yelahanka on a site measuring 291 acres. It was commissioned in the year 1984. It manufactures Wheels and Axles of various kinds required by the Indian Railways. The significant feature of this plant is that the material for manufacture of wheels is pedigree scrap mostly generated by the Railways themselves, thus leading to material conservation. The casting of molten steel into the final shape of the wheel, with controlled pressure pouring into graphite moulds followed by heat treatment to develop optimum physical and metallurgical characteristics is done in this highly automated plant. Planned to produce 5 main types of freight stock wheels of 725 mm to 1090 mm diameter and 10 types of axles representing a major cross-section of different types needed by Indian Railways for all gauges, Wheel & Axle Plant reached the targeted production level of 23,000 wheel sets during 1986-87 itself. The production crossed 30,000 axles of different types during 1989-90 and crossed 38,000 wheel sets in the year 1992-93. This plant is considered as incomparably superior to older plants which use virgin steel and employ forging technology, as evidenced by this plant achieving saving on energy to the tune of 74 percent, saving in virgin raw material like iron ore, coal and the like to the tune of 90 percent, saving in water and water pollution to the tune of 40 percent and 76 percent respectively and reduction in air pollution by 85 percent.

The plant has a total workforce of 2,246 technically skilled workers who are moderately unionized, represented by one union. The climate of industrial relations is quite cordial with no incidence of industrial conflict reported during the last five years. The overall levels of job satisfaction and commitment appear to be high with an organizational structure so designed as to facilitate moderate degrees of formalization and bureaucratization.

6. Indian Telephone Industries

Indian Telephone Industries is one of the largest public sector units established immediately after independence. It manufactures state-of-art telecommunication equipments with a market presence of close to 75 percent. It has over 10,000 employees on rolls who are highly unionized. This industry with state-of-art technology is incurring loss inspite of capacity utilization being in the range of 75 to 90 percent. The plant inspite of being unionized is characterized by cordial union management relations with Collective Bargaining being a method most effective and most frequently resorted to in resolving industrial disputes.

7. Triveni Engineering

Triveni Engineering is another highly profit making private sector Manufacturing unit. Established to produce machine components and machineries for the core sector, it employs 435 workers. In commensuration with the nature of product, more than two thirds of the workers are highly skilled with unskilled workers constituting only 5 percent of the workforce. The plant has the state-of-art imported technology and utilizes capacity around 90 percent. The plant is highly unionized with 98 percent unionization of the workforce and though at the time of study union-management relations were cordial, the plant suffered closure and suspension of work in the recent past resulting in the loss of 4,800 man days. The workforce appears to be moderately committed with moderate level of job satisfaction, though the organizational structure of the plant is conducive for higher level of morale and commitment.

8. Tata Tea Limited

Tata Tea Limited is a highly profit making unit of the well known Tata Group of Industries. Established in 1963 with a total strength of 485 workers, it operates utilizing installed capacity to the tune of 75 to 90 percent. It manufactures 136,000 kgs of tea powder per year of different grades which are popular in Indian markets and abroad. The plant has moderate unionism represented by a union affiliated to communist federation. However, the climate of industrial relations appears to be cordial with no incidence of strike during last five years. As has been in the case with all the Tata concerns, the job satisfaction and commitment among the workforce is quite high and the management is progressive in its approach and ameliorative in its outlook.

With the foregoing discussion on methods, conceptualization, field, the setting of the study and study group, which is assumed to provide the indispensable scientific and contextual backdrop as well as present a framework of analysis against which the findings of the study could be comprehended, an attempt is made in the next chapter to provide an intellectual backdrop to the study through a review of theoretical and empirical literature.

3

Review of Literature

This chapter deals with the review of theoretical and empirical literature pertaining to the social realities of WPM. It attempts to provide a theoretical foundation to the issues that are discussed in the body of the book. In other words, it is concerned with providing a theoretical orientation and empirical support against the backdrop of which the objectives of the present study could find adequate justification and the findings could seek a meaningful place in the empirical literature on WPM. A theoretical support like this is significant from the point of view of analyzing, integrating and organizing the data of present study so as to yield a fairly meaningful understanding and generalizations pertaining to social realities of PM in the context of Indian work organizations. Moreover, an empirical work such as this will be meaningless unless it has moorings in the existing knowledge which gives relevance and contextual validity to the findings. With a view to provide a theoretical support to the present study and in order to gain intellectual insights into the existing literature, significant works on WPM in industrial context are reviewed elaborately.

An attempt is made here to acquaint the study with the classic works in the field of Personnel Management and Industrial Relations focusing on WPM and to develop requisite theoretical insights to comprehend and interpret the findings of the present study through a review of relevant literature. It may be clarified here that this review is confined mainly to the Sociological literature or studies with Sociological perspective on WPM and issues related to it particularly in the context of industrial organizations. Diverse aspects of WPM, which have traditionally been the concerns of Social Scientists engaged in applied research focusing on human dimension of the enterprise have been identified to provide the core theme for this review and the chapter is divided into several sections, each dealing with one issue concerning the WPM. Thus, the works dealing with the concept, machineries, significance, forms, level, extent, areas and of WPM on the one hand and effectiveness, determinants of WPM on the other, are reviewed separately under different sections to provide a meaningful basis for the analysis and interpretation of the findings of the present study pertaining to each one of these issues which together represent the prime thrust of the present study.

Since, mention has been already made about the works dealing with concept and history of WPM in the Introduction chapter itself, an attempt is made here to review the works dealing with other aspects of WPM such as machineries, implications, forms, level, extent, degree, areas, determinants and effectiveness of WPM.

PM: GLOBAL VIEW AND EXPERIENCE

PM has generated a great deal of interest among social scientists, politicians, trade unionists and industrial managers all over the world. The concept of involving workers in the decision making process has been on trial for several decades. Various models of WPM have been tried out in large number of countries all over the world with different social, political and economic frameworks (Mankidy, 1995). The conceptualization of WPM has been different in different cultural contexts. WPM takes various shades of meaning in different politico-economic settings. It varies from one country to another country both in degree and nature according to traditions, beliefs and circumstances existing in such countries (Varandhani, 1989).

Some of the prominent models of WPM are:

United Kingdom

The idea of workers' participation in the United Kingdom began with industrialization. It was also the result of the humanitarian attitude of some of the employers who realized difficulties of the workers and tried to have informal discussions with representatives of workers. In the seventeenth century, workers constituted Shop Committees called 'Chappels'. These Committees facilitated workers to have informal discussion among themselves on common problems of their trade and welfare and representing same to their masters (Varandhani, 1989). However WPM saw a formal beginning in United Kingdom when the Whitley Committee of 1916-17 encouraged the establishment of voluntary joint consultation between the workers and the employees at Plant level. The Committee recommended Joint Industrial Councils in well organized industries and Works Committees consisting of the representatives of managements and workers in individual establishments. But these bodies failed during the inter-War period and joint consultation was revived once again when the Second World War broke out. Joint consultation now is quite common in U.K. A Joint Committee usually consists of representatives of management appointed by the Chief Executive and representative of employees being elected by secret ballot. The number of management representatives on a Joint Committee is often less than the number of employees' representatives. The Joint Committees are advisory in character. Their functions include consideration and discussion of changes in methods of production, safety and welfare of employees, work rules and personnel problems, training and education. There is a general opinion that Joint Consultation has not succeeded in United Kingdom due to indifferent and suspicious attitude of both employees and trade unions toward Joint Consultative Bodies. There have also been many other experiments in the United Kingdom in the field of labour-management cooperation such as Employee

Share Holding, Profit Sharing and Board of Directors. Collective Bargaining, which is conceptually very much different from Joint Consultation has also been an integral part of industrial relations system of United Kingdom. However, Plant level bargaining has become more prominent of late (Pylee, 1975).

France

In France, PM has been a spontaneous movement. Industrial sector of the country was very much shattered as a result of Second World War and many of the factories were abandoned by the owners. A group of workers took over such industrial units and formed on their own Production Committees. Government later legalized these Committees and named them as Works Committees. According to the Government Ordinance of 1946 all the industrial units employing 50 or more workers were required to form Works Committee, however, public sector was exempted (Michael, 1984). The head of the undertaking will be the Chairman of the Works Committee. The strength of the Committee shall be 3 to 11 according to the number of workers employed in the undertaking. Elections to the Committee are held every two years. The candidates are put forward by the recognized trade unions as representative of the workers. The Works Committees are consultative bodies, excepting the welfare activities which are administered under the supervision of Works Committees. They are responsible for the administration of canteens, libraries, housing societies, cooperatives and such other welfare services. These Committees have the right to receive information and the right to be consulted on all economic matters affecting the operation of the undertaking. In Joint Stock Companies they can even send two representatives to attend Board of Directors meetings (Pylee, 1975). Works Committees have yielded positive results in the fields of welfare and social activities. But in the case of economic and industrial relations, the Committee mechanism has failed to achieve its objectives (Michael, 1984).

United States of America

In the year 1920, partnership schemes were introduced for the development of cooperative relationship between workers and employers. WPM gained ground in the United States of America when Joint Consultation Committees were set up during the First World War to increase production (Varandhani, 1989). The Joint Consultation Committees which were set up during two World Wars with the sole object of increasing production could not survive. In U.S.A., WPM is very limited and collective agreements are very extensive in scope. Here the idea of Workers' Partnership is not appreciated much both by management and labourers. Collective Bargaining has been given prime importance. Acting through their union, workers in U.S.A. influence the terms and conditions of employment and other matters that may be included in the collective agreement with the management. A recent innovation in the field of industrial relations in U.S.A. is the creation of Joint Union Management Bodies or Joint Study Groups meant to examine complex issues which cannot be thoroughly examined at a bargaining table and issues over which it is difficult to arrive at a satisfactory decision at the bargaining table itself. After examining such issues, Joint Study Groups recommend mutually acceptable solutions. Some of the groups may even be given the authority to negotiate agreements. Such Joint Bodies exist in Steel, Automobile, Glass, Electrical Equipment and other industries. Profit Sharing Schemes which have been evolved during the last four decades or over have become another means of associating workers with the management. However Collective Bargaining is more prominent than these two forms of participation (Pylee, 1975). Quality Circles which consist of a small group of employees who meet regularly to identify, analyze and evolve ways and means to solve work related problems have also been taken off more recently in U.S.A.

Yugoslavia

Yugoslavia today provides the most classic example of

PM. It was formally instituted in the year 1922, when coalition Government passed a legislation conferring on workers the right to participate in the management of enterprises. However, due to some political problems, it could not take off effectively. It was made effective with the passing of the Basic Law of 1950 which introduced Workers' Management popularly known as Workers' Self-Management. It does not provide simply for a degree of consultation with the workers or their partial involvement in policy and decision making, but bestows upon the workers themselves the right of managing the enterprise in which they are employed. The Self-Management is carried out through a body of representatives elected and through universal suffrage of the workers' of the enterprise. The elected representatives are not accountable to some Supervisory Board for the discharge of their duties, but they are accountable directly to the workers. Workers' Council, Management Board, Director and Local Peoples' Committee are the major institutions under Yugoslavian model of Workers' Management.

Japan

The decision making process in Japan includes a system known as 'Ringi' which involves a consensual approach to decision making based on the confidence in the abilities of subordinates. Japan is known for WPM through its Quality Circles (QCs) which consists of a small group of employees who meet regularly to identify, analyze and solve problems related to work. In other words, they are voluntary and autonomous groups independently organized for the purpose of studying and solving problems chosen by the participants themselves. During the last two decades, QCs have increased at a phenomenal rate in Japan (Dey, 1988). Public sector undertakings in Japan have a system of Joint Consultation, the main aim or function of which is to smoothen communication between the management and the union to prevent the outbreak of industrial disputes concerning technological innovations (Kumar, 1992).

West Germany

The Federal Republic of Germany is well known for its unique contribution to the field of WPM in the form of Co-determination. Co-determination was mainly a product of Second World War. The Act of Co-determination of 1951 applies to all undertakings employing more than 1,000 workers in the Coal Mining, Iron and Steel industries. Co-determination, as the term itself implies gives equal rights to the employees' representatives in all the matters concerning the industrial establishment. Co-determination may be economic which relates to management policy, it may be personnel Co-determination which deals with personnel policy including recruitment, training, transfers. It may be social Co-determination which deals with working hours, vacations, sanitation, piece-rates, accident prevention (Mamoria and Mamoria, 1988). Industrial establishments in Germany are governed by Supervisory Boards. These Supervisory Boards appoint Managing Boards which include a Labour Director as a representative of workers. The workers' representatives on Management Boards who act as Labour Directors in the Coal and Steel industries are regarded by the trade unions as full-fledged members of management. The backbone of WPM in the Federal Republic of Germany is the Works Council. All the industries except Coal Mining and Iron and Steel are governed by the Works Constitution Act of 1952 which relates to the setting up of Works Council. The Act requires that a Works Council, as the representative organ of all the employees, should be set up in all units employing five or more workers (Pylee, 1975).

Israel

The credit for implementing the scheme of WPM in Israel goes to the General Federation of Labour of Histadrut founded in 1920. It is one of the largest employers employing 24 percent of the total work force of the country and it is the largest trade union affiliating fifty national unions. (Michael, 1984). There have been four distinct schemes by the Histadrut leadership to advance WPM in Israel. Works' Committees, Joint Production Committees, Plant Councils and Joint Management are these four distinct schemes. The Works' Committees which were introduced first represent the workers before the managements of the undertaking concerned in all matters falling within the scope of collective agreements. These Committees are elected periodically by the workers and are essentially Plant level bargaining Committees. Joint Production Committees introduced originally in 1945 were composed of an equal number of elected representatives. These Committees were expected to advise the management on incentive schemes, health and safety of workers, technical and vocational training. Plant Council consisting of five to ten workers' representatives and two to five management representatives was to be constituted in each undertaking. The frequency of meeting of Plant Council is once in a month. The authority of the Plant Council extended to production plans and method, marketing, training, investment and reorganization. Plant Councils, however, had a very short life. After the disappointing experience with Plant Councils, Histadrut leaders decided to go ahead with another form of WPM, that is, Joint Management. Joint Management involves worker participation at two levels that is, at the level of Central Government and in the management of the individual undertakings. Under the scheme, one third of the members of each Central Management should be representatives of workers (Pylee, 1975).

Russia

In Russia, there is participation of masses in industry, that is of the non-managerial workers. Mass Participation in industry takes different forms. One of these is supervision by the workers in a firm over the work of the management and their strict criticism of all its deficiencies. Second is the offering of suggestions through Employee Conferences and third is direct performance of administrative task by workers. Production Conferences also take place in Russia where workers take part in meetings and conferences with the main aim of increasing production. Conferences of what are called 'Production Activities' are considered of great importance in the matter of increasing production. These 'Production Actives' constitute a highly select group composed of junior management personnel, engineers and technicians and selected workers. There is also another movement concerned with production, which is known as Stakhanovite movement. It is a movement to raise production by more efficient and earnest work (Giri, 1962).

MACHINERIES OF PM: INDIA

The WPM is realized or brought into operation through diverse machineries in different industries depending on the areas of WPM, level of WPM and the skill composition of the workforce. However, there appears to be no universal pattern or uniform division of labour among the machineries of WPM. A survey of literature on the composition and functions of machineries of WPM reveals that these aspects differ from industry to industry and in the same industry over a period of time. It also appears that there exists a functional overlapping among the machineries rendering it to classify or demarcate the functions of several machineries of WPM. It is observed that JMCs, SFCs, WCs and QCs are the most frequently evolved and employed machineries of WPM and the number of such Committees operating in different industries varies with the size, complexity of structure and the type of products associated with industrial organizations. And these machineries are composed with different proportions, representing workers, managerial personnel and union representatives.

An attempt is made in this section to focus on literature pertaining to the composition and functions of these machineries of WPM.

Works Committees (WCs)

History of WPM commences from these Committees.

Soon after the First World War, the Tata Iron and Steel company at Jamshedpur set up a Works' Committee with workers co-operation. This Committee had to be wound up in a few years for it was not effective. At other places such as Ahmedabad and Calcutta also Works' Committees were set up, but with little success. The Royal Commission on Labour in India recommended Works' Committee at the plant and industrial level for consultation and resolution of disputes. The Industrial Disputes Act of 1947 vide Section 3 (1) has provided for the setting up of WCs in all undertakings employing 100 or more workers. The main objective for setting up WCs is to remove friction between the employers and the employees. It was obligatory for all units employing over 100 workers to establish WCs. Equal representation of both management and workers was provided. The number of members forming the Committee was not to exceed 20. The Committee was expected to discuss matters of common interest or concern and to promote measures for maintaining cordial relations between management and workers and it was expected to deal with following items: conditions of work, lighting, ventilation; amenities, such as drinking water, canteen, medical services; safety and accident prevention, occupational diseases and protective equipment; adjustment of festivals and national holidays; administration of welfare and fines fund; education and recreational activities; production and thrift of savings; implementation and review of decisions reached at meetings of WCs (Prasad, 1973; Michael, 1984; Sherlekar et al. 1986; Varandhani, 1989; Sharma and Chauhan, 1989; Vishwa Nath, 1992; Mankidy, 1995).

Composition and Functions of WCs

Alexander (1972) who studied WCs in Manorama Cloth Company, a Textile firm in India, says that the WC in the company, consisted of twenty members, ten elected by the workers and ten nominated by the management. Chairman of the Committee is the representative of management and Vice-chairman is the representative of the worker. WC meets on an average eight times a year and attendance in the meeting showed an upward trend. The working conditions are the major concern of WC. But on occasions it also discussed issues such as employment of temporary workers, bonus, production, efficiency which were outside the purview of WCs according to Industrial Disputes Act, 1947. Pylee (1975) who studied WC in Aluminum Industries Limited in Kundara says that, the WC in this firm consisted of equal number of members elected by the workmen and those nominated by the company. The Chairman of the Committee is selected on an alternative basis for one year. The functions of the Committee are purely related to grievances such as promotions, transfer, welfare amounts, advance, holiday, wages, housekeeping, payment of wages. Sarikwal's (1990) study of WC in Modipon Limited Co., a private sector undertaking in Modinagar revealed that the WC in this firm consisted of twelve elected members of the management and twelve co-opted members of the management. The Chairman of the Committee is management representative and Secretary of the Committee is workmen representative and the tenure of the Committee is one year. The functions of the Committee relate to welfare, hygiene, cleanliness, canteen, games, excursion, tours, festival gifts, dress and so forth. Nadkarni (1990) who studied WC in a Pune Factory says that, WC in this factory consisted of six workers' representatives and equal number of management executives. The Committee performs functions relating to wage, overtime allowances, issues of upgrading workers and the like.

Progress of WCs

In 1951 there were 1,142 WCs, their number rose to 2,574 in 1959-60, to 3,133 in 1965-66 and to 3,129 (873 in Central Sector and 2,256 in States) in 1970. Besides, there were 435 Production Committees and 370 Joint Committees in States in 1970. Thus, the total number in 1970 was 3,934 in all. Till the end of 1975, in India, there were established 2,285 WCs. Out of these 766 came under the Central Sector while 1,819

Committees were in the areas of State. The greatest number came under West Bengal numbering 870. At the end of 1983 WCs were functioning in 583 establishments and by 1990 this figure had fallen drastically to 530 (Vasudevan and Ghosh, 1985-86; Sharma and Chauhan, 1989; Mankidy, 1995).

Ineffectiveness or Failure of WCs

WCs did not function effectively. The Government of India realized it. According to the Second Five Year Plan, 1956, a major hindrance in the way of effective functioning of WCs is the lack of clear cut demarcation between their responsibilities and the responsibilities of trade unions operating in the field. The Government of India, subsequently made an attempt to evaluate the functioning of the WCs. It was revealed that these Committees were not functioning effectively, and could not achieve their expected goal. While managements were cold, the trade unions were unhappy with WCs. Nothing constructive did turn out. Factors which impeded the smooth working of the Committee in some undertakings were lack of appreciation by labour and management of the functions and significance of the Committee, illiteracy among the workers and opposition by trade unions to these Committees owing or inter-union rivalry. Other reasons for the failure of WCs are : lack of interest shown by workers; opposition by the middle management who are not represented on the WCs; general indifference by the management; incompetent workers' representatives. Thus, the idea of WCs was sound, but in practice it rarely worked out as intended by Industrial Disputes Act, 1947 (Prasad, 1975; Chhabra et al, 1977; Michael, 1984; Sherlekar et al, 1986; Vishwa Nath, 1992).

Ineffective functioning of WCs led to the setting up of some other following machineries of WPM.

Joint Management Councils (JMCs)

The Industrial Policy Resolution of 1956, adopted by the

Government of India, had sought some joint consultation between workers and management as a means for maintaining industrial peace and improving industrial relations. The resolution envisaged for a joint consultation between the workers and management. The Second Five-Year Plan sought to translate the spirit of this part of the Government Resolution in the statement on labour policy. The Third Five Year Plan opined that, for the peaceful evolution of economic system on a democratic basis, it is essential that WPM should be accepted as a fundamental principle and urgent need. To give a concrete shape to this idea of workers' participation, the scheme of Joint Management Councils was accepted as an effective measure for promoting joint consultation between the workers and the management. Indian Labour Conference of July 1957 appointed a small Sub-Committee of four persons each from the employees and workers group and from the Government to work out the details of the scheme. The recommendations of Sub-Committee were discussed by a seminar on Labour – Management Cooperation held at New Delhi on 31st January and 1st February, 1958. In order to review the progress of the scheme, another seminar on labour management was held in March, 1960. As the pilot stage was already over, it was recommended that the scheme should be extended to as many units as possible. The Third Plan, in its approach to the problem of industrial relations, elaborated the policy of associating labour more and more with management and accepted the progressive extension of the scheme of JMCs as a major programme. The Fourth Plan also declared that Joint Management ought to be the main element in the structure of industrial relations. The Government by announcing a scheme for WPM in industry at the Shop-floor and Plant level through resolution on 30th October, 1975, modified JMC and named it as Joint Council. In every industrial unit employing 500 or more workers, there shall be a Joint Council for the whole unit. Only such persons who are actually engaged in the unit shall be members of the Joint Council. The Joint Council shall function for a period of two years.

The Chief Executive of the unit shall be the Chairman of the Joint Council and there shall be a Vice-chairman who will be nominated by worker-members of the Council. The Joint Council shall meet at least once in a quarter. Every decision of the Joint Council shall be on the basis of consensus and not by a process of voting and shall be binding on employees and workmen and shall be implemented within one month unless otherwise stated in the decision itself (Mongia, 1980; Vishwa Nath, 1984; Singh and Sadhu, 1988; Vishwanath, 1992).

Composition and Functions of JMCs

Aziz (1980) who studied JMC in 8 units in Karnataka is of the view that there is equal membership for labour and management with regard to the composition of Joint Council, but there is no uniform number of representatives across the units. The Chairman of the Council is normally management representative and Vice-chairman is workers' representatives. No outsider is allowed to be a member of the Council. The functions of the Council are related to production, efficiency, optimum use of raw materials, functions of Shop Council which have a bearing on another shop, matter emanating from Shop Councils which remain unresolved, development of manpower and training, general health, welfare and safety measures, work planning, target achievement. Vishnu Gopal (1984) in his study on JMC in Diesel Locomotive Works (DLW), a public sector undertaking in Varanasi says that JMC consists of twelve members, six each consisting of management and workers' representatives. The Chairman and Secretary belong to management side and Vice-chairman belongs to workers' side. In DLW the JMC performs the functions prescribed by the Government of India which are mentioned by Aziz in his study on JMC in eight units in Karnataka. But JMC in DLW has subjected itself to certain limitations such as, the JMC will function purely as an advisory body, it will not discuss matters concerning pay-scales, allowances, disciplinary action and such other matters pertaining to individual Railway servants, the Chairman will decide whether any subject will be discussed in the meeting or not. Varandhani (1989) studied JMC in four enterprises (both public and private), three situated in Bombay and one in Delhi. The JMC in Hindustan Insecticides, Delhi consisted of six members, three being representatives of the management and three of the employees. In Pattanwala and Company, Bombay, it consisted of thirteen members, seven being the representatives of management including the Secretary of the Council and six being the representatives of workers. The functions of the Council in Hindustan Insecticides Limited related to administration of welfare measures, supervision of safety measures, operation of vocation training and apprenticeship schemes, preparation of schedules of working hours, breaks during working hours and off days, payment of rewards by company for valuable suggestions received from the employees and any other matter as may be agreed upon. In Bombay Silk Mills, Bombay, it related to improving of the working and living conditions of the workers, improving the productivity of the enterprise, encouraging suggestions from the workers and thereby creating a sense of participation in their minds and providing an authentic channel of communication between the Mill and its workers. In Pattanwala and Company, Bombay, the functions of the Council were related to absenteeism, productivity, welfare of the workers, safety measures, improved quality of goods manufactured, working hours and improved working conditions of work.

Progress of JMCs

During 1965 and 1966, a number of individual undertakings had entered into agreement with their unions for setting up JMCs and on this basis they were included in the lists of units which had set up JMCs. In most cases the Councils did not start functioning and, in 1969, the names of these units were deleted from the list. This accounted for the significant fall-in the number of JMCs from 1969. Though

Government made repeated efforts to promote JMCs, the JMCs could not progress much. The reasons attributed for slow progress of JMCs are: that workers' propensity to participate is low and/or the management and the employees indifference to participatory culture; that the JMCs are only consultative bodies and have no effective role in the vital decision making processes at the enterprise level; that the JMCs have no jurisdiction to discuss and take decision on the substantive issues of importance to workers such as wages, bonus, industrial grievances and other conflict prone issues falling within the ambit of CB; that there is an inherent conflict between the trade unions and management representatives. This consciousness of conflict and divergence of interests exists not only in the private sector but also in the public sector. Even the National Commission on Labour (1969:345) too noted the failure of the JMCs and observed: "There does not appear to be much support for the institution of JMCs in their present form. Even where the Councils existed, they are reported to be ineffective and their functioning unsatisfactory in many cases".

The field studies conducted by Mhetras (1966) and Sheth (1972) present the picture of the actual working of the JMCs in some selected enterprises. Mhetra's study covered five JMCs in Bombay which tried to present a picture of the functioning of the JMCs and their impact on labour management relations. This study brings out very clearly the reservations with which employers and workers treated the scheme and the negligible impact made by the latter on productivity, workers' welfare and the overall industrial relations situations in the plant. Based on the studies of six units Sheth concluded that the JMC experiment worked some what better where joint consultation had been voluntarily introduced before the JMC experiment than where joint consultation was introduced in the form of JMC on the basis of the tripartite recommendation.

Very few studies have reported the proper functioning or positive progress of JMCs. Report on the working of Joint Management Councils published by the Department of Labour and Employment (1965:8) says that "one remarkable result of the setting up of Joint Councils has been to see a understanding between the management and the workers in regard to several aspects of their day-to-day relationship. Both management and the workers have come to appreciate the difficulties and problems of one another. The management has become more sympathetic towards workers and willing to lend ear to their views. The evaluation studies have revealed better industrial relations, a more stable labour force, increased productivity, reduction in waste, better profits in most of the units in which Joint Management Councils have worked successfully". Further, a study by a researcher on JMC in Southern Chemicals and Fertilizers Limited says that the establishment of the Joint Management Council in the company brought in an increased awareness on the part of the employees regarding the problems of the enterprise. The questions raised by the workers usually displayed an intelligent awareness of the various problems of the industry and an earnest desire to extend cooperation by advancing valuable suggestions for their solution (Pylee, 1975; Chabbra et al, 1977; Sherlekar et al, 1986; Varandhani, 1989; Mongia, 1989; Sarma, 1990; Vishwa Nath, 1992; Kumar, 1992).

Suggestions for Making the Scheme a Success

The successful functioning of any Joint Council depends on, management's willingness to give all information connected with the working of the industry and workers' responsibility to handle that information with full confidence, establishing similar Councils at lower levels functioning like subordinate Councils, willingness on the part of the Trade Union to not to bring labour disputes in the Council, educating workers and practicing employee counseling, lively interest on the part of management, workers and trade unions and provision for the recognition of one representative trade union (Pylee 1975; Sherlekar et al, 1986; Varandhani, 1989).

Workers' Directors

When it became clear that the earlier experiments were not succeeding, the Government considered the possibility of introducing Participative Management at the policy making level of the enterprises by inducting Worker Directors on to the Boards of organizations. By this time it was probably felt that participation, to be effective and meaningful, had to be at the level where policy decisions were made. This idea was reflected in a piece of legislation enacted in 1970 as soon as the 14 major Commercial banks in the country were nationalized. The Government of India introduced a scheme for appointing workers' representative on the Board of Management in the year 1976. The scheme provided that the Council would resolve problems at the Shop-floor level but in case no consensus or agreement was reached, the same was to be referred to the Board of Management. The workers' representative is to be nominated by the recognized union in the undertaking and it is required to submit a panel of names of three persons from whom one person is to be selected for nomination as Director. A person to be eligible for nomination should have attained the age of 25 years and he should have a minimum of 5 years service in the undertaking and should not attain the age of superannuation during his term of appointment as Director (Annual Report, 1975-76; Varandhani, 1989; Mankidy, 1995).

Pros and Cons of the Scheme

One of the useful methods of motivating the workers to have sense of sincerity to the establishment is to give them the highest honour in the establishment by providing them representation on the Board of Directors. This representation will make them to realize their responsibility towards the concern. The Employee Director can serve as a desirable link between labour and management. The Employee Director can present the labour problems in the Board in the right perspective before it takes a serious form and the labour problems can be amicably settled in the Board meetings. Thus, Employee Director can represent and safeguard the labour interests and viewpoints. This method of participation will certainly protect labour interest and give a sense of security as well as justice to labour, since policy, financial and other important matters are discussed here (Sherlekar et al, 1986; Varandhani, 1989; Nadkarni, 1990).

However, a few limitations of this scheme have come to be stressed. A Worker Director would be in a minority and thus his views would carry little weight with the Board. Moreover, the Worker Director is not properly trained in the management function. Though he is an effective leader, he may not necessarily be an effective manager. As he lacks the qualities of a good manager, he will only hold an obstructing view and he may not be in a position of judiciously deciding the short-term effects and long term effects of a new proposal. Since the Worker Director is the representative of a trade union, he will always take a biased view for the benefit of the workers rather than looking the interests of the organization, which has certain responsibilities towards the society. The Worker Director will merely act as the mouth piece of the union. Moreover, once the Worker Director identifies himself with the cause of management either at the top level or down the line, he cannot act contrary to the managements' decision because of the principles of collective responsibility on the management.

Thus, employee representation on the Board is still a matter of controversy. Public sector experience in India in this direction is not quite heartening because labour has not been associated with management at all levels. Despite the Industrial Policy Resolution of 1983 not even a single public sector undertaking has implemented workers' participation at the Board level. Trade union leaders as well as the ordinary workers are of the view that the Workers' Directors are not permitted to participate in actual decision making process rather their role is that of information sharing only. The trade union leaders are of the view that the main role which is played by the unions is the protest role in order to protect the interest of the workers and Workers' Directors will betray this cause rather than further strengthening it. The appointment of workers as Director on the Board of Management involves numerous problems namely, selection of workers to the Board of Directors would lead to many complications because various pressure groups inside and outside trade union try to claim representation in the Board. The political affiliation of trade union is likely to be a vital consideration and the choice of Worker Director will create difficult situations for the labour leader as to who will occupy such position (Sethi, 1973; Chabbra et al, 1977; Lakshamanna, 1988; Varandhani, 1989).

Because of its limitations, few studies have suggested that, workers' representatives should not be involved in Boards where policy decisions are made. Experience has shown that it is difficult for them to exercise, influence and make any effective contribution in the decision making process. As such, Sethi (1973) suggests that in order to eliminate such problems, workers should be involved in a Joint Council immediately adjacent to Board so that before the Board's decisions are made for implementation, agreement with workers is obtained.

Suggestions for Making the Scheme a Success

A scheme of nominating Worker Director in the Board of Management can succeed only if the management and trade unions change their attitude toward the programme. The scheme of representation of the Worker Director will be successful only if the management provides necessary facilities and training in business management to the workers elected or nominated by the trade unions. Workers should be selected by the recognized union. Representation should be only on the basis of their educational qualifications, efficiency and sense of responsibility. The Workers' Director should be treated equal and on par with other Directors irrespective of his designation or status in the enterprise. In pursuance of the recommendations contained in the Administrative Reforms Commissions Report on Public Sector Undertakings, Government has drawn up certain guidelines with regard to the participation of Worker Director on the Board of company. The scheme envisages that the Worker Director should continue to be a workman on the Shop-floor, subject to normal rules of discipline of the undertaking concerned. He should not hold the position if he ceases to be a worker or if the union nominating him ceases to be recognized before the expiry of the full-term of such Director (Sheralekar et al, 1986; Mamoria and Mamoria, 1988; Varandhani, 1989).

Shop-floor Councils (SFCs)

One of the items in 20 Point Economic Programme (1975) relates to the introduction of schemes for workers' participation in industry, particularly at the Shop-floor level and in production programmes, in pursuance of the same, the Government announced a scheme for WP in industry at the Shop-floor and Plant level through a resolution on 30th Oct. 1975. The resolution says that in every industrial unit employing 500 or more workmen, the employer shall constitute a Shop Council for each department or shop, or one Council for more than one department or shop considering the number of workmen employed in different departments or shops. Each Council shall consist of an equal number of representatives of employers and workers. The employees' representatives shall be nominated by the management and must consist of persons from the unit concerned. All the representatives of workmen shall be from amongst the workers actually engaged in the department or the shop concerned (Vishnu Gopal, 1984; Singh and Sadhu, 1988).

Composition and Functions of SFCs

Though the resolution says that, there should be equal representation to employers and workers in the Council, Aziz (1980) in his study on WPM in eight units in Karnataka has found that there is an unequal representation on the Shop Councils - the inequality being disadvantageous to workers in some cases and to management in others. The Chairman of the Council is management representative and Vice-chairman is workers' representative. No outsider is allowed to be a member. Further, he says that the number of representatives varies not only across the units but within the unit it varies even across the Councils. Aziz has come to identify following factors as relating to functions of SFCs: productivity, elimination of wastage, achievement of targets, reduction of absenteeism, general discipline, physical conditions, safety and welfare measures, management and workers' interaction. Vishnu Gopal (1984) studied SFCs in Diesel Locomotive Works, Varanasi. His study revels that there is parity or equal representation of workers and management in SFCs. But the number of representatives varies from one Shop Council to another within the D.L.W. The Chairman and Secretary belong to management side and Vice-chairman belongs to workers' side. Tenure of the Council is two years and meetings are not held regularly. D.L.W. management has incorporated in its SFC constitution all the functions prescribed by the Government of India which are mentioned above in Aziz's (1980) work review, but it has subjected them to certain limitations not prescribed by the Government of India. They are: the SFC will function partly as an advisory body, it will not discuss matters concerning pay scales, allowances, disciplinary action and such other matters pertaining to individual Railway servants, the Chairman will decide whether any subject will be discussed in the meeting or not. Nadkarni (1990) in a study on 'The Practice of Participative Management' in a public sector drug company says that the Shop-floor Committees find the representation of six to seven members from each of the management and worker categories. Her study comes to identify following as the functions of SFCs: production facilities, storage facilities, material economy, operational problems, wastage control, safety problems, quality improvement, cleanliness, monthly targets and production schemes, cost reduction programmes, formulation and implementation of working system, working conditions and welfare measures.

Quality Circles (QCs)

The basic idea of Quality Circles originated in USA. But it was Japan which initiated real involvement of rank and file employees in QC activities. A system of Participative Management in which small group of employees meet voluntarily and regularly to identify, analyze and solve their quality problems and take corrective actions for better results, are popularly known as QCs in modern management literature. QC is a very recent phenomenon in India. QC activities started in India in the 1980s. The spectacular success of QC in Japanese industries led to the promotion of the same in the rest of the world including India. One of the Indian public sector giant Bharat Heary Electrical Limited (BHEL) in its Hyderabad unit implemented this concept first in the year 1989. BHE Ltd. which employs 18,000 workers in its various units spread over the country has about 1,600 QCs. About 200 Indian organizations have experimented this concept (Saibaba et al, 1990).

In April 1982, the Quality Circle Forum of India (QCFI) was formed in Secunderabad which is actively involved in sharing the experiences of the Indian industries in QC efforts, collection of national data on QCs, development of a suitable methodology for Indian organizations, organizations of national conventions. Quality Circle India, a quarterly Journal is being published by QCFI since Oct, 1983 (Dey, 1988).

Composition of QCs

As for as the composition of QC is concerned, it consists of members who voluntarily come together to improve their work environment by evolving solutions to their work related problems (Gupta, 1989). Bhuyan and Nath (1989) who have studied QC activity at TELCO, Jamshedpur says that, QC is a small group consisting of eight to ten workers, to perform voluntarily QC activities within the same group. Thus, there is no exact number as for as its composition is concerned. It differs from one firm to another, depending upon the number of employees volunteering themselves to join it.

Functions of QCs

Gupta (1989) in her study on 'Quality Circles - Impact on Organizational Culture' in Maruti Udyog Limited, Gurgaon comes to identify following as the functions of QC: improving the work environment, promoting the climate of team work, promoting work related discipline reflected by factors such as punctuality, cleanliness, orderliness. Bhuyan and Nath (1989) in their study on 'Quality Circle For Continuous Quality Improvement' have held view that, QC activities need not only be product related. It can be quality of process, quality of work life, quality of everything they perform. The prime objective of QC is to contribute to the improvement and development of the organization and in the process improve the quality of work life too.

Merits of QCs

The merits of QC are: it contributes to the improvement and development of the organization, improves quality of work life, leads to job satisfaction, team work, creativity, innovation, improves communication, morale, has positive impact on organizational culture (Gupta, 1989; Bhuyan and Nath, 1989; Saibaba, 1990; Hill, 1991).

Like other schemes, QC scheme is also becoming a failure in Indian Organizations. Kher (1990) who examined the working of QCs in India came to the conclusion that they have not brought about the expected results. Reasons for the failure of QCs are apathy of workers in the working of trade unions and the lack of honesty and sincerity both amongst trade unions and the management.

The success of QC scheme depends on commitment of the parties concerned and on careful ground work. It also depends on size of the Circle which should neither be too small nor be too large (Dey, 1988).

Suggestion Scheme

Management initiative to consult the workers and inviting suggestions from them to improve the production process and management practice is known as Suggestion Scheme. Novel ideas regarding improving material handling, safety measures, production planning and quality, cost control and other things will be put forward by workers. This is another mechanism of Participative Management (Chabbra et al, 1977).

Prasad (1973) says that the managements' recognition of workers' contribution creates in them a sense of participation and helps in improving the industrial relations climate. Their interest in work and the affairs of the company is also increased. In many of the public sector undertakings, Suggestion Schemes have been adopted successfully. In Hindustan Air Craft Limited, 'Cash Your Ideas Scheme' is run under the Suggestion Scheme which gives cash awards for the useful suggestions made by employees. In Dec. 1963, a supervisor invented a method by which a certain part of an aero engine could be repaired in the factory itself instead of sending it to the U.K. as was being done earlier. Hence he was awarded a prize of Rs. 2,000 under the 'Cash Your Ideas Scheme'.

Sarikwal (1990) who studied WPM in Modipon Ltd., Modingar (U.P.) states that a Suggestion Committee has been constituted in the plant in order to make the workers feel that they are part of the managerial process and as reported by the management, this Committee has been functioning satisfactorily over the years.

This type of participation is also criticized on many grounds. Since it includes written communication, motivation that comes from face to face interaction is absent. There is no joint deliberation of thinking in this type of participation. Thus, it has limited scope and value (Sherelkar et al, 1986).

IMPLICATIONS OF WPM

Irrespective of the different meanings and machineries that WPM comes to represent in the above context, there has been a universal consensus among the management and social scientists as well as among the policy makers in all the Democratic, Socialist and Welfare States about the positive consequences and hence the desirability of PM. The positive implications of PM need no emphasis in view of its being widely accepted as a positive step toward democratizing and humanizing work places and thereby contributing to the industrial development. There are several areas of industrial operation which could experience the positive effects and desired results owing to a meaningful and effective implementation of WPM. They are, productivity, climate of industrial relations, democratization of work place, morale, commitment, job satisfaction and identification.

Participation is acquiring greater importance in work organizations over a few decades in the past. During this period, the theory underlying participation and its many benefits have been transformed into actual practice and it has been proven rather conclusively that participation will work and will result in advantages to both employees and employers (Huneryager and Heckmann, 1967). It is opined that only by participation through their own organizations, can the workers' interests in terms of their employment be protected and only through participation man's labour can be made humane (Walker, 1973). Further, a number of scientific studies have emphatically concluded that industrial progress and prosperity depend on workers' devotion and dedication which ultimately depend on democratization of industrial management, allowing further right to workers' to participate in it wholeheartedly (Srivastava, 1984). In vast literature on management, participation has been hailed, on theoretical grounds, as the most appropriate solution to the problems of alienations in modern industrial societies, as the best method of facilitating the development of socially aware and public spirited people, as a stepping stone to the fulfillment of certain higher echelons of needs which are deemed to be common to all men and finally as a means of overcoming major social disadvantages which are consequent upon non-democratic modes of decision-making (Poole, 1975).

Vishnu Gopal in his 'Industrial Democracy in India' (1984) focused on the impact of participation on welfare aspect and on reduction in sense of alienation among workers. He found that, 19 percent of the workers' representatives, 10.4 percent of the mass of the workers, 55 percent of the management representatives held positive view about the impact of participation on welfare aspect. Similarly, 15.2 percent of the workers' representatives, 8.8 percent of the mass of the workers and 18.3 percent of the management representatives held positive opinion about the impact of participation for reduction in workers' sense of alienation.

Maier (1952) undertook a study to find out the effect of informal participation on a group of telephone repair workers and came to the conclusion that group participation in decision making could improve the performance of the group. It is noted that, the principle of WPM affords a self-realization in work and meets the psychological needs of workers at work by eliminating, to a large extent, any feeling of futility, isolation, and consequent frustration that they face in normal industrial setting (Mamoria and Mamoria, 1988). Keeping in view these positive implications, participation is being tried with varying aims - such as, to increase work satisfaction and decrease employees work apathy; to increase the efficiency, productivity and creativity in the enterprise; to bring the culture of democracy in the industry as an alternative model to the prevailing Collective Bargaining system (Bhatia, 1988). Further Madhusudhana Rao (1986) has identified the benefits of participation as: feeling of belongingness (37.0), sense of satisfaction in taking decision along with the managerial executives (27.8), checking implementation of irrational and one-sided approach of management (71.1), joint decision arrived at can be smoothly implemented by both the parties (37.0), checking extravagant and unproductive activities (16.0), and ensuring additional financial and non-financial benefits to the members (18.2). Stressing the positive impact of WPM, Likert (1961), Blake (1964), and McGregor (1960) have advocated that Participative Management is a management innovation capable of making positive contribution towards the health and effectiveness of the social organization of an enterprise. These findings appear quite logical viewed in the light of the psychological basis upon which employee participation rests. The psychologists have proven most conclusively that people are more creative, exhibit greater degrees of initiative, and become more responsible when they are given the opportunity to express themselves and share in the decision affecting them. This is true not only of our democratic society as a whole, but of industry as well. Therefore, industry must provide means for allowing employees to participate actively (Huneryager and Heckmann, 1967). Participation is also found to be associated with reduction in turnover, absenteeism and tardiness. Further, participation also leads to improved quality of managerial decisions. It is seldom possible for managers to have knowledge of all alternatives and all consequences related to the decisions which they must make. Participation tends to breakdown the barriers, making the information available to managers (Tennenbaum and Massarik, 1967).

Participation is especially important in motivating people to accept change, a constant pressure on all of us in our dynamic society. Participation is helpful both in planning and installing change. When employees understand the objectives and content of a change, they are confident that management has good intentions. In participation, individuals are given an opportunity to direct their creativity toward the objectives of the group. Participation encourages people to accept responsibility for an activity (Davis, 1967). Further, Likert (1967) states that, increased participation and responsibility in decision making tend to develop organizational loyalty, confidence, trust, favourable attitude towards supervisors, low absenteeism, low turnover, high productivity and so forth and thereby tends to eliminate dysfunctional behaviour.

According to Anthony (1978), the advantages of Participative Management are: better decisions, improved productivity, improved morale and job satisfaction, reduced tardiness, turnover and absences, better communication and conflict resolution, greater readiness to accept change, more peaceful manager-subordinate and manager union relations, increased employee commitment to the organization, greater trust of management, greater ease in the management of subordinates, improved quality of managerial decisions, improved upward communications and improved teamwork. The scheme has economic, psychological, social and ethical objectives. Economic objective of the scheme is to raise workers' level of motivation. The social objective of the scheme is to provide the workers with a sense of importance, pride and accomplishment, freedom and opportunity for expression, feeling of belongingness to the place of work and sense of workmanship and creativity. The ethical objective of the scheme is to develop the workers' personality and to recognize human dignity (Kumar, 1992).

Thus, there are numerous positive implications of WPM,

that have been testified by several empirical studies. An attempt is made in the following pages to review the studies that have come to identify each of these positive implications of WPM for the industry, for the workers and for the society at large.

Productivity and Participation

It is an universally recognized empirical fact that WPM leads to increase in productivity. It assures hard work and devotion on the part of workers to the industry. With WPM, there exists in the workers' mind an urge for status and importance in the organization in which he works. If he can be made conscious of this fact that his purpose of work is linked with the broad purpose of enterprise, this feeling makes him a proud link in the organization and generates in him a desire to work. This human desire to co-operate is the most promising source of productivity (Varandhani, 1989).

Aziz (1980) who conducted a study on WPM (Shop and Joint Councils) in eight factories in Karnataka, says that there are various ways of improving production and productivity in the plant and the managements have profitably used these methods in the past. But what is forgotten in the process is the need for recognizing the fact that better results are ensured if workers' co-operation is enlisted. It is in this perspective, the scheme of WPM has involved workers in decision making on the question of improving production and productivity in the shops. The listed objective of the Shop Councils is to identify areas of low productivity and to arrive at a consensus on ways and means of improving productivity in such areas.

To be productive and efficient, an organization or an industry needs the ability, initiative and cooperation of every member more than any previous system of production. Human resources are the greatest assets of an enterprise. The major incentives to productivity and efficiency are social and moral rather than financial (Drucker, 1964). Therefore, in existing set up of modern, large-scale, mechanized and rationalized industrial production, mere commands, directions, guidance and training as envisaged under scientific management schemes, will fail to achieve the maximization of production without proper utilization of labour, avoidance of loss of man days as a result of industrial conflicts and without the active, healthy and enthusiastic cooperation, collaboration and involvement of the workers. WPM is thus no longer a debatable issue. It is now the only form of industrial administration and management, which is the call of the existing socio-economic order (Vishnu Gopal, 1984).

Vishnu Gopal (1984) who has undertaken a Sociological study of the organizational structure and functioning of the new scheme of Shop and Joint Councils as working in one of the biggest Public Sector Undertakings of India, found that on an average 30.6 percent of the workers' representatives, 14.7 percent of the mass of the workers and 9.9 percent of the management representatives held positive opinion about the impact of the participation on production, productivity and efficiency.

Resenberg and Rosenstein (1980) have studied effects of worker participation on productivity in a unionized foundry and concluded that an increase in the level of participative activity was associated with an increase in productivity and was more important in this respect than a group bonus plan tied to productivity. Similarly, Coch and French's (1948) study in a Pyjama factory has revealed that participation could result in greater productivity. Experiment by Morse and Reimer (1956) also revealed the fact that productivity would increase with increased role of workers in decision making. A study by Seashore and Bowers (1963) of a Manufacturing company found that participation had positive correlation with employee productivity. In a study of ten public sector and private sector organizations by Sahu (1985), the respondents of both the sectors identified increase in productivity along with improvement in job satisfaction, reduction in waste and decrease in absenteeism as number one objective of WPM.

Pylee (1975) in his study found evidence of increased productivity since the time the Joint Council was constituted. In his study of another plant, Pylee found that with the formation of the Emergency Production Committee in 1963 there was all-round improvement in all the activities connected with production. This also supported the results of the Hawthorne studies at Western Electric Company indicating that participation is a significant factor in improving productivity (Mayo, 1941). A study of Lawrence and Smith (1955) also indicated that participative framework leads to increase in productivity.

Bragg and Andrews (1973) in their study of laundry workers in a hospital set up three groups to know the impact of participation. In one group participation was practiced and in the other two groups no participation was practiced. At the end of fourteen months, productivity had increased by almost 50 percent in the participation group and absences were reduced by 59 percent in the same group. In the two comparison groups with no participation, productivity had declined slightly during the study.

In a pioneering study in the human relations perspective, Roethlisberger (1941) and his associates sought to show the relationship of physical change in environment and output. In the course of their experiments, new relationships, many of them involving participation developed between workers and supervisors and workers and experimenters. The results indicated that these social changes improved both productivity and morale. Participation seemed to be a significant cause, though not the whole cause of these improvements. As such, Guest and Fatchett (1974) state that by giving the workers more freedom to pursue desirable outcomes, production level can be raised.

Thus, the significance of WPM in relation to productivity has been empirically documented by several studies providing justification for advocating greater areas under and extent of WPM. However, the impact of WPM has been equally strong and positive on the climate of industrial relations.

PM and Climate of Industrial Relations

The system of PM, if introduced properly, is assumed to promote industrial peace and harmony leading to rise in production (Varandhani, 1989). Vishnu Gopal (1984) is of the opinion that WPM improves industrial relations and thereby promote industrial harmony and peace. In his study on Shop and Joint Councils of Diesel Locomotive Works, Varanasi, he found that 30.9 percent of the workers' representatives, 15.5 percent of the mass of the workers and 27.1 percent of the management representatives held positive opinion about the impact of participation on industrial relations.

For achieving the goal of smooth and uninterrupted industrial growth, industrial peace based on mutual harmony between employers and employees, is very much essential. Industrial peace in turn can be built up on close cooperation and coordination between workers and employers. This calls for active participation of workers in management. In the recent times, WPM is looked upon as a modern and scientific approaches to maintain peaceful industrial relations because of inherent qualities of this approach and constant mutual contact, as well as mutual thinking between both the parties for removing all the minor and major misunderstandings between them on the spot and creating a sort of mutual good will between them. It is stated that, this scheme definitely has the potentialities of bringing industrial peace permanently in the national economy by creating the climate of mutual faith, mutual trust, mutual understanding, respects for one another and genuine interest for reciprocal wellbeing and a perennial welfare (Vishwa Nath, 1992).

Pylee (1975) who studied the functioning of Joint Management Council in the Southern Chemicals and Fertilizers Limited, found that ever since the inception of the Council and during the period the Council had functioned, there was uninterrupted industrial peace and no man days were lost due to industrial strife.

Alexander (1972) found empirical support to his hypothesis that an industrial organization in which Participative Management is institutionalized is likely to have a greater level of organizational health and effectiveness than the one in which this is not the case. As such, Participative Management could be looked upon as a lubricating mechanism which smoothens the strained labour management relations in an organization.

Anthony (1978) based on a study states that Participative Management leads to more peaceful manager-subordinate and manager-union relations. The use of participation tends to bring into the open any concerns the group might have. The firm finds that union-management relations become more peaceful as the union participates where appropriate in managerial decision making. Instead of having a strictly adverse relationship, the firm and the union work together to achieve common ends. This is also achieved through better communication and conflict resolution. All organizations experience conflict. Conflict is healthy for an organization, if it is managed and channeled to bring about needed change. Participative Management provides a communication forum for resolving conflict in the open and for channeling it for creative purposes in the organization. Instead of festering and acting in a dysfunctional manner, conflict is brought out into the open and resolved within a participatory frame work.

A breakdown in industrial relations can sometimes be a stimulus to the introduction of worker participation. Since such breakdown in industrial relations are seen as being very costly, the improvement of industrial relations and the promotion of calm and peaceful relations can be a specific objective (Guest and Fatchett, 1974).

It is believed that the social purpose of WPM is to reduce industrial disputes and to create positive conditions and atmosphere in which industrial harmony and peace can develop. It cuts at the very root of industrial conflict and removes or at least minimizes the conflict between the parties through cooperation and creates in the workers an abiding self confidence and a sense of responsibility in the work and develops in them social amity (Mamoria, 1971). Further, participation leads to increased understanding throughout the organization. People learn that others have problems besides themselves. If the workers are invited to share in these problems and to work towards common solutions, a greater degree of organizational balance occurs because of decreased misunderstanding and individual and group conflict (Huneryager and Heckmann, 1967; Tannenbaum and Massarik, 1967).

Thus, WPM undoubtedly has positive implications for the climate of industrial relations, as testified by the works reviewed.

Democratization of Workplace

WPM was initially conceived as a devise and instrument of democratizing and humanizing work place which have inherent benefits for the work organization.

Participation as a form of power equalization, gives subordinates greater autonomy which is satisfying, especially for those who have greater need for independence (Strauss, 1963). For over half a century, Participatory Management has been presented as the 'answer' to the twin problems of productivity growth and work humanization (Heckscher, 1988). Thus, participation has a broader objective that is, democratization of workplace or even an implicit objective of social ownership over means of production (Hameed, 1973). The ideological aim of workers' participation includes humanizing work, that is, ensuring the human dignity of the worker by making him feel that he is not a mere cog in a machine, but a participant in decisions affecting his work and working environment (Balundagi and Bagali, 1994). A meaningful participation of employees in management may lead to humanization of industry and provide a sense of importance, pride and accomplishment to employees. By facilitating democratization in the work processes it may offer to employees an opportunity to use their knowledge of work which may otherwise remain unutilized. By offering freedom and opportunity for expression, it may also create a feeling of belonging to the workplace and organization (Sarma, 1990). WPM may ultimately result in a permanent fight for more democracy in organizations and in society as a whole (Szell, 1990). It makes the work place more democratic by giving employees more influence over aspects of the corporate structure (Toole, 1973). By giving scope for self expression and by ensuring workers' control over the conditions under which they work, it democratizes the industrial milieu and ensures equlitarianism in the process (Vishnu Gopal, 1984).

It may further be noted that as complex organizations are pluralist entities, industrial democracy is a meaningful concept. Because pluralist bodies contain elements of conflict and consensus, power and authority, participative schemes which permit an extension of democracy, can also pursue improvements in organizational effectiveness (Hebden and Shaw, 1973). The term 'Industrial Democracy' generally refers to the democratization of industrial relations, and particularly of the relations between labour unions and management. There is, however, another aspect of industrial relations, namely, employer-employee relations. The ultimate goal of Industrial Democracy is to democratize fully the latter aspect of industrial relations in a given society. Hence, since the commencement of the industrial era, efforts have been made by management experts and behavioural scientists to evolve a system of industrial management wherein a climate of constructive cooperation between labour and management is fostered. Such efforts have led to the creation of considerable interests throughout the world, especially, during the last forty years or so in adopting democratic practices in industries in different forms-ranging from workers' control to some forms of simple information sharing, which have technically been termed as 'Industrial Democracy'. This is partly due to the understanding that democratic management does help in improving the performance of industries, and partly due to the faith that, political democracy cannot be sustained for long unless it is supplemented with democratic practices, in industrial spheres too. It is now believed that democracy in industry is not merely an utopia, but is indeed indispensable (Vishnu Gopal, 1984).

In a democratic society the demand for industrial democracy is a logical correlate of the urge to democratize all the major aspects of social life (Sheth, 1972); and the demand for WPM of the enterprises is a natural corollary of the process of democratization of industry; (Cole, 1957) which requires involvement of all ranks of employees in the process of managerial decision making and its implementation. Democratization at different levels of decision making and its implementation is expected to be a potent instrument in fostering climate of constructive cooperation within the industrial community and to improve the quality of performance of the enterprises (Vishnu Gopal,. 1984).

Industrial democracy by definition means democracy in industry characterized by equality, liberty, fraternity and social justice. It is the government of the partners in industry, for the partners in industry and by the partners in industry (Singh, 1977). It is manifested in features like self-government, power equalization and the rule of law (Pylee, 1975). Cooperation is different from Co-determination. In case of the former, the workers influence decisions but are not responsible for them, whereas in the latter case the workers have actual control and the authority for particular decisions (Shuchman, 1957). The inevitability of such cooperation lies in the fact that each party is dependent upon the other and can, as a matter of fact achieve the objective more effectively if it wins the support of the other (Chamberlain, 1951). The concept of industrial democracy in India appears in perfect harmony with the socialist ideals of the Government professing to establish an egalitarian society. The idea augurs well with the policy proclamations made out by the Government in matters relating to industrial workers (Thakur and Sethi, 1972). Far more pragmatic reason was the country's need for greater industrial productivity coupled with considerations of peaceful change in the economic system to attain the goals of a Socialist democracy. Consistent with these ideological imperatives, several attempts have been made to democratize relations between labour and management and thereby extend democracy to the work place (Srivastava, 1990; Kumar, 1992).

Morale

The results of the Hawthorne studies conducted at Western Electric Company, near Chicago, during the late 1920s and early 1930s, in order to know the impact of environmental factors on the job and work output of the employee group, indicated that participation was a significant factor in improving both productivity and morale (Mayo, 1941). Better decisions and improved productivity brought about through meaningful participation should improve morale and job satisfaction of employees (Anthony, 1978). In Hebden and Shaw's study (1977) of medium sized Textile firms in the north of England, the General Manager held the view, after only one year of operation, that the new participation scheme had a direct influence to the good on morale and communications and had contributed towards an improved profit position and in turn to employee earnings.

Participation affords a means of building some of the human values needed in a group. It can create an asset in morale so that when necessary orders are given people will respond more cooperatively because they are participating in their group (Davis, 1967). Locke and Schweiger (1979) have held the view that there are numerous mechanisms through which participation in decision making may produce high morale and performance.

WPM gives employees more power which enhances their status. This enhanced status dimension leads to improvement in morale and productivity (Blumberg, 1968).

Job Satisfaction

Job satisfaction has generally been understood as another positive outcome of WPM. Vroom (1960) says that, participation has positive effects on attitudes and motivation. It was further demonstrated that the magnitude of these effects is a function of certain personality traits of the participants. Authoritarians and persons with weak independence needs are apparently unaffected by opportunity to participate in making decision. On the other hand, equalitarians and those who have strong independence needs develop more positive attitude toward their job and greater motivation for effective performance through participation. It was also found that participation, apart from satisfying a person's needs to be valued and appreciated, gives him scope to participate in making decisions about wages, working hours and working conditions and thus to improve the work situation in these respects. Thus, participation satisfies the need for independence. Participation in making decisions increases the power of equality of the participant and thus leads to greater satisfaction for equalitarians than for authoritarians.

The study of Mann and Dent (1954) in an Electric Power Company, Jacobson (1951) in a Car Factory and Katz et al (1950) and Morse (1953) in an Insurance Company revealed that employees derive satisfaction from work if they work under employee oriented supervision.

Sahu's study (1985) rates improved job satisfaction as one of the prime objectives of WPM along with increased productivity, reduced waste and decreased absenteeism. Strauss (1963) says that participation permits members of the group to unfreeze their catharsis which may reduce the negative valence towards the task, and increase motivation for work. The Motivational Theory developed by Hergberg (1959), Hierarchy of Needs Theory developed by Maslow (1943) and Achievement Theory developed by McClelland (1965) also support Participative Management. McClelland (1965) says that an achievement motivated person seeks accomplishment for its own sake and works because of the sense of challenge.

Patchen (1970) based on his study at TVA, concluded that, along with other consequences, increased participation in institutional decision making leads to greater job satisfaction and work achievement, as well as greater individual integration into the organization. Blumberg (1968) says that, there is hardly a study in the entire literature which fails to demonstrate that satisfaction in work is enhanced or that other generally acknowledged beneficial consequences accrue from a genuine increase in worker's decision making power.

Argyle, Gardner and Cioffi (1958) compared the supervisors of 90 work groups on a number of items including five dimensions of supervisory behaviour. The result indicated that, supervisors in charge of highly productive groups were significantly more democratic and less punitive. Staff working under highly democratic leaders were significantly less likely to be absent. Therefore it appears from this study that democratic supervision is associated with high productivity and job satisfaction. Morse and Reimer (1956) studied white-collar employees in an Insurance company. A change programme in two divisions was designed to involve employees more extensively in decision making, whilst in a further two divisions hierarchical control was increased. This programme was continued for a year. As predicted, the autonomous group with democratic leadership showed an increase in job satisfaction in contrast to the hierarchically controlled group which showed a decrease. Francis and Milbourn Jr. (1980) states that Participative Management can show positive results in terms of profits and employee satisfaction. Studies further show participation to be a leading factor in getting people to accept changes. People who are consulted about changes, who are allowed to participate in decisions about the changes, are normally people who best adjust to such decisions. Hence, participation along these lines greatly facilitates individual adjustment and satisfaction (Huneryager and Heckmann, 1967). Singh and Pestonjee (1990) in their study on 'Effect of Job Involvement and Sense of Participation on Job Satisfaction' found that high participation group has shown a greater degree of job satisfaction in all areas of job satisfaction and overall job satisfaction.

Commitment

Coming to the commitment, WPM in essence is conceived as a device of sharing management authority with workmen as part of the strategy of creating a committed work force in industry (Aziz, 1980).

In a study carried out by Sahu (1985) in ten public and private sector organizations, the respondents belonging to managerial category identified 'increased employee commitment to the organization' as one of the five important objectives of participation. Further Sahu, in his study on a large Iron and Steel factories says that, the most positive gain from Joint Consultation, an important form of participation has been strengthening of the team spirit and the sense of belongingness to the organization. Siegel and Ruh (1973), from a sample of 2,500 employees in six American Manufacturing Organizations, found those who perceived greater influence over decisions affecting their jobs felt more involvement than did those who perceived less influence. A study by Lawler and Hackman (1969) of custodians indicate that a participatory framework produces significant increase in attendance over an autocratic management approach. According to researchers, this was because the group of custodians who were involved in participation were more knowledgeable of and committed to the plan and had more trust in the good intentions of management with regard to the plan.

Participation makes employees to commit themselves to the organization (Anthony, 1978). There are a number of advantages in letting subordinates participate in the decision process. Most importantly acceptance and commitment increase, since participation gives subordinates a sense of ownership in the decision, and this makes implementation of the decision much easier. Participation also increases downward communication and relieves the pressure for increased involvement that many managers receive from subordinates. Finally, letting people participate in decisions helps create a team atmosphere in which all members have increased commitment, not only to the decision but to each other (Anderson, 1984). The active involvement of the employees will lead to a firmer commitment to organizational goals with mutual benefits to the organization and to the individual (Francis and Milbourn Jr, 1980). Blumberg (1968) says that the participating worker is an involved worker, for his job becomes an extension of himself and by his decisions he is creating his work, modifying and regulating it. As he is more involved in his work, he becomes more committed to it, and being more committed, he naturally derives more satisfaction from it.

Identification

It is also noted that WPM breeds a stronger sense of closer identification. Participation means co-functioning, playing one's part in an integrative unity, contributing all that one is capable of to the good of the organization. Participation signifies workers' identification with the progress and development of business (Varandhani, 1989). The research of Huneryager and Heckmann (1967) and Blumberg (1968) have come to indicate that the level of identification increases with the degree of participation.

Thus, works reviewed above, have come to stress the positive implications and as such the desirability of WPM on the one hand and significance of WPM for the work organizations as well as the significance of an empirical study of WPM in an Indian context on the other. An attempt is made to review other works dealing with the determinants and effectiveness of WPM in the pages to follow.

It is indeed a fact proved beyond any empirical doubt that WPM has been an innovative intervention holding great promise and a practice of progressive and professional management of immense positive implications for the society and economy at large in general and each section of society associated with economic and industrial processes in particular. Having been a practice with great positive potential for management, workers and industry, it has come to be extensively researched upon by scientists across disciplines and on almost its every dimension, ramification and manifestation. Although an exhaustive review of enormous empirical literature focusing on diverse aspects of WPM in diverse contexts, particularly in a chapter of a book such as this, may appear impractical and infeasible, an attempt is made in the following pages to discuss major findings of a few landmark studies on a few aspects of WPM. Several empirical studies have focused on forms, levels, extent and areas of participation and review of the same is attempted here.

FORMS OF PARTICIPATION

The form of participation refers to the methods and systems by which workers participate in decision making (Wall and Lischeron, 1977). The 'form' or the way in which workers do participate in management varies due to differences in the level of management, the subjects or areas in which participation is sought, and the pattern of labour management relations. The forms or stages of participation refer to the same thing. The stages imply that participation proceeds from stage to stage, but in practice it is found that various forms or stages and levels of participation continue at the same time in a firm (Alexander, 1973; Vishwa Nath, 1992).

As for as forms of participation are concerned generally the distinction is made between informal and formal, direct and indirect, descending and ascending, interpersonal and institutional, interpersonal and structural, immediate and distant participation.

Barry, Peterson and Norton (1989) in their work distinguish between interpersonal participation (informal) and structural participation (formal). They say that participation may occur interpersonally (or informally) and structurally (or formally). Interpersonal participation refers to a system in which superiors are personally responsive to the ideas and suggestions of subordinates and such participativeness is informal in the sense that it is not defined in the charter of rules of the organization. Structural participation on the contrary refers to a system in which rules explicitly establish decision-making procedures or structures through which members contribute to decisions. Employees who vote their stock or who elect representatives to the Board of Directors of their firm illustrate the highest degree of formal participation.

Lammers (1967) has suggested a useful distinction between direct and indirect forms of participation. Direct participation, customarily entails that the subordinate participants speak for themselves about work or matters related to work, in general, aims, rules and means are not codified and external influences are normally absent. Indirect participation on the other hand implies that the subordinate participants speak for their constituents with top managers about the general policy of the organization, procedures are finalized, and outside agencies often do influence to some extent what goes on. Wall and Lischeron (1977) have also suggested a useful distinction between direct and indirect participation. The former includes any or all of the situations in which workers participate personally in decision making. The latter includes any or all of the ways in which workers are represented by others in decision making process. Poole (1975) also speaks of direct and indirect or representative participation. In direct participation, all the members of a given work group influence decision making process. But at times, managements have turned to less direct forms of WPM as they are generally been keen to ensure that ultimate powers of decision remain in managerial hands and have not infrequently demanded an embargo on a number of sensitive issues, notably on commercial, business and wages questions.

Walker (1973) speaks of descending and ascending participation. In descending participation, workers may be given power to plan and make decisions about their own work. In ascending participation, they may be given an opportunity to influence managerial decisions at higher levels, through their elected representatives to the Board of the enterprise. They may participate through Collective Bargaining. They may also participate informally when, for example, a manager adopts a participative style of supervision or workers apply unofficial restrictive practices.

Roy (1973) distinguishes between interpersonal participation and institutional participation. Interpersonal participation occurs in the web of the face-to-face superior-subordinate relationships in the small groups, which constitute the organization. Institutional participation, on the other hand, denotes the structures and forums designed in industry, such as the Joint Management Council, Works' Committee and so forth.

Mehtras (1966) has given five forms or stages of participation: informative participation, consultative participation, associative participation, administrative participation and decisive participation. Informative participation is the slightest form of participation and decisive participation is the highest form of participation where sharing of decision making power is complete and the delegation of authority and responsibility of managerial function to such a body is maximum. According to Alexander (1973) the important forms in which workers could participate in management are: collective bargaining, joint administration, joint decision-making, consultation and information sharing. Odaka (1975) has identified four forms of participation: participation by suggestion, participation by consultation, participation by workers or their representatives and participation by self-government.

Having discussed about the various forms of the participation, another important aspect of WPM sought to be discussed here is the levels of participation.

LEVELS OF PARTICIPATION

Workers can involve themselves in the conduct of enterprise affairs at various levels, i.e., Shop-floor level or Middle Management level or at the Board level. The level of participation depends upon the nature of functions, the strength of the workers, variety of departments, attitudes of trade unions and the management. The areas and degrees may differ very considerably at different levels of management (Vishwa Nath, 1992).

A participative situation has to be analyzed through a two variable approach i.e., spheres that express participation, and levels that indicate the degree or depth of participation in each sphere. This means that even in an organization there may be a high level of participation in certain spheres, whereas the level of participation in certain other spheres may be low (Alexander, 1972).

Aziz (1980) who undertook a study on WPM in Karnataka states that workers' participation at the Shop and Plant levels is preferred more than Board level participation. He further says that the low preference shown to this form is not a vote against the Directorial level participation and in favour of Shop level participation as such. In principle the workers do like to participate at the Directorial level but their objection is to the form in which it is practiced in Karnataka. It was pointed out that nominating one or two worker leaders to the Board of Management and then taking decisions on the principle of majority would hardly made the functioning of the Worker Directors effective. That is the reason why workers prefer Shop and Plant level participation. It is suggested that in order to make the Worker Director scheme a success, their should be numerical equality in the matter of representation on the Board. Thus, participative schemes can operate at many different levels simultaneously. In view of the important changes needed in attitudes, skills, and abilities, participation will probably spread gradually upwards from Shop-floor levels and downwards from Board levels, and in both cases only slowly (Broad and Beishon, 1977).

Walker and Bellecombe (1967) of the International Institute of Labour Studies have, however, visualized four levels of participation in decision making, that is, participation in the decision of the Board Room, participation in the decision of the manager, participation in the decision of the executives, and participation at supervisory level. Empirically, it has been found that the level of participation (that indicates the degree or depth of participation) varied from situation to situation even in the same organization (Vishnu Gopal, 1984).

Thus, participative situation is attempted to be analyzed in this study in terms of spheres as well as levels of participation.

Possibly the aspect of workers' involvement in decision making which, on the one hand, has the most dramatic and superficial appeal and, on the other, raises the most unreasonable and ill-founded fears is that of involvement at the highest level in the enterprise. The Board Room supporters of this idea see it as a means of both establishing and demonstrating a greater degree of harmony in the enterprise. Through the medium of workers' representation on the Board, it is suggested that the decisions taken by the Board will, in fact and appearance, be more in line with workers' interests and ideas and therefore more acceptable (Daniel and McIntosh, 1972). These arguments are, however, subject to sharp criticism from representatives both of organized labour, and of capital or shareholders. Most opposed to the idea of Workers' Directors were those whose position would be most challenged by them, that is, managers. These were the group who felt 'cut out' by worker representation at Board level (Bendix, 1956; Dahrendorf, 1959; Brannen et al, 1976; Hammer and Stern, 1986).

Sahu's (1985) study of ten Manufacturing and Production organizations, both public and private situated in Karnataka, Orissa and Bihar revealed that workers in both public and private sector organizations had shown some interest for Board level participation whereas same was not the case with management personnel. The management personnel's support was least for parity in the Board. The responses of office bearers/executive body members of Central/State level trade union organizations and management associations revealed that Central/State level trade union leaders had maximum desire for Board level participation preference being more parity in the Board whereas office bearers/executive body members of management associations had least preference for Board level participation.

The opponents of Board level participation claim that, placing an employee at the lower end as a representative at the Board of Directors' level can make him feel helpless in that basically he does not have the background knowledge required for policy decisions at this highest level. Thus, whilst participation has its advantages, it can be only effectuated in terms of the situation and the level which makes it meaningful. For example, to participate effectively in a decision making situation, the participants must have the necessary knowledge and the required analytical skill to contribute to the decision making process (Davar, 1974). Another argument put forth by opponents of greater participation is the claim that workers are not capable of participating in certain levels of decision making in organizations, either because they lack the intellectual ability or because they lack the technical knowledge and skills to understand, for example, accounting procedures or business practices. It is usually argued that participation must therefore be limited to workplace levels where workers can understand the issues (Broad and Beishon, 1977).

Further those, who believed that participation would promote efficiency through the use of Shop-floor knowledge, were among those most strongly in favour of Worker Directors. Worker Directors would reflect the Shop-floor, not represent it (Brannen et al, 1976). But again, as the Worker Directors are in a minority their voice will have no effect. So they may develop inferiority complex or may be completely suppressed or frustrated and may create nuisance for the company. That is why trade unionists wish to maintain their present independent status and this way they can better act as a check on the management. In countries where the trade unions are very strong as in Britain, U.S.A. and Scandinavia, the trade unions definitely reject the idea (Chhabra et al, 1977).

While the great majority of employers continue to oppose Board representation and other forms of participation in management, they now tend to take a more positive attitude to workers' participation in the organization of their work and the determination of their conditions of employment (Cordova, 1982). The Shop-floor participation is meant to mobilize the lower workers at their work situation. The workers are encouraged to take part in the decision making process on the issues which are reached by the agreement between management and the trade union. It is materialized through representatives of workers who will have right to negotiate, consult and observe the group activities for the overall efficiency and productivity of the enterprise (Sahai and Misra, 1990). It is apprehended that workmen would not be in a position to participate effectively at the Board level and that participation should be initially at the Shop-floor and Plant level and there should be a system of graduating from lower level to the Board level (Singh and Singh, 1993). This is supported by Poole (1975) who says that, so far as the ordinary worker is concerned, participation at Shop-floor has had impressive results. In view of this most of the effort that has gone into increasing participation among people in organizations has now tended to be concentrated on the Shop-floor worker or his equivalent; that is to say, that it has been the plight of the man at the bottom of the organization that has aroused attention (Cherns, 1973).

Coming to focus on the structure of organizations as variables, Hebden and Shaw (1977) state that organizational decision making may be seen as a hierarchy, shaped like an inverted pyramid. At the top lie the wide-ranging strategic decisions with a broad sweep of implications for people operating throughout the organization. They are followed by a middle range of decision making of more limited in application which is required for the implementation of the strategic decisions. This in turn is followed by still narrower decisions down to the level of the individual task. The most dramatic form of indirect participation is probably the appointment of worker representatives to the Boards of

Directors of companies. Worker directorships extend participation by permitting a greater range of people to exert influence over organizational decision making. Representation at Board level is a form of power sharing and a ready means of obtaining an extension of industrial democracy. But strategic decisions require information from all parts of the organization. Board level participation without a similar involvement at lower levels will reduce the effectiveness of the Board representatives in obtaining and using accurate information for strategic decisions. Participation at Board level will be a paper exercise if it is not followed through by greater levels of involvement at middle range and operational levels of decision.

Hammer et al (1991) who have studied worker representation on Boards of Directors as a form of employee participation in organizational decision making in 14 U.S. firms in the early 1980's say that, the effectiveness of worker participation is dependent on a set of integrated participative structures that tie Shop-floor, Board level and trade union participation into a unified whole. They further say that, although the assignment of worker representatives to the Board is theoretically a substantial shift in an organization's formal authority structure, previous empirical research leads to the conclusion that without a well developed system of participative structures and sufficient political or economic power in the hands of labour to use the structures, Worker Directors have limited influence on decision processes and outcomes. They are often cast in the role of Shop-floor experts and are kept outside informal discussions that affect Board decisions. In view of the studies reviewed, an attempt is made in this study to ascertain the various levels at which WPM takes place and to what extent and with what amount of effectiveness.

EXTENT AND DEGREE OF PARTICIPATION

Extent of participation is another important variable pertaining to WPM and it is indeed one of the most realistic measures of WPM and wherever WPM is introduced, maximum efforts are put in seeking to it that it stabilizes at a higher extent.

It is rather a universal consensus to view the success of WPM, as the function of its extent, that is, extent of participation by workers is the sole yardstick of the success of the schemes of WPM, though, its effectiveness and the extent to which the decisions arrived at through WPM are actually implemented are also considered as the indices of the meaningful success of the scheme. Further, many a time it is rather difficult to measure effectiveness and impact of WPM with valid and reliable accuracy owing to lack of scales and instruments for the same, whereas, the extent of participation is somewhat less complex, more amenable for measurement, and places where WPM is recently introduced as a positive intervention, extent is viewed as a measure good enough to ascertain the working success of the schemes, particularly in such cultures where, participation of workers in the decision making process in itself is viewed as a positive departure and a welcome change in the administrative and human milieu at place of work leading to democratization and humanization of work organizations. As such, there are several studies focusing on the extent of WPM.

Extent of participation is measured by the proportion of workers who take part, on the one hand, and by how much they participate on the other. Indirect participation through representatives involves less participation by individuals than could occur in direct participation (Walker, 1973).

Cherunilam, (1989) states that the form and extent of WPM vary widely. In some cases it is limited to making suggestions on certain matters whereas on the other extreme workers are represented in the Board of Directors, so that they become a part and parcel of the decision-making and administration. In some other cases, even the whole management of the enterprises is rested with the workers.

The extent to which participation takes place has widened so that now a days issues which would have been considered as coming under the heading of managerial prerogatives have become subject to joint regulation of various degrees (Hebden and Shaw, 1977). VishwaNath (1992) in his pioneering study of WPM in public and private sector units operating in Iron and Steel, Textile and Sugar industries traced inter industry differentials in the extent of participation. His study reveals that the private sector units provide better scope and hence experience greater extent of WPM than their counterparts in public sector. This association was particularly pronounced in Steel industry. Further in terms of type of industry, the extent of WPM again was found to be highest in Iron and Steel industry, irrespective of sector and lowest in the Sugar industry, presumably because of the workforce being seasonally employed. The study also testifies to the fact that the extent of WPM is positively associated with the climate of industrial relations and thereby with the productivity and performance. Similarly Bhatnagar (1990) in her study on 'impact of technology on propensity among worker to participate in management' found that Textile industries provide a more conducive climate for participation than the Fertilizer industries.

In a study by Aziz (1980), the worker leaders and trade unionists categorically stated that they were interested in real participation in the sense that they should have substantial share in decision making and administration. The relative amount of control the workers should ideally exercise, as stated by both management and worker leaders, is found to increase as one moves from the management prerogatives to worker-management cooperative issues and from there to workers' welfare programmes. In other words, workers would like to take decisions more and more on issue which directly concern them and the issues, which can be resolved with their cooperation. Kher (1988) says that participation varies in degrees if not in kind. The difference in information sharing and consultation is very complex and not easily realized by the participants. For instance, workers may be merely informed about a new system to be brought into the work life. At the most, their views might be asked without giving any due consideration.

It is assumed that where the authority in the decision making is almost complete, participation will be negligible and where the authority is relatively small, participation will be minimum. Extent of participation will depend on the cooperation involved and the delegation of authority in decision making and their implementation (Varandhani, 1989). It also depends to a significant extent upon workers' propensity to participate and the managements' acceptance of workers' participation. Workers' propensity is a function of their attitudes, their perceived power to participate and workers' capacities to participate (Bhatnagar, 1991). Despite the actual setting up of certain institutions for workers' participation, the extent to which participation actually occurs is determined by the strength of the parties' propensity to participate and the participation potential in the situation. It should be noted that propensity to participate depends both on ability to participate and willingness to participate. The participation potential, on the other hand depends on four principal factors-like autonomy of the undertaking, technological limits that might exist, size of the undertaking and the limits set by the form of workers' participation (Balundgi and Bagali, 1994).

Coming to the extent of participation viewed in terms of the depth or intensity, Brannen and others (1976) observed that those who hold the view that 'workers alone should control the plants' represent the smallest category compared to those who opine that 'workers should be consulted'. However, the extent where workers and managers take a decision jointly appears to be on the rise. It was also noted that realizing the notion of 'Worker Director' could be a distant reality with half of the managerial personnel and over a one-third of the Directors themselves being opposed to the notion.

Attempting to conceptualize extent of participation, Anderson (1984), for a change, takes to the model envisaged by Vroom and Yetton (1973) in which the emphasis is on the style of management which determines the extent of participation. The styles of management range from autocratic where the manager makes the decision to consultative where the manager and group share decision responsibilities, to delegation in which the groups actually make the decision.

Butteriss (1971) in her study of 'Worker Representation on Management Boards' in Reynolds, (Bycycle industry, Manchester), Glacier Metal (Metals, USA) and Scott Bader (Business) found that the involvement of Worker Directors in decision making follows the Vroom, Yetton model.

Thus, in the present study the extent of participation is ascertained and analyzed to understand it as a function of personal and contextual factors.

Although the extent of participation is taken as akin to the degree of participation, the degree of participation is purely meant how far workers influence managerial decision, on a scale extending from complete unilateral control by management at one end to complete unilateral control by workers at the other (Walker, 1973). In other words, at the one end of the scale management can make decisions unilaterally and at the other end, much more rarely, workers decide unilaterally. Between these extremes there is a range of intermediate point, such as, management communicates decision to employees, management consults employees before making final decision, management joins with employees in making decisions (Armstrong, 1988). An area in which the so called managerial prerogative predominate, where the manager feels unwilling to permit the workers to share in the making of such decisions and expect them to accept his decision with grace, managerial action involves only a limited degree of participation. Some times a manager discusses a pending decision with the workers before finalizing it. Under these circumstances he is ready to modify his proposed decisions, reconsider it or substitutes another for it, depending upon the considerations which arise in the course of the discussion. A situation like this involves a high degree of participation. A still higher degree of participation is involved where the manager presents to the workers the problem facing him and requests them to help him find the best solution to it, and if he finds the solution to be workable he accepts it. A situation arises where the manager, having made the decision, discusses with the workers the best way of implementing it within the given alternatives. Such a situation involves a comparatively high degree of participation (Varandhani, 1989).

In the words of Salamon (1987) there is an overriding element to be considered namely the degree of participation. The existence of participation must depend ultimately on how far employees are able or are allowed to influence management thinking and contribute to the determination of decisions irrespective of the form of participation, the process of interaction used may range, in practice, from only management information giving through consultation and negotiation to committed joint decision making.

Robert Tannenbaum and Schmidt (1958) have presented a continuum which demonstrates the degree of participation. The underlying assumption of Tannenbaum and Schmidt's continuum of leadership behaviour is that the manager should decide where to operate on the continuum - whether to announce a decision instead of trying to sell his idea, whether to invite queries or let subordinates decide an issue. An important element of their continuum is the implied utilization of situational analysis.

According to Bhatia (1988), the bigger the range of problems which employees help to solve, and the larger the proportion of employees who can play some constructive part, the greater is the degree of participation. The technology, tasks and condition of work affect the potential degree of workers' participation. Some technologies and tasks provide scope for delay while matters are discussed or negotiated. Technologies also differ in the amount of tolerance that can be allowed in the performance of a task. When such limitations operate WPM may be necessarily limited to the setting of general policies and objectives and the conditions under which such tasks are carried out (Pylee, 1975).

AREAS OF PARTICIPATION

There are so many potential areas on which workers may have or do have a measure of decision making control, from technical 'on-the-job' problems to questions covering welfare and safety, wages and working conditions, production, commercial and economic issues. Shuchman (1957) endeavored to classify these areas and tried to relate these areas of workers' participation to the levels in which they are confined. At the enterprise level, the main areas of workers' participation may be: personnel decisions such as the hiring, firing, promotion and transfer of workers; social decisions including matters such as health and safety, form and administration of pension funds; economic decisions which includes technical aspects such as new methods of production and the introduction of new machinery; and 'business' issues which refer to marketing and financial questions.

Vishnu Gopal (1984) has categorized areas of participation as economic, personnel and social. Satya Raju (1993) states that, the areas of participation are shown under four classes of decisions such as, issues relating to technical matters, areas relating to employment and personnel, decisions relating to the economic and financial policy of the undertaking and general policy decisions.

Vishwa Nath (1992) is of the view that, scope of real

participation covers not merely such issues which may theoretically lead to developing satisfaction and contentment amongst workers and development of cooperative work-team and performance of job without frictions and grumbles, but has to cover in real sense and true spirit all such issues which lead to optimum utilization of the human resources, with the faith that workers have necessary will and ability to participate in decision concerning the increase in output, reduction in cost, full utilization of manpower, elimination of wastage, reduction in absenteeism and maintaining discipline.

A research study conducted by Ramsay (1976) makes it clear that the items such as organization of your own work and fixing of work standards, which particularly relate to the control over the job itself, where participation was found to be most in demand, receive high but not the highest scores in the 'ideal' picture. Marchington and Loveridge (1983) who undertook research on participation in a Furniture firm say that employee involvement was accepted by management in those areas which were of lesser importance to them, one's in which decision making was not seen to be a priority for them. In other words, joint decision making was confined to the relatively 'safe' aspects of the business whilst unilateral decision making continued in those areas felt to be crucial to the future well-being of the firm. The British writer Jacques (1968), has pointed out that the interest of the worker in and his ability to contribute something to management is confined to the 'area of his job'. Participation of each person should be strictly confined to the filed in which he is competent and with which he is concerned (Balundgi and Bagali, 1994).

It is stated that, workers' participation is meaningful in areas where they are directly concerned. In other words, workers' participation is meaningful in such management decisions which concern the workers and on which they will have opinions to express or suggestions to make. Thus, diverse areas of management have been viewed as coming under the purview of WPM depending on the socio-economic and politico-cultural milieu.

Several empirical studies focusing on the determinants and effectiveness of WPM have also been undertaken, a brief survey-cum-review of the same appears to be warranted here with a view to provide an academic and empirical backdrop for the discussion of the findings of the present study in subsequent chapters.

DETERMINANTS

Having come to recognize the desirability of WPM as an intervention in the work organizations, the researchers seem to be preoccupied with the factors that facilitate or retard the process and in the process have come to identify several determinants of extent and effectiveness of WPM.

Based on the Open System Approach to Participative Management of Optner (1965), and Emery and Trist (1960), the implication is that in an organization there must be identified conditions both internal and external which impinge on Participative Management and its effectiveness.

The factors affecting the WPM can be categorized into two broad headings, namely external and internal.

External Factors

Under external factors, we can include the social environment, general attitude and belief in the society in authoritarianism or democracy, class distinction, conception of superior and inferior, level of general education in society, economic environment, the socio-economic order and the general economic climate (Clarke et. al., 1972). The same view is held by Vishnu Gopal (1984) who says that participation requires democratic social environment and spirit of industrial democracy and relatively higher position of labour market.

In addition, the political system refers to political democracy ensuring equal rights to all citizens without any discrimination. The legal environment refers to democratic judiciary exercising justice without any distinction of caste, creed, religion, position and wealth. And the legislative environment refers to its democratic constitution and its power to control and supervise the working of industrial enterprises both in public and private sectors.

Internal Factors

There are several internal factors which affect WPM. These can be classified as organizational and human factors.

Organizational Factors

WPM will be possible and effective in an organization if the following conditions exist. The management must have freedom and autonomy to arrive at final decision without reference of final authority and the technology is simple; the character of the task and work is such that workers can influence managerial decisions by putting pressure on it; the character of the work and the conditions under which it is performed is such that the workers may communicate with one another easily and may develop consciousness of common interest; payment of wages is on piece system; the location of the enterprise is in an industrially localized area giving opportunity to the workers to develop class interest as the result of communication with workers in other industries; the size of the concern is smaller (Clarke et. al., 1972; Suri, 1973; Walker, 1973; Pylee, 1975); the structure of the concern is such that there is delegation of authority and power to the lower rank and the managers have rights of participation with their own superior; the organization is less hierarchical (Morse and Reimer:1956); it works from bottom to top; if it provides for total participation (Coch and French, 1948); if the managers instead of imposing their superiority, permit free and frank expression of the views of the worker to perceptibly influence the setting of actual goals (Lawrence and Smith, 1955); if the form of participation is not merely based on human relations but is based on human resources model too and if the contents of participation relate to all subjects and issues which are important for workers' job perception and attitude and affecting their motivation, expectations and fulfillments, then the participation will be effective (Roy, 1973; Vishnu Gopal, 1984).

Clarke et. al., (1972) observed that firms which are strongly unionized tend to be ready to enter into consultation and negotiation with their employers. Vishnu Gopal (1984) is of the opinion that in Capitalistic countries trade union's attitude toward participation is not favourable. Trade unions in such countries consider the schemes of WPM with suspicion and as a device to deprive them of control, guidance, and organization of the workers. On the other hand, in Socialist countries like Russia and Yugoslavia, where the entire economy is under their control, trade unions not merely fully participate in management but make provisions for giving necessary training to the workers to understand the complications and techniques of management and bearing its responsibility.

Athreya (1973) has come to focus on organizational climate, organizational structure and organizational process as three important organizational determinants of participation. Cherns (1973) in his attempt to trace the effective conditions of participative democracy agrees that a cultural climate which permits the goal of quality of working life, the support of unions, Government and employees, systemic change in organizations and a conducive value system are the organizational variables determining the effectiveness of participation. Dhingra (1973) probes into the determinants of dispositions and identifies managerial status, line and staff affiliation, age, educational attainments as personal variables and size of firm, organizational climate and operating status as the organizational variables determining the managerial disposition towards participation and through that the actual process of WPM. Continuing to focus on organizational dimensions Huneryager and Heckman (1967) opines that degree of centralization, delegation of managerial authority, style of supervision and management's orientation are the factors impinging upon the extent of Participative Management at work place. Argyris (1967) while emphasizing the importance of Participative Management looks at the process from the perspective of Sociology of Organizations and argues that the executive feelings and attitudes towards Participative Management, existence of small informal groupings and personal policies in operation are the three crucial factors in making Participative Management work and to this he adds organizational structure as the fourth supportive factor.

Human Factors

In addition to organizational factors, researchers have identified several factors associated with the actors participating in the process, which could be termed in general as human factors. These can be categorized into two broad categories as Workers' Propensity to Participate and Managements' Acceptance of Workers' Participation. The Workers' Propensity to Participate includes workers' attitude towards participation, capacity to participate and perception of power. Workers' attitude towards participation refers to kind of participation liked by workers and the eagerness and enthusiasm to work in participative organizations. The workers' attitude depends not only on their ideologies and values but also on sex, age, education, training, skill, experience, family background, migratory character, possible benefits from participation and the like. However, attitudes, may alter as conditions change. Further, the capacity to participate involves education, understanding and experience of business matters, technical matters concerning production processes and other relevant aspects of management. It requires proper training on the part of workers. Perception of power refers to power enjoyed by workers to influence managerial decisions by giving their opinion, views and suggestions in a free and frank manner and the confidence that they will be respected by the management. Similarly, Managements' Acceptance of WPM includes management attitude, managerial capacities and perception of power. Management attitude depends upon whether managers consider participation as a significant procedure or a mere wastage of time, manager's participative predisposition which is influenced by their ideology, the social stratum from which they come, degree of their professionalization and past traditions of industrial relations as well as the authority structure. Managerial capacities involve training and moulding of behaviour to sit across a common table with workers' representatives for participative decisions. Managements' perception of power refers to the consideration that managers alone do not have the monopoly of authority and power but the workers too enjoy power, giving rise to the question of balancing of the power. Thus, the amount, form and character of participation in a particular situation depends upon the combination of Workers' Propensity to Participate and Managers' Acceptance of Workers' Participation. When there is a lack of congruence between the character of workers' participation wanted by workers and its acceptance by management, workers' participation takes forms different from those provided for in the organization structure. In case where workers' propensity to participate is lower than managers' acceptance of participation, workers are apathetic towards authorized forms of participation (Walker, 1973; Pylee, 1975; Vishnu Gopal, 1984).

Bhatnagar (1991) in her study on 'Workers' participation in BHEL at Tiruchi', notes that the presence of structural mechanism is necessary to facilitate participation, but by itself it is not sufficient to ensure participation. Actual participation would ultimately depend upon the organizational climate, cordiality and mutual trust between management and workers. In other words, it depends upon the workers' propensity to participate and management's acceptance of participation. Similarly Balundgi and Bagali (1994) in their study found that the extent of workers' participation in management decision making in various types of undertakings depends on the propensity to participate on the part of both the 'managers' and the 'managed' and on the participation potential. Propensity to participate in turn is influenced by the possibility for the Works Council to show effective results, the degree of geographic mobility of the workers, the level of education of the workers, the level of management at which workers' participation is exercised, the level of wages and the degree of responsibility for the organization assigned to the worker. The participation potential, on the other hand depends on four principal factors, such as, the autonomy of the undertaking, the technological limits that might exist, the size of the undertaking and the limits set by the form of workers' participation.

Further, when it comes to human factors, social profile of actors is considered as another important determinant. For any Sociological study, the analysis of social background of the respondents would be helpful in enquiring into the complex nature of social phenomena and in gaining insights. An individual in a society is subject to various socio-personal situations and is exposed to various stimuli in the environment, which in turn, reflects his personality and behaviour in day-to-day life (Vishnu Gopal, 1984). Beynon and Blackburn (1972) have emphasized the significance of social characteristics of incumbents working in an organization in influencing their orientation to work. Argyris (1964) observed that years of experience with varying degrees of frustration, conflict, dependence, apathy and failure influence and become part of working class culture. Then the prevailing conditions of any society make it imperative to study the cultural conditioning of the human personality and its implication for participatory predisposition (Krech and Cructchfield, 1948; Whyte, 1951; Harbinson and Myres, 1959; and Abegglen, 1958; Vishnu Gopal, 1984).

Coming to the Indian Context, the social characteristics of industrial employees are significant in determining the Participative Management. Therefore, Vishnu Gopal (1984) tried to analyze the specific background factors such as age, caste-status, religion, marital status, level of education, ecological background, type of family, monthly income, service, experience, category, skill and trade union membership and so forth for their influence on participatory process. His study further reveals that mutual trust and confidence between the workers and the management, cordial management and worker relationship, managements' readiness to encourage maximum participation of the mass of workers, readiness to sincerely understand each others views and problems, adequate emphasis on suggestion and persuasions in place of restraints and coercions, clear understanding of the basic objects of participative committees are some of the prime factors which are responsible for promotion of WPM.

Coming to the attitudinal determinants of WPM Athreya (1973), has observed that bio-social characteristics effect every sphere of individual's life, including participation which is a social-psychological phenomenon. Walker (1973) found that workers' attitudes to participation are shaped by values and ideologies (culture) as well as by factors such as age, sex, skill, education and experience. Tanic (1969) is of the view that success of participation depends upon social, cultural, and biological conditions of the participating parties. He stressed that higher economic status enables a worker for developing potentials for democratic participation and the level of general as well as industrial education is also a determining factor for active participation. Further Narayana and Moorthy (1970) are of the view that factors such as level of education, caste, age, category of worker, length of service, income and distance of workers' residence from work-place have considerable bearing on the level of workers' participation. Further, Michael (1979), who studied workers' participation in five Textile Mills in Bombay says that, age group and educational level of workmen have a direct impact on their attitude towards workers' participation. This association was supported also by Butteriss (1971). Goldthorpe and his associates in their Luton investigation found that age, education and environment have significant influence on an individuals propensity to participate (Goldthorpe et. al., 1968).

Hebden and Shaw in their 'Pathways to participation' (1977) have identified external and internal factors relating to work environment, which could determine the extent of participation. The cultural background, the sub-cultural features and the general economic milieu are the external factors whereas technology, degrees of bureaucratization as manifested in the degree of structural complexity, centralization and formalization, size, occupational structure, the tradition of industrial relations and managerial attitudes represent the internal factors. These factors have been focused and hypothesized as determinants of WPM in this study as well. Similarly, Guest and Fatchett (1974) in their study on 'organizational and individual constraints on participation' have come to identify the level of individual skill, capacity, inclination and individual background as the individual determinants and personality traits as the individual factors, whereas, size, technology, organizational environment and organizational structure as the organizational constraints determining the extent of direct participation in organizations.

Alexander (1972) in a study of two Mills hypothesized that the institutionalization of Participative Management in an industrial organization is contingent upon the motivation of workers to participate in management on the one hand, and upon the motivation of management to encourage WPM on the other. The study also revealed that an exceptionally large proportion of the rank and file workers and a large proportion of the activists wanted workers to participate in management. Alexander further states that the propensity of workers to participate in management was contingent upo.

their status in the plant community, their attitudes towards management and trade unions, as well as the area in which opportunities for participation were provided. It was also noted that the interest of the workers to participate in management did not vary with the different areas of management. The influence of various socio-personal characteristics on workers' propensity to participate in management was examined and it was found that workers' interest to participate in management was related to their level of education. Antagonism towards management was another force that motivated workers to seek participation in management. It was also found that workers' interest to participate in management was also related to their attitude towards trade unionism. Workers who held more favourable attitude towards unionism were more interested in participating in management.

Varandhani (1989) states that success in the various modes of Participative Management including the Joint Management Council greatly depends upon the outlook and attitude that the parties bring to the Council and the atmosphere in which a free exchange of thoughts and opinions take place. The management's initiative, the support of trade unions, the cooperation of the workers and supervisors, a proper organization and suitable administrative procedures, the effectiveness and importance of the issues deliberated, implementation of its conclusions and decisions, adequate training and experience in Joint Management Councils, and wide publicity to the experiments, are some of the preconditions for success. Thus, any idea of WPM at any level in running the enterprise depends on the behavioural attitude of the parties. Aziz (1980) states that, among other things, the extent to which power of decision making is passed on to the workers is largely influenced by the frequency of the meetings, the nature of the issues discussed, the extent to which the resolutions passed are implemented, the extent of cooperation from the trade unions, the extent to which the worker leaders are equipped to participate in decision making.

Kumar (1992) states that Workers' participation depends on the workers' own efficiency level in respect of participation and on the workers' belief in the logic and rationale of participation. He further says that functional literacy directly conditioned the workers' response to participation, and affected their inclination.

Sexena (1979) taking lead from the earlier studies identifies permissive socio-cultural environment, institutionalized fora of participation supported by a network of regulatory norms and the requisite value orientation and behaviour patterns among participative groups to lend functional realism to the concept of participation as the determinants of WPM. Nadler (1980) and SubbaRao and Narayana (1992) have come to identify management commitment, union involvement, distribution of authority, involvement of workers, communication and information sharing, industrial relations climate, union ability as the factors affecting workers' participation.

Broad and Beishon (1977) are of the view that demographic influences will have profound influence on workers' participation. We may expect individuals from rural surroundings to be satisfied with less involvement than those from urban areas, because of their greater deference to authority. Workers who have become experienced in making decisions about their jobs, or in conceiving of issues in a wider context, may be keener about participation. Workers who expect to remain with their present employment for a long time may be more committed to participation and increased efficiency.

It is further noted that the environmental factors have an influence on WPM. Enterprises in stable environments tend to adopt 'mechanistic' types of relatively static, rigid, and sharply defined authority structures. In more volatile environments enterprises tend to evolve 'organic' forms of organization of a more fluid character better suited to the need for constant adaptation (Burns and Stalker, 1961; Emery and Trist, 1969).

Drago and Wooden (1991) in their study of 'Determinants of Participatory Management' have attempted to develop and test a general model of participation. They state that, that model is closely related to the Industrial Democracy in Europe (IDE) model developed by International Research Group (1979, 1981). They seek to extend and apply the IDE model to account for potential linkages between the participation and employee desires for it. They used data from survey of employees at twenty three work places in Australia and three in Newzeland conducted during mid 1988. Based on this study they conclude that formal participation programmes often achieve the objective of enhancing employee influence over management. However, as earlier studies indicated employees generally desire greater amounts of participation than firms are providing. They found variety of contextual variables such as age, gender, job tenure, job technology, firm size and work incentives as having important implications for the extent of participation.

Roy (1973) in his study identifies and classifies determinants of participation in to two broad categories as environmental conditions and organizational features. The environmental conditions include political system, the bureaucracy, the legislature and public opinion and organizational features consist of organizational tradition, leadership and communication, managerial and supervisory autonomy, industrial relations situation and in conclusion he states that the organizational groundwork and a favourable attitudinal milieu would facilitate these determinants to be in operation. On the contrary, Anthony (1978) comes to focus on the negative determinants of WPM, which he terms as the barriers. To begin with, he identifies the organizational barrier such as organizational tradition, philosophy and values on the one hand, quality of personnel, policy and procedures on the other.

Several studies have also revealed that attitude towards participation varies in accordance with the cultural conditions of human personality (Krech and Crutchfied, 1948; Whyte, 1951; Roy, 1973; Vishnu Gopal, 1984).

Managers' Orientation

Walker (1973) has noted that even in Socialist countries ideologically committed to workers' participation, managers vary in the extent to which they accept and actively facilitate participation. Haire, Ghiselli and Porter (1966) have observed that in non-socialist countries, many managers acknowledge the necessity for democratic styles of supervision, but most of them have a low opinion of the average person's initiative, responsibility and desire for autonomy.

Dhingra (1973) in his study found that, among the top level managers, the incidence of non-participative predisposition was higher than that of participative predisposition and 'line' managers had a stronger non participative predisposition than 'staff' managers or those managers who were handling simultaneously both 'line' and 'staff' functions. Among the managers, the proportion of those with participative predisposition increased with each lower level of managerial hierarchy. Derber (1970) observed that as managers become more professional, their professionalism interposes a barrier against involving employees in decision-making, except in an information giving or cooperation seeking context. Strauss and Rosenstein (1970) have pointed out that managers are reluctant to give out 'confidential' information. Dingra (1973), however, has noted that a great proportion of managers who had undergone professional training evinced participative predisposition than those who had no such training.

Walker (1973) opines that even though managers may hold unfavourable attitude towards participation, they may accept it, if they consider that balance of power is against them.

Anantaraman (1980) states that the skill required to manage participatory groups cannot be assumed to exist or willed into existence by flat or pious hopes. Management has to devote a lot of time and effort to tap the resources of creativity and develop teamwork to achieve success through participation. It is also supported by a study in India which has reported that, contrary to the official belief, it is the management, particularly the top management that needs education for the success of the participative scheme (Suri, 1973).

Thus, in conclusion it may be stated that, participation does not occur in a vacuum. It is implemented in a preexisting social system and attitudes towards such an innovation will necessarily be coloured by the institutions and experience of that preexisting social system. The social system of the organization conditions the expectations of all the participants and limits the extent to which participation is deemed legitimate or relevant by the various parties (Hebden and Shaw, 1977).

EFFECTIVENESS AND THE DETERMINANTS OF EFFECTIVENESS OF WPM

Coming to the less researched upon aspect of WPM, that is, the effectiveness and the determinants of effectiveness, there appears to be lack of consensus and universal indices of effectiveness of WPM.

Sahu (1985) in his study conducted at Karnataka, Orissa and Bihar to know the existing and desired level of effectiveness of different Joint Committees functioning in the organizations identifies nine parameters like increasing production, improving quality of product, reducing cost of production, eliminating waste, reducing accidents, improving two-way communication, reducing work stoppages, improving labour management relations and satisfying workers' urge for self-expression as the measures of the effectiveness of functioning of different Joint Committees. Further, a comparison between public sector and private sector revealed that, existing level of effectiveness in both the sectors was very low and there was no marked difference in the scores of the two sectors. In both the sectors, the desired scores were quite high and there was no marked difference between the desired scores of the management personnel of both the sectors whereas workers' desired score in public sector was significantly higher than that of workers in private sector.

Alexander (1972) who studied Participative Management in English Textile Mills and Manorama Cloth Company came to the conclusion that WPM was more effective in ETM than in MCC. The effectiveness of WPM depends on the motivation of management to encourage WPM, which was more prevalent in ETM than in MCC.

Misir (1983) who studied WPM in the Sugar, Rice and Bauxite industries in the public sector of Guyana, found that in the enterprise, the level of commitment to the values and interests of worker participation by the politicians and managers will determine the level of institutionalization, and the more institutionalized worker participation becomes, the greater is its potentiality of emerging as an effective system.

Michael's (1979) study on workers' participation in the reputed Textile mills of Bombay attempts to measure the effectiveness of the present form of workers' participation in India. The study has thrown light on various important and interesting aspects regarding the present system of workers' participation. The study reveals that the ordinary workers are not interested in the present system. Hence, the practice of workers' participation has not produced substantial results. It was primarily because most of the workers, and those who actually deserve to participate, do not get an opportunity to express themselves.

According to Sherlekar and others (1986) conditions for effective participation are: subordinates must be educated and competent to take active and intelligent interest in planning and decision making processes, they must have strong drives to express and assert themselves and to exercise their own judgment, the desire to participate and co-operate must come from within, management at all levels must be committed to practice participation honestly and there must be mutual trust and confidence and open communication between employees and management. Alexander (1972) and Pylee (1975), in their studies on schemes of WPM with special reference to JMC have emphasized the need for sound organizational structure for its effective functioning. Further, Mehtras (1966); Tanic (1969); Alexander (1972); Pylee (1975) and Leberman and Leberman (1978) on the basis of their studies of the functioning of the various participative management bodies have emphasized the importance and the need for regular meetings and proper agenda for effective functioning of the bodies of WPM.

Monappa and Saiyadain (1996) in their study found that the effectiveness of participative decision-making can be enhanced if some key parameters are taken into account. They identified following variables significantly associated with the effectiveness of participation: the degree of effectiveness varies directly with the degree with which the participation meets the motives of the participants, the greater the clarity of goals, the higher the effectiveness, provided conformity to goals is a strong motive among the participants, settlement of relatively difficult issues leads to greater effectiveness, the higher the viability of the activity of participative decision-making, the greater the effectiveness,

effectiveness varies inversely with the urgency of the decisions, effectiveness varies directly with the number of administrative levels subsumed by the programme, finally, the amount of useful information influences the effectiveness of participative decision making; the more useful the information, the greater the effectiveness. Sharma (1976) states that the success or failure of any scheme of WPM depends on the attitudes of both the parties, i.e., management and workers.

The studies conducted by Kennedy (1966) Subramanian (1967), Nair (1970) and Warrier (1978) indicate that a system of Collective Bargaining is a base for the success of WPM. According to Mamoria (1971) the success of JMC depends upon the attitude and out look that the parties bring to the Council and the atmosphere in which a free and frank exchange of thoughts and opinions takes place, establishing the Councils through the voluntary efforts of the parties, not imposed by law, genuine desire to work together on the part of management and labour, wide publicity to the idea of participation, ensuring real participation, suitable framing of workers' education scheme and lastly, a good and efficient management, a strong, stable and responsible trade union; a belief in the very idea of JMC and full faith in the usefulness of the machinery for that purpose and above all a fair record of industrial relations are the necessary prerequisites for successful working of joint management schemes.

Sharma and Chauhan (1989) and Mamoria and Mamoria (1988) have come to identify some of the following factors which lead to success of workers' participation in industry. Form, coverage, extent and levels of participation should grow in response to specific environment, capacity and interest of the parties concerned; participation must work as complementary body to help Collective Bargaining, which creates conditions of work and also creates legal relations; institutional participation should be discouraged but such participation should be encouraged through changes in leadership styles, communication process, and inter-personal and inter-group relations; there should be single strong trade union; a peaceful atmosphere should be there wherein there are no strikes and lock-outs, for their presence ruins the employees, harms the interest of the society and puts employees to financial losses; authority should be centralized through democratic management process; programmes for training and education should be developed comprehensively; management should be prepared to give all information connected with the working of the industry and labour should handle that information with full confidence and responsibility, the follow-up action on the decisions of the participating forums should be ensured and finally effective two-way communication is a must for the success of the programme.

Managerial philosophy and organizational climate are the two important factors which separately or in combination determine the extent to which a Participative Management can be successfully implemented. When managers are unwilling to delegate authority, no true participation can take place. Those who choose to hold on to their authority do not fully understand the nature of the managerial task or the objectives of delegation. However the reasons for success or failure of a management system can seldom rest with only one of the variables. In the final analysis the success of a participative approach is dependent upon the appropriate combination of the elements which determine leadership style. In other words, the success of Participative Management is a function of the situation, the leader and the led (Francis and Milbourn Jr, 1980).

Sheth (1973) in a study of six units seems to have reached the conclusion that the JMC can be expected to function effectively if there is one strong union in a unit and there is no overlap of tasks among various consultative fora. Similarly, it can be said that if the managers and the workers develop proper attitudes towards each other, they may realize the importance of joint consultation and may not need any Government persuasion. Schregle (1976) in his study concludes that worker participation initiatives, to be successful, must come from all levels and from all sides simultaneously.

Focusing on the pre-conditions for a meaningful success of any WPM scheme, particularly in Indian context, Saxena (1979) states that, the presence of reasonable degree of mutual understanding and good will on both sides; the existence of strong and representative trade unions; the inclusion of major subjects such as wages, norms of efficiency and so forth within the scope of the joint consultative machinery; sound business practices, including sufficient degree of autonomy; and adequate training of workers' representatives are rather imperative.

Aggarwal (1973) focusing on the cultural milieu as a determinant of WPM suggest that to make Participative Management meaningful, first, Participative Management must be decentralized. Second, real power and responsibility must be given at every level. Third, incentives should be built-in in the form of recognition and monetary rewards for outstanding performance. Fourth, workers should be considered partners in the enterprise and not mere wage-earners. Fifth, communication should be in the language of the workers, and efforts should be made to disseminate information about the enterprise widely and in a form easily understandable to workers. On the contrary, Hameed (1973) while indicating to the fact that the studies dealing with effectiveness of Participative Management seldom use a conceptual framework, suggests that instead of blaming factors such as lack of Government leadership, loss of confidence among workers and lack of management initiative, the studies should focus on the environment which may or may not permit the actors to develop goals, attitudes, and perception of roles necessary for successful functioning of Participative Management. The conceptual framework envisaged by him incorporates the economic, social, political and legal environment of a country, goals among the union, management and Government and the degree of role conflict for the actors in the mechanism or technique under consideration. These factors according to him provide a meaningful conceptual framework for the analysis of effectiveness of machineries of WPM.

Vishwa Nath (1992) in his study of effectiveness of WPM in Iron and Steel, Textile and Sugar industry found different factors responsible for differential degree of effectiveness of WPM in different industries. The restructuring of organization and communication channels with greater degree of autonomy were the factors found to be contributing to higher degree of effectiveness of WPM in Iron and Steel industries. Further training programmes and seminars for a qualitative change in the attitudes of management and workers were found to be contributing to the development of consultative management style in Textile industries whereas educational standards or literacy levels and solving the problems of egoism were the factors influencing effectiveness of WPM in Sugar industry. Similarly, Hebden and Shaw (1977) found that training can contribute to the quality of representation by role analysis as well as through the development of specific skills of representation.

Further, Panakal and his associates (1979) have also come to stress the role of training in the effectiveness of WPM. They opine that WPM is not a machine that can be installed easily at any work organization. They state that transition to the participative system of management involves a new style of working together on the basis of a new set of values requiring breaking the barriers of traditional attitudes, values and structures which could be brought about by an effective training for the actors of WPM. The existing approaches to training for Participative Management according to them are inadequate to guarantee the degree of effectiveness desired, as these training programmes are directed at only few selected levels in the organization and emphasize imparting skills only rather than attitudes and values. As such, they recommend for a research based training imparted to all levels in the organization to inculcate new attitudes and values on the one hand and structural changes in the desired directions coupled with imparting skills on the other. This alone can ensure and enhance the effectiveness of Participative Management. And an attempt is made in this study to come out with recommendations based on the findings that could out line the right kind of programme and structure for training workers in WPM with greater effectiveness.

Thus, the area of WPM has been empirically focused upon by numerous researchers through multidisciplinary perspective and interdisciplinary approach dealing with diverse aspects of WPM such as, concept, forms, degree, areas, levels, extent, machineries, determinants, effectiveness and implications. The foregoing review, as set-out in the opening remarks seeks to provide a necessary intellectual and empirical backdrop against which the findings of the present study, in Indian setting, could be meaningfully analyzed and discussed. Hence, in the chapters to follow, an attempt is made to draw upon the foregoing review in the analysis and interpretation of the data generated to place the findings or generalizations based there upon in their proper perspective. In view of this, the present chapter could be viewed as an important portion of this book.

4
Social Profile

An attempt is made in this chapter to present a social profile of the actors who participate in the machineries of WPM. In doing so, the socio-economic background, the family milieu, educational attainments and the professional career of the respondents have been focused upon. It is logically assumed that the socio-cultural milieu the respondents come from, the process of their socialization and professionalization and their upbringing in formative years are of significant relevance in understanding their disposition toward and participation in the machineries of WPM. Particularly in Indian social setting, with its traditional and rigid social fabric, the interaction and interplay between different social categories and the outcome of these could be the function of the socio-economic and cultural background of the participants in the process of WPM. Apart from assuming the dispositions and the experiences of the respondents as the functions of their socio-cultural makeup, these personal background variables have been employed in analyzing the extent, effectiveness and the nature of WPM in Indian context. As such, this chapter is primarily aimed at presenting the social profile of the actors in PM, provide a necessary socio-cultural backdrop for the depiction of the process of PM as well as identify explanatory or independent variables to help analyze the extent, effectiveness and nature of WPM.

The chapter seeks to focus on the personal background variables such as, age, sex, religion, caste, education, family background traits like family occupation, rural-urban background, marital status, income, professional background traits such as, career pattern, span of work career, occupational mobility and it also seeks to focus on social origin and so forth of the respondents. An attempt is made in this chapter to identify the differential manifestations of these socio-cultural traits among the different categories of participants, that is, managerial personnel, trade union leaders and workers. However, it may be noted at the same time that, such an analysis would enable us to understand the general traits of the actors who operate the systems of WPM.

PERSONAL BACKGROUND

Age

Age is one of the most important traits when it comes to the portrayal of the social profile of respondents in social research. It is so, logically, because, age speaks of an individual's maturity to perform a role, experience of and exposure to work life, span of career as well as it relates an individual to a particular stage in the evolution of work culture. The data pertaining to the age of respondents reveal interesting and quite meaningful pattern in the sense, managerial profession is represented by people who belong to wider age groups than the categories of workers and trade union leaders.

It may be observed from the table 4.1 that about one-third (33.9 percent) of the managers are in the old age group with only 15-16 percent of the workers and union leaders being in this age group. Similarly, there is none among workers below the age of 30 years, whereas, as many as 4 percent of the managerial respondents are below the age of 30 years. The category of trade union leaders seem to be in between the two extremes noticed above. It may thus be stated that the category of managers has a better age mix to suit the temperamental requirements to participate in the machineries of WPM than it is in case of workers and trade union leaders. This phenomenon may also be attributed to the fact that among managers, even the younger ones get designated or assigned to represent management in the machineries of WPM, whereas among workers and to some extent among trade union leaders, it is those with longer span of career and longer stint at collective bargaining and hence relatively more aged are chosen to represent their respective categories.

TABLE 4.1

Category-wise Age Distribution of the Respondents

Age	*Category*			*Total*
	Managers	*Trade Union Leaders*	*Workers*	
Young	02 (3.6)	01 (1.8)	—	03 (1.3)
Middle Aged	35 (62.5)	46 (82.1)	108 (84.4)	189 (78.8)
Old	19 (33.9)	09 (16.1)	20 (15.6)	48 (20.0)
Total	56 (100.0)	56 (100.0)	128 (100.0)	240 (100.0)

X^2= 13.70, DF=4, Significant at 0.01 Level, C=0.23

Sex

The study further revealed that, WPM is still a male domain, with not a single woman being found associated with the machineries of WPM in the industries selected for the study. Although women constitute a minority of industrial workforce, the trend is toward increasing participation of women in all types of enterprises, particularly in Electronic, Telecommunication and Tertiary industries. Inspite of this trend it is rather significant to note that no woman in the sample of industries selected is associated with the process of WPM, not even as managerial representatives. It may speak of the general situation in Indian context. Women are less frequently called upon to take part in decision making process as well as management of important affairs, within the domestic sphere as well as outside of it. It is observed that less and less number of women make it to the managerial profession and women from working class appear to be thought of as not endowed with requisite expertise and aptitude to be associated with the process of decision making and managing the affairs of a large-scale enterprise. A serious thought and sincere effort appear to be warranted in order to involve women in the process of WPM so as to render the decisions and management responsive to and appraised of the women's perspective and their specific needs.

Religion

Coming to the religious background of the respondents, the study reveals that an overwhelming majority of the workers are Hindus (93 percent) followed by Christians (6.3 percent) and Muslims (0.8 percent) and a still bigger majority of trade union leaders (98.2 percent) are Hindus followed by Christians (1.8 percent). The religious composition of the respondents, chosen randomly, reveals that it is Hindus and Christians who take to employment in industries rather than preferring business or other kinds of self employment. It may be noted here that the proportion of Hindus in the population at large is much less than it is found in the sample and Muslims appear to be very much underrepresented supporting the statement made above. It could also be so that Muslims may not be willing or keen to be associated with these machineries.

Caste

However, it is the caste background of the respondents which could be of more significant implications for the patterns of participation than is religion. In Indian context, a social analysis of any phenomenon could rather be considered as incomplete without having a reference made to the caste factor. For all the purposes of Sociological inquiry into Indian society, caste is considered as providing a singularly most important perspective and insight into intricate patterns and realities pertaining to statics and dynamics of Indian society. The caste background of different sections of society could as well be of significance in the analysis of work life and non-work life and extent as well as nature of participation therein.

A cross tabulation of caste with the category of respondents reveals interesting distribution pattern. The data appear to be indicating to a more cosmopolitan composition of those associated with the process of WPM than it is in the population at large. It is interesting to note that the proportion of those coming from high castes is expectedly much higher among the representatives of management (55.4 percent).

TABLE 4.2

Category-wise Caste Distribution of the Respondents

Caste	*Category*			*Total*
	Managers	*Trade Union Leaders*	*Workers*	
High	31 (55.4)	22 (39.3)	35 (27.3)	88 (36.7)
Intermediate	19 (33.9)	24 (42.9)	68 (53.1)	111 (46.3)
Low	06 (10.7)	10 (17.9)	25 (19.5)	41 (17.1)
Total	56 (100.0)	56 (100.0)	128 (100.0)	240 (100.0)

X^2=13.55, DF=4, Significant at 0.01 Level, C=0.23

It may be observed from the table that the lowest proportion of those from high castes is found among the representatives of workers and the lowest proportion of those from low castes is lowest among the representatives from the management. The data seem to support one general assumption that the managerial profession even today is within the reach or is a monopoly of those coming from high castes, but at the same time negates the general opinion that the workers are normally led by the high castes in their movement or furtherance of working class interests through trade unions. Incidentally, it was also noted that a significant majority (83 percent) of the trade union leaders were workers themselves negating the existence of high incidence of high caste outside leaders, which again is so vehemently lamented.

The table, however, seems to indicate that in tune with the occupational prestige and hierarchy generally accepted, the workers had lowest proportion of those coming from high castes and had the highest proportion of those coming from low castes. Conversely among the managerial category, those coming from high castes constituted highest proportion and those coming from low castes constituted the lowest proportion and the trade union leaders were placed between the two in terms of caste composition. However, the fact that over 80 percent of the workers coming from high or intermediate castes could be indicating to a shift in the rigid traditional occupation structure allowing little deviation from traditional caste occupations. It may be suggesting to a recent trend, necessitated by the forces of social transformation towards higher caste people willing or being compelled to take to jobs in industries or work organizations as operatives. One more inference that could be drawn from the caste composition of the workers' representatives is that, it is those coming from high castes who are normally identified or chosen or eventually emerge as representatives of the workers to participate in PM machineries mainly because they have to negotiate, bargain and participate in the process of decision making with the representatives of the management, who, more often than not, as observed from the table, happen to be from the higher castes. It could be like fielding their members who are compatible with the actors from other categories so as to have a bargaining or decision making process that could be more balanced. However, caste may not be the sole factor determining the expertise and effectiveness in participation. Other factors like educational level, span of work career, rural urban background and the like may also be of significance in determining the nature and effectiveness of participation by the parties to the process of WPM. However, the fact that the caste composition of the different categories associated with PM appears to be in tune with the occupational prestige associated with these categories, as it is observed that as many as 56 (55.4) percent of the managerial respondents come from high castes whereas the corresponding proportion among the workers' representatives is 27.3 percent, which is less than half of what is found with the managerial respondents.

With regard to the social profile of the respondents, another trait that is significant from the view point of WPM is the educational background. It is logically assumed that the level of educational attainment of the participants could be conditioning the nature, extent and the effectiveness of WPM in industries. As such, as stated above, education could be a factor facilitating the extent and quality of participation.

Educational Level

The data pertaining to the educational background of the respondents, quite logically, indicate that it is the managerial respondents who represent a much better educated lot than are their counterparts from operatives as well as trade union leaders.

It may be observed from the table that as many as 84(83.9) percent of the respondents from the managerial category are educationally better off, whereas, the corresponding proportion among the workers is as low as 8(7.8) percent. Conversely, those with low educational level constitute only 4(3.6) percent among the managers whereas they constitute 16(16.4) percent among the workers. Further, the trade union leaders are educationally placed between these two categories with 23(23.2) percent and 11(10.7) percent of them having high and low educational levels respectively. The data appear to be logical in the sense, high prestige, highly responsible and better paid jobs of managerial status call for higher levels of educational attainment and on the other hand to work as an operative higher levels of education may not be imperative. Further, it may also be true that to serve as a trade union leader, which involves and requires familiarity with labour and industrial laws, representing workers on diverse bipartite and tripartite fora as well as technical and legal correspondence in English, at least a few of the leaders in the union need to have at least moderate level of education. The data presented in the table seem to suggest precisely the same logic.

TABLE 4.3

Category-wise Distribution of Educational Level of the Respondents

Educational Level	*Category*			*Total*
	Managers	*Trade Union Leaders*	*Workers*	
High	47 (83.9)	13 (23.2)	10 (7.8)	70 (29.2)
Moderate	07 (12.5)	37 (66.1)	97 (75.8)	141 (58.8)
Low	02 (3.6)	06 (10.7)	21 (16.4)	29 (12.1)
Total	56 (100.0)	56 (100.0)	128 (100.0)	240 (100.0)

X^2=110.91, DF=4, Significant at 0.01 Level, C=0.56

However, the fact which is pertinent to note here is that, even among the representatives of the workers, the level of education appears to be much higher than it is among the working class at large. It may be noted from the table that over three-fourths (75.8 percent) of the workers' representatives are moderately educated, which is much higher than such proportion that could be observed among the work force at large and if we add those having higher education to this proportion, the data indicate that about 84 (83.6) percent of the operatives or workers associated with the machineries of WPM have moderate to high level of educational attainments which is incomparably high taking into consideration the educational level of the working class in general. The implications of levels of education for the extent, nature and effectiveness of WPM are analyzed and discussed in the subsequent chapters.

Coming to the other social traits of the respondents which could have less important implications for the process of WPM but nevertheless important from the point of view of portraying the social profile of the respondents, the income, family occupation, rural-urban background and marital status are focused upon. However, social origin, which is considered the single most important composite variable in the analysis or presentation of social profile, is discussed at the end of the chapter after a note on the career patterns of the respondents.

FAMILY BACKGROUND

Family Occupation

Coming to the family occupation, the data indicate that, more than two-thirds (68.2 percent) of the managerial respondents had the family occupation which could be classified as high prestige, high status occupations. On the other hand, the corresponding proportion among the workers (30.6 percent) and the trade union leaders (39.5 percent) was considerably less. However, an overwhelming majority of the trade union leaders come from the families that had pursued occupations, which could be classified as intermediate.

Rural-Urban Background

With regard to rural-urban background, the findings indicate to a higher urban background (87.5 percent) of the managerial respondents, followed by the workers (61.7 percent) and trade union leaders (55.4 percent). It is assumed that, particularly among the workers, those with urban background tend to be more actively associated with the process of WPM. Further, it is interesting to note that rather than workers, it is among the trade union leaders that the proportion of those with rural background is highest. It is normally assumed that the trade union leaders, in view of the nature of responsibilities involved and the type of skills required tend to be picked up from among better educated urban members. However, the urban composition in this study is found to be in favour of workers. It could be so, owing to the workers with higher levels of educational attainments and with urban background could be chosen specifically, to represent workers in fora of WPM.

Marital Status and Income

Coming to the marital status, the overwhelming majority of the respondents in all categories, that is, in excess of 95 percent are married and are with dependents. With regard to income, it is interesting to note that workers are relatively better off than are their counterparts among trade union leaders and managers. However, it may be noted that different scales were used for different categories, as it is impractical or illogical to use the same scale for all the categories coming from different occupational background. It was observed that over 80 (81.3) percent of the representatives from the workers had high income, corresponding to their category, whereas, such proportion among managerial respondents was as low as 5(5.4) percent. Further, trade union leaders, who are generally drawn mainly from the workers themselves, also had about 45(44.6) percent of those having high income. It was further noted that the workers and managers operating in private enterprises were better paid and better off than their counterparts from public sector. However, income is important as a constituent variable of the composite variable social origin, which is discussed later in the chapter.

PROFESSIONAL BACKGROUND

Career Patterns

Coming to the occupational life, an attempt is made here to focus on occupational status, span of career, occupational mobility and the like to have a general idea about the respondents work life. With regard to the occupational status of the workers, the data reveal that about 90 (89.8) percent are operatives, about 7 percent are supervisors and the remaining 3 percent of the worker respondents are from clerical jobs. It may be deduced from the observation made above that it is the operatives who are preferred to supervisors and clerks, to represent the workers in different fora of WPM. It could be so because of the closer exposure to the working conditions and realities therein, which may stand them in good stead in presenting or representing views and aspirations of the working class better than the supervisors and clerks. Thus WPM appears to be in the real sense a forum for the operatives to participate in the management. This statement is further supported by the fact that, even among the trade union leaders over two thirds (69.6 percent) are operatives at present or at one time before they took to trade union leadership as a vocation. However, it is also interesting to note that there are trade union leaders (3.6 percent) who also once held managerial positions and have taken to trade union leadership later. It is also pertinent to note that the proportion of those from clerical cadres is much higher among the trade union leaders than it is among the workers. Coming to the managerial respondents, it is significant to note that over three-fourths (76.8 percent) are high ranking managerial personnel and only about 5 (5.4) percent are from the junior managerial cadres. It may thus be stated that, the management tend to take part in the machineries of WPM rather seriously and hence assign such responsibilities and assignments to rather senior and high ranking officials, especially from the HRD or Personnel and Industrial Relations departments. This could be taken as a welcome sign because, when the senior managers get involved in the process of decision making in the WPM fora, the decisions arrived at could be viewed seriously by the management and it would be rather easy to implement such decisions without further need for scrutiny or approval as they have been taken with the consent of quite senior officials in the organizational hierarchy and in addition, it lends the sanctity to the forum as well as of the outcome of its functioning.

Span of Work Career

Further, span of career is considered as another important professional trait that could be of significance in the analysis of the dispositions, experiences and performance of the respondents with regard to the WPM. It is normally assumed that, longer the association with the industrial sub-culture and association with the machineries, more definite are the dispositions and higher the probability of the actors being more proficient with the machineries of WPM. An attempt is made in the chapter on attitudes and dispositions to probe into the relevance of span of career in the analysis of attitudes and dispositions.

The data on span of career reveal that, quite logically it is the trade union leaders who have on an average, longer span of career as compared to the managerial respondents and even the workers. It could be assumed that it takes quite some time for the workers to rise to the ranks of union leadership as it calls for longer association and active involvement in the working class movement to be picked up for the task of leading a union, and even after taking to union leadership quite a few continue to be operatives or supervisors as the case may be and as a result come to have a relatively longer span of career by the time they come to represent unions in the WPM fora.

TABLE 4.4

Span of Work Career of Respondents by Category

Span of Work Career	*Category*			*Total*
	Managers	*Trade Union Leaders*	*Workers*	
Short	11 (19.6)	02 (3.6)	11 (8.6)	24 (10.0)
Medium	20 (35.7)	24 (42.9)	49 (38.3)	93 (38.8)
Long	25 (44.6)	30 (53.6)	68 (53.1)	123 (51.3)
Total	56 (100.0)	56 (100.0)	128 (100.0)	240 (100.0)

X^2=8.78, DF=4, Not Significant

It may be observed from the table that, the highest proportion (19.6 percent) of those with short span of career and lowest proportion (44.6 percent) of those with long span of career are found with managerial category. Conversely lowest proportion (3.6 percent) of those with short span of career and highest proportion of (53.6 percent) those with long span of career are associated with respondents from trade union leaders. Even in case of the workers' representatives on the machineries of WPM, the composition is not much different from that of trade union leaders, indicating that as in the case of education, operatives with longer span of career are preferred to those with short span of career, emphasizing need for maturity, familiarity with industrial sub-culture and experience on work life in order to represent workers on machineries of WPM. It may also be stated here that inspite of having the largest proportion of those with short span of career, on the whole, the managerial respondents have among themselves 80 (80.4) percent with moderate to long span of career, again indicating to the fact that management has drafted on the fora for WPM, quite senior officials, that is, those with higher responsibilities in the organization and those who have enough powers to take decisions on the spot with enough sanctity to implement them. On the other hand it also testifies to the fact that the management takes the WPM quite seriously and assign the responsibility for the same to the officials of higher ranking, that is, in case of workers and trade union leaders, longer span of career is by necessity, whereas, in case of management it is by choice which could be taken as a positive sign.

Occupational Mobility

With regard to the occupational mobility among the respondents, the data reveal a distribution which is in favour of management. This finding is quite logical in view of the fact that, a bulk of representatives from workers are operatives with a small minority being supervisors or clerks, and so is the case with the trade union leaders. The proportion of those having experienced upward mobility is 7.6 percent, 9.0 percent and 31.5 percent among the workers, trade union leaders and the managerial respondents respectively, from which it may be concluded that it is the upwardly mobile executives or managers who tend to associate themselves with or tend to be associated with responsibilities relating to WPM.

SOCIAL ORIGIN

Lastly, in this chapter on social profile an attempt is made to ascertain the social origins of the respondents, which is, as explained in the section on conceptualization, a more rational and realistic estimation of the socio-economic standing of the respondents, and as a composite background variable could provide us with insights into social realities or determinants of WPM.

The data pertaining to the social origin of the respondents presented in the table indicates to a significant association between the social origin and the category of the respondents.

TABLE 4.5

Social Origin of the Respondents by Category

Social Origin	*Category*			*Total*
	Managers	*Trade Union Leaders*	*Workers*	
High	48 (85.7)	27 (48.2)	29 (22.7)	104 (43.3)
Low	08 (14.3)	29 (51.8)	99 (77.3)	136 (56.6)
Total	56 (100.0)	56 (100.0)	128 (100.0)	240 (100.0)

X^2= 63.79, DF=2, Significant at 0.01 Level, C=0.45

It may be observed from the table that about 86 (85.7) percent of the managerial respondents come from high social origin and on the contrary, over three-fourths (77.3 percent) of the workers come from low social origins. It may further be noted that as a class or section of society in between the two above, the proportion of those coming from high (48.2 percent) and low (51.8 percent) social origins is almost equal among trade union leaders. The distribution of the respondents on social origin is in tune with the logical assumption relating to composition and social statics and social dynamics of Indian society more than it is in case of any other single background variable discussed so far. Social origin, which is made up of respondents' score on caste, family income, family occupation and level of education could definitely be taken as a better measure of an individual's socio-economic standing in social hierarchy and other traits and properties that go with it.

The managerial class, in the modern sense of the term, though is of recent origin in Indian context owing to the recent origin of industrialization, industrialism and industrial sub-culture, it appears that it has followed the traditional pattern of social distribution of occupations with high ranking, high prestige and better paid jobs being cornered by the more privileged sections of the society, and the less privileged settling with least prestigeful and most arduous occupations. It may be stated that in spite of universalization of education, liberalization and globalization of the economy, the forces of Westernization and Modernization having their play and over fifty years of democracy, the social distribution of occupations, privileges and other material and non-material, objective and subjective criteria of class still by and large have not changed so much as to make big difference. It is again the so called cream of society that enjoys the cream of positions and opportunities in society and those at the rock-bottoms of the society tend to be denied not only positions but even the means through which they scale and attain these positions. Five decades of protective discrimination in the form of reservation may be taken as not having made a big dent at the traditional cultural superstructure or have provided those sections of society with leverages to move up the social hierarchy for whom they are meant. The reservation in educational, employment opportunities, meant for the weaker sections of the society appear to have not done great good to these sections warranting a serious as well as systematic and scientific analysis by social scientists. Thus those sections of society who have traditionally been associated with more prestigeful occupations tend to be associated with the more prestigeful modern occupations as well in the contemporary setting indicating to a routinization of traditional patterns in the modern context.

Further, in case of trade union leaders, the findings seem to suggest that it requires a better mix of both the worlds to make up the mettle neaded for trade union leadership. It may be indicating to the fact that it requires trade union leaders to be drawn neither from high nor from low social stations but from somewhere in between. They are required to lead the masses of workers and as such need to be of a notch above them and in order to be not identified with the antagonist class of exploiters, tend be a notch lower than those captains of industry. A sense of class consciousness and the fire and desire to uplift the oppressed as testified every now and then, has been a trait of middle classes rather that of the upper or lower classes. And more often than not it is those from the middle classes that are in the vanguard of labour movements.

Thus, the findings with regard to social origin of the respondents appear to be just in tune with the logical assumptions about the rubric and fabric of Indian society and the overall social profile of the respondents presented in the chapter, too, appears amenable for logical deductions from social realities pertaining to Indian society. However, how significant the social profile happens to be in the analysis of the functioning of the machineries of WPM, and to what extent, the nature, effectiveness and implications of WPM could be the functions of the social profile of these actors involved in the process would be dealt with and analyzed in a subsequent chapter.

5

Machineries of PM: Structure and Functions

Having ascertained empirically the social profile of the actors of PM, that is, the human component of WPM, an attempt is made in this chapter to provide a structural and functional profile of the machineries of PM in operation in Indian industries. Thus, the chapter deals with the types, composition, forms and structural features of these machineries on the one hand and the areas and levels of WPM and the actual functioning of these machineries on the other. For the purpose of analysis, in this study, however, only the major machineries which are generally or commonly found to be operating in most of the work organizations, if not all, are focused upon. This chapter, in short, seeks to provide the necessary backdrop and develop composite explanatory variables, which would be of empirical relevance in the analysis of extent, determinants and the effectiveness of WPM in the subsequent chapters.

TYPES OF MACHINERIES

As has been discussed in the chapter on Introduction and Review of Literature, the history of PM abounds with diverse machineries, institutions and structures of WPM in diverse socio-cultural settings. History of WPM in every country deals with the evolution of such structures and machineries and records the functioning and experiences, advantages and limitations of these machineries.

However, some of the commonly found schemes or machineries of WPM are the Joint Management Councils (JMCs), Workers' Councils (WCs), Shop-floor Councils (SFCs), Production Committees (PCs), Worker Directors (WDs) and Quality Circles (QCs). The constitution, powers and functions of these machineries appear to be varying from country to country and within the same country from one plant to another depending on the objectives enshrined in their documents of establishment. An attempt is, thus, made in this chapter to identify and explain the structural and functional features of diverse types of WPM machineries in operation in Indian industries.

With regard to the types of machineries of PM in operation, the findings indicate that wherever these machineries are adopted and employed, the practice is to have more than one machinery working in the organization, rather than adopt only one machinery. It may appear quite logical that those plants that are in favour of WPM need to have several machineries operating at different levels with varying functions, areas and powers since participation at different organizational levels requires different types of skills and rapport with different set of people and different functional areas of management come to be associated with different levels of responsibility and authority commensurating with them. It was observed that, all the eight industries studied had several machineries of WPM in operation concurrently, and the most commonly found machineries in operation were Joint Management Councils (JMCs), Shop-floor Councils (SFCs), Workers' Councils (WCs), Production Committees (PCs) and Quality Circles (QCs). However, there were other machineries established with worker and management components, to deal with issues concerning the plant in general, and such could be in a way, considered as machineries of WPM. Works' Committee, Wage Negotiation Committee, Welfare Committee, Grievance Committee and even Canteen

Committee and the like were found to be operating with worker and management components and in a way could be considered as contributing to democratic milieu in the plant which is the aim of WPM in the final analysis. That is, if PM is aimed at democratizing the workplace through decentralization of decision making process and delegation of organizational authority, then these other machineries may be considered as furthering this organizational goal. These machineries, as their names themselves suggest deal with wages, education, welfare, amenities and grievances pertaining to the workers and their working lives. Their constitution and level of participation vary with sector, type, size and nature of management. In quite a few industries these subsidiary or secondary machineries are the off- shoots of major machineries in course of time, when the issues to be dealt with by these machineries come to be too numerous and complex and warrant a separate committee consisting of persons with requisite aptitude, orientation, exposure and expertise to deal with these issues. Hence, committees like Wage Negotiation Committee, Technical Committee, Education Committee, Welfare Committee and the like come into existence. Such proliferation of committees was found to be more conspicuous in large, private sector manufacturing organizations. And the experience was found to be rather rewarding, having a positive impact on the climate of industrial relations in general as manifested in the scant and very sparse industrial disputes breaking out in strikes or lockouts. The establishment and functioning of these bodies was taken as indicators of the democratic milieu in the work organizations, which has been taken as an explanatory variable in the extent, nature and effectiveness of the other machineries of WPM in the subsequent chapters.

An attempt, thus, is made here to focus on the constitution, powers and functioning of the major machineries of WPM such as JMCs, SFCs, WCs, and QCs. As mentioned earlier, these machineries were found operating in the plants in different combinations with QCs and SFCs being the most frequently employed machineries.

For the purpose of analysis the data were attributed to the respondents representing industries with specific machineries in operation, composition of the machineries, the frequencies of meeting, areas of management dealt with by the machineries and the like, and with 30 respondents from each plant, in all the total respondents to whom the organizational variables were attributed were 240. The findings are based on the analysis so undertaken.

Joint Management Councils (JMCs)

In all five out of eight industries representing about three fifth of the universe studied had JMCs in operation. Establishment of JMCs, as discussed in the Review of Literature, is a statutory requirement in the industries employing workers in excess of 500. This statutory managerial obligation is found to be well adhered to by all the industrial establishments. Further, the review of the findings based on research elsewhere seems to suggest that JMCs are the main workhorse of WPM process in Indian industries, having been found a place in statutory books and also having wider scope and broader span of organizational stretch than any other machinery. As the name itself indicates, the JMCs have been looked upon by the employees and unions as a forum for raising any issue that concerns them and the organization for a bilateral decision. Whereas, other machineries, like Quality Circles, Welfare Committee and Wage Negotiation Committee have narrow and specified issues to deal with limited sphere of competence. Thus, a majority of issues concerning most of the areas of management are dealt with by JMCs and only a few other more complicated issues that warrant intricate skills and expertise or those issues that are not of very high functional importance come to be dealt with by other subsidiary or ancillary committees. It may thus be stated that the JMCs are the major thrusts, main instruments of WPM in Indian industries and are synonym of the spirit, ideal, practice and movement of wPM.

In terms of sector, it was observed that public sector units had JMCs almost as a rule whereas, in private sector units the JMCs were substituted by other machineries. Thus, the presence or absence of JMCs significantly varied with the sector of industry. Further, the findings also revealed that it was in the large units that JMCs were found to be operating more often than they were in the smaller units. However, in terms of the age of the industry, the presence or absence of the JMCs was found to be independent, with old and newly established industries having the JMCs depending on size and sector.

With regard to the structural dimensions of the JMCs, the study revealed that, the size of the JMCs varied extensively from one industry to the other, ranging between four members to seventeen members. However, the average size of the JMCs was 11.2 members, which also varied significantly with the other characteristics of the organization. The findings further indicate that the size of the JMCs varies significantly again with the size and sector of the industry. The large units were found to be having larger JMCs, with membership drawn from diverse categories of workers and unions than compared to the smaller units with limited representation. Further, with regard to the sector, it was observed that the JMCs in public sector units were of larger size than those in the private sector units.

Further, more than size, it is the composition of JMCs which could be of functional relevance to the process of WPM. In the literature on WPM, it is frequently lamented that the failure of WPM is mainly due to the machineries of WPM being management biased, whereby, incase of a stalemate or dead lock, the managements can still steal the show or their opinion would come to prevail. Another lacunae of

WPM, frequently noted is the lack of management representation from higher organizational levels owing to which, the representatives of the management in the WPM machineries tend to be devoid of requisite authority backed by required managerial support, rendering them unable to take a final decision requiring them to seek approval of the top management before committing anything in the deliberations of the JMCs. Another bottleneck in the functioning of these machineries is the apathy and scorn of top management toward the functioning of these bodies, wherever they are involved, owing to social and organizational distance between them and their worker counterparts. As such, it is the composition of the machineries of WPM, which is of immense functional significance in the process of WPM.

The findings with regard to the composition of JMCs reveal that, composition is either worker biased or balanced and seldom it is management biased.

TABLE 5.1

Composition of JMCs

Composition of JMCs	*Frequency*	*Percentage*
Balanced	90	37.5
Management Biased	00	00.0
Union Biased	30	12.5
Worker Biased	30	12.5
Non Existent	90	37.5
Total	240	100.0

As such, the much lamented lacunae of management representatives out numbering the worker representatives and thereby over ruling the worker opinion appears to be rather unfounded and hence unwarranted. In one half of the organizations studied the JMCs had equal number of representatives from the management and the workers which is as per the statutory requirements where as in other units, the composition is in favour of workers, either due to separate representation for unions, workers and supervisors or due to worker component being larger than that of the management. However, the practice of having elected worker representatives was found to be not in vogue and workers' representation was normally through the union leaders, who in turn were elected by the workers to the union offices. The practice of electing the workers' representatives directly by workers through election, as stipulated in the legislation elsewhere appears to be not favoured by the working class and unions in the Indian context. Even unions may be in favour of this representative participation of the workers in the management through the unions as it enhances the bargaining powers of the unions on the one hand and lends a greater degree of sanctity to the charter of demands and grievances submitted by the unions to the management as these issues could be raised in the JMCs in their routine meetings. However, one apprehension about the constitution of machineries of WPM in such a way as to marginalize the workers from the decision making process, particularly relating to important issues, is not supported by the findings of this study.

It was further noted that the composition of the JMCs varies significantly with the sector. The public sector units were found to be having more often an equitable base as compared to the JMCs operating in the private sector units, where the composition was either worker biased or sometimes representation of managerial component was through the supervisors. However, the age of the industry appeared to have no significant impact on the composition of the JMCs.

With regard to the establishment of JMCs, it was also noted that, it is the public sector industries in which this machinery was established earlier than in the private sector units, taking into consideration the date of establishment of the industries themselves as the reference points.

The other dimension of internal structure relate to the division of and delegation of power among the different officials and designating members to different offices. More often than not, the JMCs have a Presiding Officer and a Convenor and likewise a Joint Presiding Officer and a Joint Convenor to act on behalf of Presiding Officers and Convenors in their absence. Sub-committees of the JMCs are constituted to deal with different areas of participation depending on their expertise. The members constitute committees like Production Committee, Discipline Committee, Welfare Committee and the like to have some semblance of division of labour among the members to deal with different areas of management in as expert a manner as possible. However, these committees were not formal bodies representing watertight compartments and represented semi formal committees set up to deal with diverse areas of management, with inputs from every other willing member from the JMCs. There are also provisions and practices of having Joint Committees to deal with issues that come under the purview of more than one committee.

The system of communication in JMCs is more of an informal nature with written communications reserved to situations of less cordiality. Otherwise the decisions in the form of proceedings and resolutions are recorded and referred to for implementation. The communication, however, appears to be more formal with formal procedures to follow in the conduct of the deliberations of JMCs in such units where the industrial relations are relatively less cordial.

Similarly, wherever the JMCs are in operation, they invariably have a letter or document of their establishment, that is the constitution which clearly state the aims and objectives, areas of competence, jurisdiction of operation, the constitution, powers and functions of various members and office bearers, the rules of business, frequency of meetings and the like and represents tl• normative order of the JMCs.

These norms include the procedure for nomination and election of the management and workers' representatives and the tenure of such nomination and election, tenure of office for the office bearers. Thus, though the JMCs have a formal structure on paper and constitution, they are found to be functioning less formally. They do have a structure, in principle and spirit, that of an elected or democratic administrative structure, however with quite less formalism.

The study further focused on the functioning of the JMCs in terms of the frequency of meetings, areas of management addressed, the extent and nature of participation of workers' representatives, workers' say in the actual decision making process and so forth. However, these aspects of PM in general are dealt with separately in the chapter on attitudes and experiences of workers, union leaders and managerial personnel in a subsequent chapter, based on interview of all the above categories of participants. An attempt is made in this section to portray the functioning of each one of these machineries at the level of industries.

The findings with regard to the frequency of the JMC meetings indicate that on an average, the JMCs meet once in three months though in a small minority of industries the meetings are less frequent as quarterly and as more frequent as once in a month. In short, however, it may be stated that the frequency of the meetings of the JMCs is moderate to high. It was also testified by both parties that the frequency of the meetings was quite adequate to deal with the work load and cases that come up before the JMCs and did not see the need or justification for increasing the frequency of the meetings. Further analysis reveals that the JMCs in private industries meet more frequently than do those in public sector units. On probe it was found that the higher frequency of JMC meetings in private industries was not due to commitment, genuine concern or favourable disposition of the management, but due to the necessity which arose out of frequent disagreements or differences of opinions and difficulty in giving effect to the agreements arrived upon through JMCs. It may however be stated that the frequency of JMC meetings was not a cause of concern in the process of WPM.

Another important aspect of PM is the area of management that come to be dealt with by the machineries. The findings pertaining to the areas of management dealt with or major concern of JMCs indicate that JMCs have a wider scope than any other machinery of WPM. The findings with regard to the areas of management dealt with by the JMCs indicate that almost everything connected with the industrial administration and management come under the purview of JMCs. Production, training, working conditions, rewards, promotions, discipline and welfare are the areas of management that are taken up by the JMCs. Except for recruitment, sales and finance matters, all other areas of management come to be dealt with by the JMCs. Even among these broad areas, production, working conditions, discipline and welfare were the most frequently and commonly dealt with areas of management by the JMCs. If at all these areas are divided into different categories based on the interest, such as 'management interest', 'workers' interest' and the 'joint interest', it is interesting and significant to note that no JMCs deal with issues that can be classified exclusively as 'workers' interests', whereas, in about 20 percent of the cases, the JMCs deal with the issues that can be exclusively taken as representing the 'management interests' such as productivity, discipline and the like.

The data however reveal that in 80 percent of the cases, the JMCs deal with the issues that could be termed as those concerning the 'joint interest'. It is rather paradoxical to note that, a machinery established with a view to provide workers with greater say in the management, could in reality be dealing exclusively with issues to promote or further management interests.

TABLE 5.2

Management Areas Dealt with by JMCs

Management Areas Dealt with by JMCs	*Frequency*	*Percentage*
Management Interests	30	20.0
Workers' Interests	00	00.0
Both	150	80.0
Total	180	100.0

Further analysis reveals that it is the JMCs operating in the private sector that are prone to have management orientation and the public sector units have the JMCs with worker orientation. Although a statistically significant association was not found to be existing between the areas of participation and sector, it at least appeared that in private units, the managements' interests are more likely to be protected than they are in case of JMCs operating in the public sector units.

Similar trend could also be found between the size of industry and the areas of participation, with larger units having JMCs furthering the interests of the workers and on the contrary, the smaller units tend to have the managements' interests protected by the JMCs operating within. As in case of the analysis of other variables, the age of the industry was found to be of little significance in explaining the areas of participation as the industries both old and new conformed to this pattern of areas of participation alike. In view of the above, it may be stated that generally the areas of management dealt with by the JMCs do focus on both the issues that are in tune with the interest of the workers as well as the management. However, if at all there is any deviation, it could be in favour of management rather than the workers' interest. It may be noted here that, production and discipline are the issues that are invariably dealt with by JMCs in all the industries, irrespective of sector, size and age of industry, whereas, the issues such as welfare, working conditions, promotion and the like which could represent worker interests may some times be not on the agenda of JMCs. Thus, the very purpose or goal of WPM, which seeks to have a greater say of workers in the matters affecting their working lives appears to be not taken as seriously as the issues that are in the interest of the management. However, it is rather gratifying to note that, in 80 percent of the cases, the issues representing both workers' and managements' interests are dealt with by the JMCs.

The study further seeks to focus on the nature and extent of workers' participation in the JMCs and their say in the final decisions that come out of JMCs. It may be recalled here that the extent and nature of workers' participation and the amount of say they have in the decisions affecting their lives in various machineries of WPM are taken together to ascertain the extent and nature of WPM in the industry at large.

With regard to the extent of participation of workers' representatives in the JMCs, the data indicate that it is reasonably high.

TABLE 5.3

Extent of Participation by the Workers' Representatives (JMCs)

Extent of Participation by the Workers' Representatives	*Frequency*	*Percentage*
High	60	40.0
Moderate	90	60.0
Low	00	00.0
Total	150	100.0

It may be observed from the table that in 40 percent of the cases the participation is high and in the remaining 60 percent of the cases it is moderate with none of the industries studied having low level of participation by the workers' representatives in the JMCs. This finding may negate the general opinion regarding the workers' apathy in the machineries of WPM, which is so widely lamented. Almost every work and report on the status of PM in India has come to hold workers' apathy as the bane of this positive and innovative intervention at place of work, whereas, the participation of workers' representatives in the main forum of WPM appears to be quite gratifying and encouraging. This may also be indicating to a positive trend in the recent past, which the earlier studies could not come across.

The study further indicates that the extent of workers' participation in JMCs varies significantly with other organizational variables such as sector, size and the age of the work organizations. As in case of the frequency of meetings and the areas of participation, even in the case of the extent of workers' participation, the public sector units appear to be having an edge over the private sector industries.

TABLE 5.4

Extent of Participation by the Workers' Representatives by Sector

Sector	*Extent of Participation by the Workers' Representatives (JMC)*		*Total*
	High	*Moderate*	
Public	60 (100.0)	60 (66.7)	120 (80.0)
Private	—	30 (33.3)	30 (20.0)
Total	60 (100.0)	90 (100.0)	150 (100.0)

X^2=69.33, DF=2, Significant at 0.01 Level, C=0.47.

The data presented in the table appears to be much against what is presumed, that is, the private firms being more professional like and more enlightened than the public sector units when it comes to the application of principles and extension of practices of modern science of management and reap the benefits of the high level of commitment, identification and job satisfaction among the workforce and the peaceful industrial relations which could be achieved through, at least in principle, by giving more heed to the participatory needs of the workers and bringing about a democratic culture at work place. The data presented in the table reveal that, in none of the industries studied, the extent of the participation of workers' representatives in JMCs was low and it ranged between high to moderate. However, all those with high level of participation were the public sector units with private units having only moderate level of participation. Even with regard to the nature of participation of workers' representatives in JMCs, the findings indicate to a more favourable situation prevailing with the public sector units vis-à-vis the private sector units. It was noted that all the public sector units were associated with participation of workers' representatives in JMCs that could be considered as active, whereas, in case of the private units, the participation at best, could be considered as moderately active. It may be noted here that the statutory requirement of having WPM in the industries is being more closely adhered to by the public sector units as against the private ones, who take the statute as an external constraint or an obligation required to be met with as a mandatory practice. It may also be attributed to the fact that workers in public sector units are less afraid of discrimination and victimization on countering and contradicting the management than are their counterparts with private sector. It may also further be attributed to the fact that, the public sector units by nature and tradition are more adherent to the statutory requirements than are their private sector counterparts, even, sometimes, at the cost of the profit and economic viability of the plant itself. Further, the public sector units are viewed more often stressing the means more at the cost of the end, and the end being the profit and means being humane work organizations as the responsibility of a Welfare State. On the contrary, the private sector units more often than not, are result oriented and the question of survival in an extremely competitive business world would rather render them conscious about the ends and undermine the means. But, in the process, they may also loose sight of the positive benefits that accrue to the firm as a result of WPM.

Similar trend could also be observed with regard to the workers' say in the decisions of JMCs. It speaks of how much say the workers' representatives have in influencing the decisions of the JMCs which was ascertained through an analysis of workers' inputs and arguments incorporated in the decision vis-a-vis that of management representatives.

TABLE 5.5

Workers' Say in JMCs by Sector

Sector	*Workers' Say in JMCs*		*Total*
	Much	*Somewhat*	
Public	120 (100.0)	—	120 (80.0)
Private	—	30 (100.0)	30 (20.0)
Total	120 (100.0)	30 (100.0)	150 (100.0)

X^2=154.66, DF=2, Significant at 0.01 Level, C=0.62.

The analysis revealed that, all those cases in which the say was considered as 'much' belonged to the JMCs in public sector undertakings and all those cases where the extent of say was considered as 'somewhat' came from the private sector units. Just as in the analysis of other aspects of JMCs functioning, the greater extent of workers' say in public sector units could be attributed to the antagonism of private sector to WPM, so widely discussed in the literature as well as to the public sector complacency about the functioning of the firms and in the process end up giving more scope for workers to have their say in the making of the decisions. Thus, if workers' say on the final outcome of the functioning of JMCs is to be taken as an important indicator of WPM, then even on this count, the situation is in favour of the public sector units. It may be stated here, to emphasize the significance of workers' say in the decision, that, the composition of the machineries, the frequency of the meetings, the areas of participation as well as the extent and nature of participation of workers' representatives could all be taken as a means to achieve the end of having greater say of workers in the decisions and greater adherence of these decisions with the needs and aspirations of the workers at large. Thus, how much of say the workers have in determining the final outcome of WPM machineries has been employed as an index of the extent of WPM and the findings, as in the case of other aspects of JMCs in operation, seem to reflect the same trend.

The data further, interestingly indicate that, it is rather larger organizations where the JMCs tend to represent the opinion of the workers more closely than do the JMCs operating in small organizations. It is normally assumed that smaller organizations provide a more conducive milieu for participation owing to closer personal ties among the members. However, the findings of the study seem to indicate that it is the size of the workforce, that is the numerical strength that matters more in the decision making process by JMCs. Stated in other words, larger the workforce that is going to be affected by the decisions, greater will be the say of workers' representatives in the process of decision making in the machineries of WPM.

Shop-floor Councils (SFCs)

Although less pervasive when it comes to the management areas of participation, a more popular and more universally found machinery of WPM is the Shop-floor Council (SFC) which is also known in some organizations as Workers'

Councils. However, a more widely prevalent and employed term, 'Shop-floor Council' is chosen to designate this machinery in the study. As such, the analysis on SFCs also includes the WCs.

Compared to JMCs which were operating in 62.5 percent of the work organizations, SFCs were found to be operating in 75 percent of the organizations having some machineries for WPM. The SFCs are normally conceived as machineries for democracy at grassroots, where actually the workers, the operatives in the work shop or at floor level participate in taking such decisions that affect their working lives. These machineries are often glorified in the literature on industrial relations as springs of democracy or the nurseries of industrial democracy and in a way, they train workers in the art or science of negotiation and bargaining which can stand them in good stead as they mature, to negotiate at higher levels culminating in representation at Board level.

Coming to the composition of the SFCs, it was noted that deviations do occur in terms of size as well as the internal categories. The size of the SFCs varies from nine to twenty members. It was also noticed that each workshop or division or department in the plant has an independent SFC. For example, the ITI had seventeen such Shop-floor Councils operating whereas Triveni Engineering had just one SFC. It appeared that the number of SFCs varies with the size of the organization as well as the degree of division of labour or specialization in the work process. However, the number of SFCs did not appear to vary with the sector and age of the work organizations.

Coming to the composition of membership in SFCs, there were again diverse patterns. In one third of the organizations, same number of workers, union representatives and management representatives constituted the SFCs. In another one fifth of the organizations, the workers' representatives were twice as many as the managements' representatives. In the remaining industries, the managements were represented by the supervisors with equal number of workers' representatives and unionists. Inspite of areas of participation being less compared to the JMCs, the SFCs were larger in size than the JMCs.

However, taking into consideration the nature of composition at large, it appeared that one third of the industries where the SFCs were in operation, they appeared to be management biased.

TABLE-5.6

Composition of Shop-floor Councils

Composition of Shop-floor Councils	*Frequency*	*Percentage*
Balanced	60	25.0
Management Biased	60	25.0
Worker Biased	60	25.0
Non Existent	60	25.0
Total	240	100.0

The study revealed that the SFCs which were balanced, worker biased and management biased in terms of composition were equal in proportion and in one fourth of the organizations studied there were no SFCs. Compared to the composition of JMCs, SFCs appeared to be more management oriented, which was not a very welcome situation. In fact, SFCs being the instruments of industrial democracy at grassroots, they ought to have been with more worker orientation to enable them to protect the interests of the workers against the possible exploitation, particularly in matters pertaining to working conditions and nature of supervision. Thus, it appears that there is a need for rendering the SFCs with a strong worker orientation and provide workers with greater opportunities and sense of participation in determining the conditions of their working lives.

Although the SFCs functioned more informally than the JMCs and the meetings were rather loosely scheduled and held as per need or as and when the occasion demands, the meetings of SFCs were found to be more frequently held than the meetings of JMCs.

TABLE 5.7

Frequency of Meetings (SFCs)

Frequency of Meetings (SFCs)	*Frequency*	*Percentage*
High	150	83.3
Moderate	00	00.0
Low	30	16.7
Total	180	100.0

The data presented in the table reveal that in more than 80 (83.3) percent of the industries where the SFCs exist, the meetings are as frequent as once in a month or more, whereas in about 17 (16.7) percent of the industries the meetings are sparse and far between as once in three months or still less frequently. On the whole it may be stated that the frequency of SFCs meetings is quite high. It may be due to the fact that all the members of the SFCs are normally present on floor almost everyday and convening a meeting on demand does not entail any extra effort. Although these meetings are required to be scheduled at an interval specified by the rules of their establishment, on the whole it appears where these SFCs are active, the frequency far exceeds this statutory requirement and where they are not active, this statutory requirement is not met with or is met with for formality or for records.

The meetings normally take place after shift hours and those industries, which work, on three shifts, the meetings are held between the day shifts. The meetings are normally convened by the Convenor, who is most often a union representative or a worker representative and more often than not these meetings are presided over by the management representatives and in their absence the meetings are presided over by the supervisors or the unionists. The meetings tend to take place on the Shop-floor itself and only in a few cases in canteens or other specified places. The proceedings and resolutions are recorded in a logbook for reference and follow-up action. Emergency meetings are convened if warranted by the exigencies - more frequently in case of retrenchments on disciplinary grounds, increase in production targets or problems of serious nature pertaining to the working conditions. Meetings are held with short notice or on the spot and the decisions are sent to the Industrial Relations Cell or Personnel office in the form of proceedings.

With regard to the major concerns of SFCs in operation, the findings seem to indicate that, as in the case of JMCs, the issues that concern both the workers and the management figure in or are dealt with by the SFCs. In more than 80 percent of the cases, the SFCs deal with the mixed issues.

TABLE 5.8

Major Concerns (SFCs)

Major Concerns	*Frequency*	*Percentage*
Management Centered	00	00.0
Worker Centered	30	16.7
Mixed	150	83.3
Total	180	100.0

Just as in case of JMCs, where there were no industries with JMCs purely dealing with workers' interests, there are no industries with SFCs dealing only with managements' concerns. Over 80 (83.3) percent of the industries studied however, had SFCs dealing with issues concerning both workers and management and in case of the remaining industries, the SFCs dealt only with issues concerning the workers' interests. It appear quite logical in the sense that, at the Shop-floor, issues concerning workers figure more prominently as the very purpose is to have cordial and harmonious working relations between the workers and the managements. It is observed that mainly at Shop-floor, the issues concerning workers get manifested and crystallized and move up to higher levels of management as necessary inputs or feed-backs for policy making at plant level, whereas issues concerning management, except those relating to productivity and compensation, are discussed and decided upon at higher levels of management. Moreover, discussing issues concerned only with management is also against the spirit and philosophy based on which the SFCs come into existence. As such, the SFCs end up dealing mainly with the issues concerning the workers and serve principally as vehicles for the furtherance of workers' interests. However, some vital issues concerning the managements such as, productivity and discipline do figure in the agenda of SFCs.

Further, these SFCs were found to be operating with considerably high degree of effectiveness in dealing with issues coming before them. In two thirds of industries studied, the SFCs dealt with issues with high degree of effectiveness and in another one third of the cases the effectiveness was moderate. In none of the industries the working of the SFCs was poor. In view of the general level of education among the workers being not high, the traditional out look of life and the recent origin of the industrialism and the concept of industrial democracy or PM, the degree of effectiveness with which the SFCs were found to be operating could be considered as reasonably high and much higher than what is normally assumed. This high degree of effectiveness could be attributed to the very active participation of the workers in the SFCs.

TABLE 5.9

Participation of Workers' Representatives in the SFCs

Participation of Workers' Representatives in the SFCs	*Frequency*	*Percentage*
Active	150	83.3
Somewhat Active	30	16.7
Not Active	00	00.0
Total	180	100.0

The data reveal that the participation of workers is somewhat more active in SFCs than it is in case of JMCs. However, it is heartening to note that in none of the cases, the participation was found to be poor or inactive either in JMCs or in SFCs. It may be argued that workers or the workers' representatives are more active at SFCs than they are on JMCs and workers feel more at home or ease with the machineries of WPM at lower level. It may appear logical that workers are better appraised, more conversant, better seized of and more interested in the issues that are of immediate concern to them and hence tend to participate more actively and effectively in the machineries that come to deal with such issues and further these machineries, because of the active participation of the workers, are relatively more effective in dealing with the issues concerning the workers. As such, the widely held opinion regarding the workers apathy toward WPM machineries, workers' inability to cope-up with the kind of efforts required to participate in these machineries and the resultant poor functioning of the machineries of WPM appears to be rather unfounded or unwarranted and the situation with regard to the functioning of the WPM machineries is not as poor as lamented. However, the degree of positive implications of such WPM which is expected as the natural outcome of the effective functioning of the WPM machineries are discussed in the subsequent chapters.

Quality Circles (QCs)

Coming to the other machineries of WPM in operation, the study found that Quality Circles (QCs) are found in all the organizations having WPM and serve as subsidiary bodies to the main machineries like JMCs and SFCs, though not directly under the control of them. QCs are far less formal than the other machineries discussed so far and have quite a limited sphere of activity. However, the QCs do not restrict or confine themselves to issues relating to promotion of quality alone as it appears going by the name of machinery. They deal with host of other issues which may have indirect implication for the quality of goods and viability of the firm at large such as waste reduction, pilferage proofing, keeping time schedules, motivating workers for commitment, quality or creation of quality consciousness, standardization of work procedures for uniform quality, improving and providing necessary working conditions for the general improvement in the quality, standard and the like. However compared to other machineries of PM, the QCs have very limited scope and sphere of competence but are of considerably more significant implications for the competitive and economic wellbeing of the firm, particularly in view of increasing stress on quality and sophistication of the goods being produced and marketed. May be it is in recognition of their such important role in the health of the firm that all the industries have QCs operating in them. Even in the final analysis, it was observed that, it is in these Quality Circles that the workforce get exposed to the skills and know how of quality and the importance of quality control. Particularly in industries like electronics and the heavy engineering the quality is the key to success and survival in increasingly global and competitive world of business, and as such a quality conscious work force could be taken as an asset beyond value. Thus, the QCs that could be taken as agencies of socialization to quality culture, are the ones most favoured by the parties to the production and more so by the managements.

The data pertaining to the QCs reveal that, as stated earlier, they are found operating in all the industries studied and accordingly, the literature on the machineries of WPM testifies to the fact that they are the most universally found machineries of WPM, irrespective of economy being Capitalistic, Socialistic or Communist as quality is the universal concern of all the economies. But, their role as machineries providing workers a say in the management of industry is more important to be ascertained in this analysis as it would focus on twin objectives like democratizing and humanizing the workplace on the one hand and improving the productivity of the organization on the other.

The size of these QCs varied from industry to industry depending on the size of the organization, the type of technology employed and the degree of specialization. The size varied from as small as four members to as many as twelve members. Further, in a few industries, these QCs within themselves had further division of labour like the subgroups responsible for improvement of techniques, arrangement and maintenance of tools and fixtures, house keeping, cost reduction, elimination of waste, quick changeovers, technical up gradation and the like. However, on an average, these QCs were much smaller in size in comparison with the JMCs and SFCs, of course, quite logically owing to limited sphere of competence.

Further, coming to the composition of the QCs, it was observed that in all industries, irrespective of the sector, size and other organizational variables, the composition was neither management biased nor worker biased. It is quite logical to expect the management being equally interested in the QCs and in many cases it is at the initiative of management that QCs were established and it is but natural to find them being interested in the functioning of QCs and be concerned about their continued existence. However, what is positive development to be noticed is its being endorsed by the workers as well by their membership. It is quite gratifying to note that the managements have given due importance to the role of workers in maintaining higher standards of quality and workers have taken the matters relating to quality as important as the managements. The constitution being balanced in all QCs in all industries is an indication of its being viewed as an important machinery in the interest of both.

Coming to the frequency of meetings, the findings reveal that, where the issues being deliberated upon and discussed about were related to quality and allied issues, the frequency of meeting was rather not formally fixed in most of the industries (80 percent).

TABLE 5.10

Frequency of Meetings (QCs)

Frequency of Meetings	*Frequency*	*Percentage*
High	150	62.5
Moderate	90	37.5
Low	00	00.0
Total	240	100.0

Quality was considered as an everyday concern as well as long term concern if it has to deal with the change in technology or the product range. Thus, in most of the industries, the QCs met as and when the need arose. But in a few (20 percent) industries the frequency was fixed ranging from once in a month to once in three months. However, the actual functioning of the QCs revealed that about two-thirds (62.5 percent) of the QCs met at a high frequency, that is, more than once a month and in case of another one third, the frequency of the meeting was moderate, that is, once in one-two months. Looking at the nature and diversity (low) of issues being dealt with, the frequency observed could be considered as reasonably high. It is also significant to note that, none of the QCs were associated with low frequency of meetings.

With regard to the effectiveness of dealing with the issues, the findings reveal that about two-thirds (62.5 percent) of the QCs exhibited high degree of effectiveness in dealing with the issues and the remaining about one-third (37.5) of the QCs were found to be moderately effective in dealing with the issues allocated to them.

TABLE 5.11

Effectiveness in Dealing with Issues (QCs)

Effectiveness in Dealing with Issues	*Frequency*	*Percentage*
High	150	62.5
Moderate	90	37.5
Low	00	00.0
Total	240	100.0

It may be stated that, to have the QCs dealing with the issues with this level of effectiveness, that too, in a country with so short a history of industrialism could be viewed as quite promising. In the sense, no QC was found to be ineffective in dealing with issues relating to quality in itself could be taken as a welcome development.

It is further significant to note that, the level of effectiveness varied significantly with sector and quite significantly, it is the public sector units in which the QCs operate more effectively than they do in private sector. All those QCs which were operating with high level of effectiveness belonged to the public sector units and similarly all the QCs which were operating with moderate degree of effectiveness were from the private sector units. Viewed in the light of general opinion that the private sector is more quality conscious and the public sector branded as quality complacent, the findings of the present study are the deviations from the general opinion and seem to be indicating to a welcome change in public sector units. The actual contribution of these QCs to the quality improvement in the plants is a different matter, but at least a sincere and effective involvement in the process aimed at achieving this objective could be viewed as a positive step. The general opinion that could be formed through the observations on the field is that, the quality of products is the concern of all alike, and every worker and management is for improving the quality of goods produced and services rendered by them. And as such, it does not need much of persuasion or motivation to get the personnel committed to quality. However, when it comes to putting this commitment into practice, they appear to be lacking. In the sense, they seem to be less careful in minimizing cost, elimination of waste and striving to improve the skills that can contribute to the overall improvement in quality of the products and services. So, in short, it may be stated that, though not as pervasive in their scope as other machineries of WPM, the QCs have come to be taken as part of the industrial culture and way of industrial life in Indian context and have been contributing not only to the democratization of workplace but also in improving the quality of products and services.

In addition to JMCs, SFCs and QCs, there were several other bodies or mechanisms of PM in operation in the selected industries but not in so many industrial organizations as to warrant separate discussion on each of them. The Grievance Committees or Councils (GCs) were found operating in one fourth of the industries studied. They were constituted of primarily the union and management representatives, vested with the responsibility of processing, channeling and disposing the grievances registered by the workers. Wherever, they were found in existence, their functioning was just moderate in the sense, moderately effective in dealing with the grievance handling. The limited success of these bodies was found to be partly owing to the management apathy and partly owing to the unreasonable or unfounded grievances of the workers.

Further, there were Production Councils, Welfare Committees, Canteen Committees and Suggestion Schemes, which had different functions as noted by their nomenclature and served in one way or the other, to some extent at least as the machineries of WPM. However, they were not found in many organizations and also had very limited scope of participation in the management.

Hence, in the present study, the functioning of only JMCs, SFCs and QCs are taken to represent the extent, nature, effectiveness and determinants of WPM and the findings of the present study are confined, in principle only to the combined functioning and its impact on the general situation of WPM.

Thus, having focused on the structure, composition and functioning of the machineries of PM, an attempt is made in the next chapter to deal with the attitudes and dispositions of those who participate in these machineries.

6

PM: Dispositions and Experiences

This chapter deals with dispositions, attitudes and orientations of the main actors in the machineries of PM on the one hand and the experiences of these actors and expectations with regard to the process of PM on the other. Hence, an attempt is made in this chapter to ascertain empirically the attitudes of workers, managerial personnel and trade union leaders toward the structural and functional pattern of the major machineries of WPM in which they participate, their disposition toward various components and conventions of PM and their orientation and approaches to process of PM. Further having ascertained these attitudinal aspects of WPM, an attempt is made to probe empirically into their experiences of working within these machineries and their exposure to the process of PM.

It is assumed that the dispositions and experiences of the participants in the machineries of WPM could, in a way, have implications for the extent, nature, effectiveness of their participation in the machineries of WPM and as such, could be viewed as, in a way, the determinants of the extent, nature and effectiveness of WPM.

DISPOSITIONS

Operationalization of Concept

As mentioned in the framework of analysis and the conceptual scheme, the disposition and experience of the actors in the process of WPM are the composite variables made up of the scores of respondents on diverse variables pertaining to their views and experiences as significant partners to the process of PM. The composite variable of disposition was made up of in all, seven variables such as, their opinion regarding the need for PM in the present context, importance of workers' say in the decision making process, expansion of scope of PM, its assumed implication for the climate of industrial relations, productivity, workers' morale, organizational climate and the like.

The findings with regard to each of these variables indicate that, an overwhelming majority of the all the three actors in the machineries of WPM have favourable disposition toward the WPM. With regard to the need for WPM in the present context, there appeared to be consensus among all the actors in the process of WPM about its necessity and desirability.

TABLE 6.1

Need for Workers Having a Say in the Management in the Present Context by Category

Need for Workers for Having a say	*Category*			*Total*
	Managerial Personnel	*Trade Union Leaders*	*Workers*	
Much	39 (69.6)	43 (76.8)	93 (72.7)	175 (72.9)
Somewhat	12 (21.4)	10 (17.9)	23 (18.0)	45 (18.8)
Little	05 (8.9)	3 (5.3)	12 (9.4)	20 (8.3)
Total	56 (100.0)	56 (100.0)	128 (100.0)	240 (100.0)

With regard to the need for having a say of workers in the management of industry, an overwhelming majority of the workers seem to be favourably disposed toward the same. Over 90 (91.7) percent of the respondents favour much to moderate need of such a say of workers and the trade union leaders appear to be relatively more in favour of workers having a greater say in the management of the industrial establishments. Though not statistically significant, the managements appear to be less inclined to accept that the need for having workers' say in the management is a priority area. However, it is rather gratifying to note that in general, a considerably large majority of the respondents perceive moderate to much need for workers' say in the management.

TABLE 6.2

Positive Implications of PM for Various Aspects

Positive Implications	*Aspects*					*Cumulative Total*
	Productivity	*Climate of Industrial Relations*	*Organizational Climate*	*Morale*	*Job Satisfaction/ Commitment*	
Much	149 (62.1)	171 (71.3)	141 (58.8)	127 (52.9)	118 (49.2)	706 (58.8)
Somewhat	58 (24.2)	50 (20.8)	55 (22.9)	62 (25.8)	72 (30.0)	297 (24.8)
Little	33 (13.8)	19 (7.9)	44 (18.3)	51 (21.3)	50 (20.8)	197 (16.4)
Total	240 (100.0)	240 (100.0)	240 (100.0)	240 (100.0)	240 (100.0)	1200 (100.0)

Similarly, with regard to the implications of the WPM on various aspects of industrial process and milieu, the actors in machineries of WPM appear to be favourably disposed, in the sense, state that the PM has more positive implications than the negative, when its comes to the productivity, climate of industrial relations, morale, job satisfaction and the like. The respondents were asked to mention the implications of WPM for each one of these aspects of industrial process. It is also significant to note that the respondents are more convinced about the positive implications of WPM for the industry rather than for the workers as individuals, though positive implications for individuals eventually may result in positive implications for the organization at large.

The conceived or observed implications of PM on the various aspects of industrial process and the work of the actors in the process of PM taken together appear to be rather desirable and positive. Five important aspects of industrial milieu, which could be influenced by the WPM, have been included in the study and the data pertaining to the same are presented in the table. The respondents believe that, the climate of industrial relations is an area which is most benefited by the PM and the job satisfaction among the workers is the least influenced area of industrial milieu by the PM. However highest proportion of those who negate the positive implications of WPM are found in the case of morale with nearly one fourth of the respondents believing that WPM has little to do with the morale of the workforce. It is further significant and gratifying to note that the perceived positive implication of WPM on productivity is quite high with nearly two-thirds (62.1 percent) of the respondents claiming that WPM has very strong positive impact on productivity. The organizational climate which is considered as a composite variable made up of scores dealing with such traits of the organizations like the degree of centralization, formalization, departmentalization, bureaucratization, communication and authority patterns is another important component of industrial milieu on which the WPM is supposed to be having a positive impact. The data accordingly reveal that WPM, in fact, does have a favourable or desirable impact on the organizational climate, though not as significant as it is in the case of productivity and climate of industrial relations.

As mentioned earlier, a closer observation interestingly reveals that the PM has greater positive implications for the work organizations at large than it has for the individuals associated with the process of WPM, in the form of enhanced morale and increased job satisfaction. As such, based on the findings it may be stated that WPM as a process contributes to the health of the organization and could be taken as an instrument of improving the organizational effectiveness rather than as a means of improving conditions of working and living for the organizational members. Thus, it may also be stated that, PM as a positive organizational intervention is in the interest of the organization and thereby in the interest of the management as a mechanism of enhancing productivity, improving climate of industrial relations and facilitating a better organizational climate, on the other hand, as individual benefits to the workers in the form of higher levels of job satisfaction and greater control on one's own working lives. Hence, the managements need to be aware of the fact, according to the workers and trade union leaders about the positive impact of WPM and need not be averse about or afraid of apprehensive of the WPM. This finding is, however based on the assumed outcome of and as a dispositional ramification of WPM which needs to be validated in the subsequent chapters dealing with the extent, determinants and implications of WPM. But nonetheless it goes without saying that the implications of WPM assumed and expected by the actors in the actual process is not expected to be far from the actual reality.

However, the main thrust of the present chapter is to identify and ascertain empirically the dispositions and experiences of the workers, trade union leaders and managerial personnel pertaining to the WPM. The respondents were classified as those with 'favourable' or 'unfavourable' disposition toward WPM based upon their scores on each of the seven constituent variables. The combined scores of the respondents on the seven variables was the basis for such classification of the respondents. Suitable coding and scoring techniques were employed to ascertain the total scores of the respondents based on which they were classified as those with 'favourable' or 'unfavourable' dispositions.

The dispositions of the respondents ascertained based on the method and criteria mentioned above would be analyzed for their determinants and co-variates in the subsequent pages of this chapter. An attempt, further, is made here in this chapter to discuss about the procedure of ascertaining the components of the composite variable of 'experiences' of the actors about the PM in their respective work organizations.

As in the case of dispositions, the 'experience' of the respondents was ascertained on the bases of their scores on several variables pertaining to the functioning of the WPM machineries in their respective work organizations and their role in the process. The variables identified to ascertain the experience of the respondents were, the nature and extent of participation by workers' representatives, managements' response to the scheme of WPM, frequency of using WPM machineries, workers' response to WPM scheme, perceived aptitude and skills of worker representatives, length of association with the working of machineries, and relevance and significance of the issues raised by the participants. The scores of each respondent on the above variables were combined to ascertain their over all experience with the functioning of WPM and the same was classified as 'favourable' or 'positive' and 'unfavourable' or 'negative'.

The findings with regard to these constituent variables of the WPM experience were quite significant as these could be taken as the conditioning factors in the actual process of WPM and may be of relevance in the discussion on the extent, determinants, effectiveness and the implications of WPM in the subsequent chapters. However, a brief analysis of the findings pertaining to these constituent variables is attempted here.

It is assumed that the response of the managements, workers and the trade union leaders to process of WPM constitutes the basic, grass root experience that may have determinate role to play in the functioning of the WPM machineries, as the working of any scheme for that matter would depend on the response of the beneficiaries and benefactors and mediators. The findings with regard to the responses of these variables have been discussed in brief in the following section.

TABLE 6.3

Response of Workers, Trade Unions and Managements to the PM

Response	*Category*			*Cumulative Total*
	Management	*Trade Unions*	*Workers*	
Favourable	165 (68.8)	182 (75.8)	194 (80.8)	541 (75.1)
Unfavourable	75 (31.3)	58 (24.2)	46 (19.2)	179 (24.9)
Total	240 (100.0)	240 (100.0)	240 (100.0)	720 (100.0)

The data presented in the table seem to indicate that, it is the workers who have most favourable response to the PM and the machineries that put it into practice or operation (80.8 percent) followed by the trade union leaders (75.8 percent) and managements (68.8 percent). It appears logical that the workers' representatives are the ones who are the chief exponents of WPM as it is this practice that can elevate their status at work place and enable them to have a say in taking decisions that have bearing for their working lives. On the other hand, the trade union leaders, as it is in the case of Western economies like France, Germany and UK, are not all that in favour of PM as it could have adverse impact on trade union movement. It is argued that the rise and popularization of the notion of WPM has been universally and rather invariably accompanied by declining influence of trade union movement, dwindling union membership, weak bargaining position of the trade unions as the machineries of WPM are taking over the functions and responsibilities once exclusively discharged by the trade unions. At least in the West, workplace democratization and workers' direct involvement in the administration of the industry and bargaining process have been viewed as a threat to the monopoly and movement of trade unions as such practices could lead to by passing the trade unions in the settlement of disputes, negotiation of deals, and signing of pacts or agreements. The trade unionists every now and then raise the issue of workers not being equipped with the skills and endowed with the aptitude and knowledge that are indispensable to bargain and participate in a decision making process on equal footing with the well educated, trained and economically powerful management. Particularly in India, where the general level of education among the working class masses is considerably low, level of awareness about their rights and privileges is quite minimal and the traditional and rather rigid social structure prevails, workers find themselves in a disadvantageous position to deal with management as equals on intricate and complex economic, legal and political issues involved in negotiations.

Similarly, the managements were found to be having rather least favourable response to the PM in Indian industries among all the three principal actors of PM. It is but natural that the management take administration of a firm as their prerogative and justified sphere of activity and others sharing this privilege could be seen as an encroachment on their rightful domain, and as such are likely to be having less favourable response to the process and notion of WPM. The kind of resistance, the notion and practice of WPM faced in the initial stages of its inception by the management can just be an indication of the managements' disposition and response to this innovative intervention in the management of work organizations. It is in the recent past, particularly after the rise and popularization of human relations perspective in the management of industry and human resources that the managements have come to realize the positive outcome and impact of WPM on productivity, morale, job satisfaction, commitment and climate of industrial relations and all the progressive and professionally managed industries have come to adopt WPM and employ such machineries to realize this practice.

However, it is significant to note that over two-thirds (68.8 percent) of the managements are in favour of WPM and respond favourably to the process of WPM in their respective industries, as evidenced by the experience of the respondents. And a still higher proportion (75.5 percent) of the trade unions respond favourably to the practice of WPM. Coupled with this, over 80 percent of the workers having favourable response to the WPM, could be taken as quite a comforting situation and a situation which could be taken as highly promising.

TABLE 6.4

Relevance of Issues Raised in the Machineries of PM by Category

Degree of Relevance	*Category*			*Total*
	Managerial Personnel	*Trade Union Leaders*	*Workers*	
High	40 (71.4)	33 (58.9)	97 (75.8)	170 (70.8)
Low	16 (28.6)	23 (41.1)	31 (24.2)	70 (29.2)
Total	56 (100.0)	56 (100.0)	128 (100.0)	240 (100.0)

Coming to the relevance and significance of the issues raised by the participants in WPM which was taken as another indicator of WPM experience of the respondents, the data seem to indicate that again it is the workers' representatives who have experienced high relevance in dealing with issues in WPM machineries followed by the managerial respondents and trade union leaders. In other words, the representatives of the workers appear to be more happy and feel satisfied with the issues raised in the machineries of WPM than are their management and trade union counterparts.

The data presented in the table 6.4 reveal that among the respondents belonging to the worker's category about three-fourths (75.8 percent) consider that the issues raised in the machineries of WPM are of high relevance and significance in achieving the general objectives of WPM and the proportion of those who experience this sense of relevance is as low as 59 (58.9) percent among the trade union leaders. On the other hand, however, over 70 (71.4) percent of the respondents coming from managerial categories opine that the issues raised in the machineries of PM are relevant and significant from the point of view of achieving the over all objectives of PM. Although the differential relevance experienced by the respondents belonging to different categories is not statistically significant, a trend could be observed which could be indicative of differential approaches of different categories to the areas of management dealt with by the machineries of WPM. It is indicative of the fact that different participants of WPM have different priorities and expectations from the WPM. It was noticed in the chapter on structure and functioning of the WPM machineries that, productivity, discipline, working conditions and rewards are the most frequently raised issues in the machineries of WPM, which are the major concerns of the workers and managements. So long as the issues concerning the productivity, worker discipline, working conditions and compensation packages are successfully negotiated and resolved through the participation of workers, the workers and managements appear to be happy and satisfied. Trade unions, on the other hand with ideological considerations and overtones appear to be less satisfied with issues that are normally being dealt with by the machineries of WPM. It is but natural that the machineries of WPM seldom deal with and are seldom established to realize the goals of working class unity, workers' ownership of the firm, breeding class consciousness and furtherance of working class interest, which are the prime concerns of trade unionism and as such, it is but natural that the trade union representatives are not as satisfied with the issues the machineries of WPM primarily concern themselves with. It is however significant to note that still a majority of the trade union leaders consider the issues coming before the machineries of PM as relevant and significant and in all, 70 (70.8) percent of the respondents in general view the machineries of WPM as dealing with issues of high relevance and significance for the general well-being of the major parties involved in the process of production. Thus, in all, it may be stated that the process of WPM appears to be geared to the needs of the workers and management, though not catering to the ideological needs of the trade unionism.

Further, coming to the conception of the participants of WPM of the skills and aptitudes of workers' representatives to participate effectively in the machineries of WPM, a similar pattern with regard to the relevance and significance of issues raised was observed. In the sense, an overwhelming majority (85.9 percent) of the workers did not feel handicapped in dealing with the intricacies of PM and participating effectively in the machineries of PM. On the other hand among the respondents from trade union leaders, who considered that the workers' representatives are equipped good enough with skills and aptitude to meet the demands placed on them as the actors in the process of WPM constituted a relatively small proportion (62.5 percent). However, the conception of the management regarding the workers' ability, skill and competence in performing their roles in the machineries of WPM appears to be more encouraging and favourable than that of the trade union leaders (71.4 percent). It is, therefore, quite gratifying to note that the managerial personnel find the workers as capable of making positive, creative or constructive contribution to the process of WPM quite more often than not and more often than do the trade union leaders. Indeed it is the management conception and assessment of workers' ability to meaningfully and effectively participate in the management of the industry which is more important than that of the trade union leaders as it is more often the management acceptance of workers as partners in decision making which goes a long way in improving efficiency of the WPM machineries. This is a considerable extent independent and inspite of the trade union leaders' views regarding the same. However, more gratifying thing is the self-confidence, and a positive self appraisal the workers' representatives have about their skills and competence in dealing with and discharging their responsibilities in the process of WPM. An issue that is frequently debated when it comes to the WPM in Indian context is the cultural milieu, socio-economic background of the workers and incompatibility between roles required to be played by the working class and the level of preparedness at which the workers find themselves. It is heard from several quarters that the kinds of experiments in industrial democracy carried out in the West are out of place, out of context and premature in Indian context owing to the recent origin of industrialism, absence of the kind of industrial subculture required, traditional social structure and the characteristics of Indian labour. Even, the management's apathy toward PM, many a time, is attributed to their lack of confidence in the working class about their capabilities to make a positive or constructive contribution in the management of firms.

Hence, in view of the general opinion prevailing as stated above, the proportion of workers and managerial personnel considering the workers' representatives having requisite skills and aptitude to participate in the management of industry may be seen or taken as considerably high. Furthermore, the apprehensions being nursed about the workers' limited capabilities in the managerial and trade union circles, academic circles, among the policy makers and the exponents of WPM appear to be rather out dated and unwarranted.

Thus, the experiences of the actors are ascertained on the bases of their scores on several constituent variables and based on their total scores on these variables, they are classified as those with 'positive' and 'negative' experience of WPM just as the dispositions of the respondents have been ascertained and classified. An attempt, hence, is made in the following pages to discuss the findings relating to the respondents' dispositions and experiences as well as the factors that condition and determine their dispositions and experiences so as to know whether they vary significantly with organizational, contextual and personal variables which in turn may hold key to the understanding the extent, determinants and effectiveness of PM in subsequent chapters.

TABLE 6.5

Dispositions of the Respondents by Category

Dispositions of the Respondents	*Category*			*Total*
	Managers	*Trade Union Leaders*	*Workers*	
Favourable	51 (91.1)	50 (89.3)	97 (75.8)	198 (82.5)
Unfavourble	5 (8.9)	6 (10.7)	31 (24.2)	42 (17.5)
Total	56 (100.0)	56 (100.0)	128 (100.0)	240 (100.0)

X^2= 8.63, DF=2, Significant at 0.05 Level, C= 0.18

Coming to the composite variable of dispositions, the data reveal that an overwhelming majority (82.5 percent) of the respondents have a favourable disposition toward the WPM process in general, which could be taken as considerably high in view of factors referred to above which are assumed to be retarding the process of PM. It is logical to state that the partners to the process of PM need to be favourably disposed toward the practice in order to have commitment, conviction and allegiance to the spirit and philosophy supporting it. It may also be assumed that the willing participation and inclination to support the scheme depends to a large extent on the how favourably disposed are those who are the integral part of the process. On this count at least, the finding that over 80 percent of the respondents being favourably disposed toward the scheme of which they are an integral part could be taken as quite positive and healthy development.

It is quite interesting to note that the findings indicate to a highly favourable disposition of managerial personnel toward the PM process and practice. As many as 91 (91.1) percent of the managerial respondents exhibit a favourable disposition followed by trade union leaders (89.3 percent) and the workers (75.8 percent). The situation could be taken as highly conducive from the point of view of managerial personnel and may be taken as a realization on the part of management about the positive impact of WPM for the industry at large. It may further be stated that to have only three-fourths (75.8 percent) of the workers favourably disposed toward PM is much less than what could be expected in view of the corresponding score among other actors to the process of PM. It may be also stated that inspite of having higher score on a few components of the composite variable of dispositions, the overall score on disposition is rather low for workers, even in comparison with the trade union leaders who are generally believed to be less favourably disposed toward WPM scheme or practice. It is rather much less than expected as, the WPM is a positive intervention contemplated specifically for the furtherance of workers' interests and through this, as a natural corollary, the interests of the management, industry and society at large. The statistical analysis reveals that the association between the dispositions of the respondents and the categories to which they belong is statistically significant at .05 level, stating that the dispositions the respondents have could be the functions of the category they belong to. Nearly, one-fourth of the workers (24.2 percent) having unfavourable disposition toward WPM could be a matter of concern for the exponents of this positive management intervention, particularly in view of the fact that the scheme is, more often than not, and more than anybody else, in the interest of workers themselves. This phenomenon may be taken up for a more detailed research to know whether the traditional cultural milieu in which the workers are born, brought up, work and live has anything to do with their apathy toward the PM or whether it is the complacency and contentment with rewards from and life on work that makes them less craving and wanting a scheme that aims at a better treatment on work and scope for participation in taking decisions that affect their working lives. Whereas, on the other hand, management and trade unions have come to emphasize the role of PM in improving industrial situation and have come to endorse it as a healthy practice through a favourable disposition toward the same. And it is because of the favourable attitude of these actors, the total reception to the WPM as a practice on the whole appears to be quite high and favourable.

Determinants of Dispositions

Further, as mentioned in the beginning of the chapter, an attempt is made here to see whether the dispositions of these actors are conditioned by other background, contextual and organizational variables, as it is assumed that the dispositions and individual exhibits could be shaped by diverse components of work milieu in which one works and lives on the one hand and by the personal background variables, which could be as diverse as social, economic, cultural, educational, emotional and demographic as well.

Coming to the age of the respondents, the findings seem to indicate that as one advances in age, the disposition toward

PM turns to be more and more favourable, indicating to a sportive association between favourable disposition and age.

TABLE 6.6

Disposition of the Respondents by Age

Dispositions of the Respondents	*Age*			*Total*
	Young	*Middle Aged*	*Old*	
Unfavourble	1 (33.3)	38 (20.1)	3 (6.3)	42 (17.5)
Favourable	2 (66.7)	151 (79.9)	45 (93.8)	198 (82.5)
Total	3 (100.0)	189 (100.0)	48 (100.0)	240 (100.0)

X^2= 5.61, DF=2, Significant at 0.02 Level, C=0.15

It is observed from the table that, over 90 (93.8) percent of the respondents in the old-age group have favourable dispositions toward WPM as compared to the respondents belonging to younger age-group among whom the corresponding proportion is just one-third (33.3 percent). On the other hand among those respondents belonging to the middle-age group also, the proportion of those having favourable disposition is as high as about four-fifths (79.9 percent). The association between dispositions and age was found to be statistically significant at 0.02 level with 'C' value being 0.15.

There could be two explanations possible to explain the phenomenon. One, that the respondents as they advance in age, come to realize the realities pertaining to human nature, come to realize the advantages of co-determined peaceful existence vis-à-vis the hostile claim of one's rights. Having longer exposure to the functioning of firms and with a longer experience of dealing with human factor in the process of production they tend to be in favour of WPM and be favourably disposed to the process. On the other hand, the younger respondents could be less conservative and less compromising when it comes to negotiated decision making being less aware of the general advantages of codetermination. The other explanation could be based on the chronological developments in the history of WPM. It is quite obviously apparent if we look at the industrial relations situation all over the world that the euphoria or nostalgia that was once so conspicuously associated with the notion, philosophy and spirit of WPM is on decline and waning to be a weak movement. Particularly, in the West, disillusionment widely experienced by all the parties to WPM owing to limited success and less than expected positive implications for the workers, industry and society, has eroded its popularity, acceptance and subscription. Such a realization might have negatively influenced the dispositions of the third generation participants of WPM, who find themselves in younger age groups. A rational audit and assessment of the achievements of PM in diverse cultural contexts do not present a very encouraging and gratifying account of WPM in operation resulting in a sense of disillusionment, resignation and resentment among those who have entered the arena in the recent past.

However, irrespective of age, over 80 (82.5) percent of the respondents still having a favourable disposition toward WPM in itself presents a ray of hope and testifies to the fact that inspite and irrespective of limited success it has met with since its inception and a steady decline of faith in WPM in other cultures, PM in Indian context, by and large is looked upon with hope of promise of better industrial civilization and better working lives for the masses and as a harbinger of industrial, and in general, economic progress and development.

Further, a similar but less definite association was also found existing between the dispositions and the educational level of the respondents. The association was however not unidirectional in the sense, though highest proportion of those with favourable disposition was found to be with those who were highly educated, correspondingly, highest proportion of those with unfavourable disposition was not found among those with low educational level, but such proportion was found with those who were moderately educated. Thus, though educational level was found to be significantly associated with the type of disposition among the respondents, a definite pattern could not be observed. However, one explanation that could be attempted here is that, in case of categories of respondents it was noticed that the management personnel had the highest proportion of those with favourable dispositions, and it is but natural to assume that the managerial respondents tend to have higher levels of educational attainments and the data revealing that those with highest levels of educational attainments having the highest proportion of those with favourable disposition could be viewed as logical and expected. However, those with moderate levels of education exhibiting relatively less favourable disposition needs to be further probed into. At the best it may be assumed that there being not much difference between the educational attainments of workers and trade union leaders as most of the trade union leaders are drawn from the rank and file, lower levels or moderate levels of education would not make much of difference for the dispositions. It may be recalled here that, in the analysis of the constituent variable of disposition and experiences, it was the trade union leaders who had least favourable disposition and experiences of WPM. In view of this fact, it may further be assumed that the trade union leaders are a trifle better educated than the operatives or the workers whom they lead, particularly the outside leaders who are still found in good numbers in Indian trade unions and they are expected to be educationally better equipped to discharge their duties as mediators, arbitrators, adjudicators and dealing with intricate legal matters. As such, a relatively educationally better-off respondents mostly represented by the trade union leaders, having a relatively less favourable disposition toward

WPM, again could be taken as logical. It may further be argued that a higher level of education could orient the respondents to the constructive and creative advantages of PM leading to a favourable disposition toward PM among such respondents. However, the findings seem to indicate to a rather vague pattern of relationships between disposition and level of education of the participants.

With regard to the caste background of the respondents, it is interesting to note that, the proportion of those with favourable disposition is highest among those belonging to the low castes (90.2 percent) whereas the proportion of such respondents is lowest (77.5 percent) among the respondents coming from intermediate castes. Such proportion among the high caste respondents is higher again at 85 (85.2) percent.

It may be assumed here in view of the data presented above that for those coming from lower castes, participation in decision making process could be a highly respectful and status elevating factor. To be the part of management, administration and decision making process could make them feel important, particularly in view of lower castes they belong to in the non-work world. On the other hand, for those belonging to intermediate and higher castes, such a participation may not mean a very ennobling and empowering experience. Further, if we look at the caste composition of occupational groups, high ranking, high status occupations tend to be predominantly associated with high castes and occupations with moderate responsibility and of intermediary secretarial nature come to be increasingly associated with the intermediate castes with low ranking, manual and physically taxing occupations tend to be pursued by the lower castes. In support of this, the caste composition of the various categories indicate that workers, trade union leaders and managers predominantly belong to low, intermediate and high castes, respectively and the distribution of disposition observed in case of different categories supports the distribution of disposition observed above. However, no statistically significant association could be found between caste and dispositions indicating that the dispositions of the respondents are independent of their caste background and caste does not play an important role in determining the attitudes and orientations of the operatives, union leaders and managers toward the system process and practice of PM.

Similarly, span of career was found to be of no significance in determining the dispositions of the respondents. No statistically significant association was found between the two. It was logically assumed that the length of exposure to work culture, work situations and prolonged interaction with the components of industrial milieu would, in a way, influence one's attitudes and orientations toward such important aspects of industrial relations as WPM. Further, as the age was found to be significantly associated with the dispositions, it was logically assumed that, since age and span of career are found to be positively correlated, as in the case of age, longer span of career was expected to be associated with favourable disposition. However, such association or correlation was not revealed by the data analyzed.

Coming to the preferred area of participation, the findings indicate to a closer correspondence between the preference for production as an area of participation and favourable disposition.

It may be observed from the table that those who consider productivity and improvement in technology as the preferred areas of WPM are more favourably disposed toward WPM (89.4 percent) than are those who consider wages and working conditions (76.0 percent) and those who consider welfare and grievance as the preferred areas of management. As observed in the chapter on machineries of PM, it appears that those issues that are more in tune with management tend to be preferred issues in the machineries of WPM and even in terms of the dispositions of the actors, it is those who consider issues that are the major concerns of management are more favourably disposed toward WPM. It may be argued on the bases of these findings that WPM as a practice, process and an institution is more in tune with management interests and cater to the needs of productivity, discipline rather than dealing with workers' interests like wages, working conditions, welfare and grievance. As such, it needs to be analyzed and ascertained whether PM has been a scheme in the interest of the worker or industry or the management, though it is propagated and advocated to ameliorate the working conditions, to democratize and humanize work places and to foster more peaceful, harmonious and organic milieu of industrial relations which are viewed as being in the larger interest of the workers.

TABLE 6.7

Disposition of the Respondents by Preferred Area for PM

Dispositions of The Respondents	*Preferred Areas for WPM*			*Total*
	Working Conditions / Wages, Bonus, DA	*Grievance, Welfare, Personnel*	*Production, Development Planning, Technology*	
Favourable	19 (76.0)	78 (76.5)	101 (89.4)	198 (82.5)
Unfavourble	6 (24.0)	24 (23.5)	12 (10.6)	42 (17.5)
Total	25 (100.0)	102 (100.0)	113 (100.0)	240 (100.0)

X^2= 7.00, DF=2, Significant at 0.02 Level, C= 0.16

Further, coming to the most important composite variable pertaining to the social background of the respondents, that is, social origin, quite interestingly and surprisingly, no association could be found with the dispositions. It is quite logical to assume that the dispositions of the respondents could be varying with the social origin, a composite variable made up of respondents' caste, income, family occupation and educational attainments, as the attitudes or orientations have been found to be influenced by these background variables in many studies, and an important aspect of one's working life such as WPM to be not influenced by these variables is rather significant deviation from the general expectations. However, the findings of the present study rather emphatically, negate any such association between social origin and the disposition of the respondents. Further, much against, those coming from high social origins tend to be more favourably disposed toward the WPM (86.5 percent) than are those coming from low social origins (79.4 percent). Even this observation could be against what is logically assumed or expected because, among those coming from high social origin, an overwhelming majority are from managerial class and among those coming from low social origin, workers constitute a bulk of the whole and it is but natural to expect workers to be in favour of WPM and management to be less inclined to share their prerogatives and be in favour of PM. But the findings of the study all along seem to be negating this rational or logical expectation. The management to be in favour of WPM more than the workers themselves, with no significant association between their social origin and dispositions is contrary to the expectation.

Thus, with regard to personal background variables as determinants of the dispositions, the findings indicate that except for age and education, other variables do not seem to be significant in determining the attitudes of the respondents. Particularly significant fact to be noted is that, caste, span of career and the more realistic estimation of respondents' social standing, that is, social origin which are more often assumed to be shaping the dispositions of persons towards the components of work milieu in general and an important aspect of industrial relations such as WPM in particular have little to do with the dispositions of the actors or participants in the process of WPM.

Though strange, the study based on the data supports the fact that personal background factors, except age and educational level have little role to play in determining the dispositions of the respondents. Thus, having ascertained the dispositions in the light of personal background variables, an attempt is further made to analyze the dispositions in the light of contextual and organizational variables.

TABLE 6.8

Disposition of the Respondents by Size of Organization

Dispositions of the Respondents	*Size of Organization*			*Total*
	Small	*Medium*	*Large*	
Unfavourable	16 (26.7)	6 (10.0)	20 (16.7)	42 (17.5)
Favourable	44 (73.3)	54 (90.0)	100 (83.3)	198 (82.5)
Total	60 (100.0)	60 (100.0)	120 (100.0)	240 (100.0)

X^2= 5.88, DF=2, Significant at 0.05 Level, C= 0.15

Dispositions viewed in the light of sector of industries where the machineries of PM were in operation, the study indicates to no statistically significant relationship between the two. It may be recalled here that in the last chapter on the structure and functioning of machineries of WPM, the findings seem to suggest that the public sector industries provide a better structural and functional milieu for the operation of WPM. But however when it comes to the dispositions, no such trend could be observed in the sense, difference between the dispositions of respondents coming from public sector units (83.3 percent) and private sector (81.1 percent) was just marginal in favour of the former. It may thus be stated that irrespective of the structural and functional features of the machineries of PM in public and private sector units, the dispositions of the actors in these two sectors were favourable to a similar extent.

However, another important organizational variable, that is, size was found to be significantly associated with the dispositions of the respondents.

The data presented in the table seem to indicate that respondents coming from organizations with medium size are more favourably disposed toward PM than are their counterparts from small and large organizations. In the selection of sample of units for the study, size was one of the main criteria assuming that, for the machineries of PM to be in operation meaningfully, minimum size of organization is rather imperative and the sample of industries was selected accordingly. However, the findings seem to indicate that it is neither very small nor the very big organizations but those organizations which are of moderate size are the ones where the dispositions of the participants of the process of WPM tend to be more favourably disposed toward the practice. It appears in tune with the argument that, unless the organization of some minimum size, the workers, union leaders and the management find PM as a cumbersome practice, requiring the establishment of machineries, formulating rules of their operation and finding a consensus among the members representing diverse interests and not worth experimenting. On the other hand, it may also be argued in case of too big organizations, in which the non-managerial participants may find it rather difficult to have an integrated idea or conception of the organization, departmentalization, divisionalization, division of labour, functional coordination between such diverse constituent parts of the organization. The organization may appear to them rather too complex and intricately structured pattern for them to make constructive and meaningful contribution to the management of the same.

This could be the reason for those respondents coming from too large organizations to be relatively less favourably disposed towards PM than are their counterparts from organizations of moderate size. It is also significant to note that even among the large and small organizations, it is the larger organizations from where we get relatively more number of respondents (83.3 percent) than those coming from the small organizations (73.3 percent). Based on this finding it may be suggested that the size of the organizations may be kept to the optimum, that is, neither too small nor too big, if possible, to have the participants to be favourably disposed towards the WPM.

A more definite relation could be found, between the age of the industry and the dispositions of the respondents.

TABLE 6.9

Dispositions of the Respondents by the Age of Industry

Dispositions of the Respondents	*Age of Industry*			*Total*
	Before 1960	*Between 1960-1980*	*After 1980*	
Favourable	108 (10.0)	69 (23.3)	21 (30.0)	198 (17.5)
Unfavourable	12 (10.0)	21 (23.3)	9 (30.0)	42 (17.5)
Total	120 (100.0)	90 (100.0)	30 (100.0)	240 (100.0)

X^2= 10.04, DF=2, Significant at 0.01 Level, C=0.20

It could be observed from the table that, older the industry more favourably are the respondents disposed toward the WPM. The proportion of the respondents who are favourably disposed toward WPM increases from 70 percent among the new industries to 77 (76.7) percent among those coming from moderately old industries and the corresponding proportion further rises to 90 percent among the respondents coming from old industries. The respondents coming from young industries being relatively less favourably disposed than their counterparts in older industries is rather unwelcome finding because, as the time passes by, the concept of WPM could have become more popular, acceptable and more welcome practice leading to the participants becoming more favourably disposed. The findings seem to be indicating to a rather contradictory trend. However it may also be argued that respondents from industries established in the recent past are yet to be convinced about the positive implications of WPM on the one hand and are yet to familiarize themselves with the process, principle and practice of WPM on the other, resulting in their being less convinced about the positive outcome and being less sure about its desirability. On the other hand, in older industries where the WPM machineries have been in operation ever since this statutory requirement was made obligatory on the part of industries employing workers in excess of a specified number, the respondents or the workers at large have come to realize their utility and have been the part of these machineries for quite some time. They may, further, have been the actual beneficiaries of the PM practices themselves in the past owing to which, they could be more positively disposed toward the WPM at large. However, whether PM is loosing its relevance with the passage of time is an important research question to answer because of the declining popularity of the WPM in the developed countries in the last decade. This may also be indicating to the fact, as it was found earlier that public sector industries have a relatively better industrial relations climate either owing to WPM or greater propensity to have WPM owing to better climate of industrial relations and since these public sector industries have been relatively older establishments, it might be the spillover of the better structures and functioning pattern of WPM which could be contributing to the respondents coming from older units having more favourable dispositions toward the WPM. The fact, however remains that, the age of the industry is significantly associated with the nature of dispositions of the respondents and such relationship being significant at .01 level.

Coming to the operating status, the findings indicated to a positive association between the two, which was rather quite expected. However, such an expectation was for that matter supported by the facts.

TABLE 6.10

Dispositions of the Respondents by Operating Status

Dispositions of the Respondents	*Operating Status*					*Total*
	Incurring Heavy Loss	*Incurring Loss*	*Making it Even*	*Profit Making*	*Highly Profit Making*	
Favourable	19 (90.5)	56 (93.3)	21 (70.0)	49 (81.7)	53 (76.8)	198 (82.5)
Unfavou-rable	2 (9.5)	4 (6.7)	9 (30.0)	11 (18.3)	16 (23.2)	42 (17.5)
Total	21 (100.0)	60 (100.0)	30 (100.0)	60 (100.0)	69 (100.0)	240 (100.0)

X^2= 10.62, DF=4, Significant at 0.05 Level, C= 0.20

The data presented in the table indicate that a positive operating status is associated with the positive disposition toward PM. It is indeed a finding of applied value, the analysis of which would be taken up in the next chapters dealing with the extent and effectiveness of PM and the implications of PM for the industry.

It may be assumed here that positive disposition toward WPM induces more sincere and effective participation in the machineries of WPM and which could in turn lead to positive implications for the productivity, capacity utilization, better climate of industrial relations and thereby contribute to the overall health of the organization which in turn manifests itself in the profitable operation.

Whether positive disposition could eventually or ultimately result in greater extent, greater effectiveness of WPM and positive implications would be a subsequent question sought to be answered but, at least favourable disposition being associated with a healthy operating status is gratifying as it supports one of the most important expected outcome of PM. The said relationship between disposition and operating status is significant at .05 level and it is but natural that those who have positive disposition toward WPM could as well be striving to achieve its stated and assumed aims of which improved operating status is one and in most of the industries the major focus and area of participation is productivity and discipline and improving working conditions and these are expected naturally to result in a positive operating status.

But it is quite interesting to know that there was no association whatsoever between the dispositions and the climate of industrial relations. It is normally expected that, the organizations that come to be associated with peaceful and harmonious industrial relations climate tend to provide a conducive forum for PM to be in operation. It is indeed quite natural to expect that the units where the labour and management are in good terms with each other with a sense of trust and goodwill for each other, the participants in the WPM machineries and even others in plant could as well be having a positive disposition and inclination toward WPM. In the literature on WPM, it has been time and again reiterated that for WPM to be meaningful and a success, harmonious industrial relations is one of the most important pre-conditions. With such preconditions that promote willingness and voluntary acceptance of WPM, it is but natural to expect that the participants of this process are favourably disposed. But surprisingly the findings of the present study indicate to no such relationship existing between climate of industrial relations and disposition toward WPM, which may mean that a harmonious industrial relations climate is not all that indispensable a precondition for favourable attitude and dispositions to develop among the people concerned about PM.

However, counter argument could be that, where the industrial relations situation is very peaceful and harmonious and where the interests of the workers are protected voluntarily and willingly by the management and where there is no scope for bargaining for benefits with the management as these needs and demands are being accepted and conceded by the management before the other party asking for them and where the opportunities for realization of the aspirations of working class are made available in plenty, the PM as an ameliorative scheme looses its relevance and as such, PM could not be a pressing need and strongly desired practice. Such a situation could as well be responsible for not a very favourable disposition toward WPM.

On the other hand, a positive correlation was found between the industrial performance and the dispositions.

TABLE 6.11

Dispositions of the Respondents by Industrial Performance

Dispositions of the Respondents	*Industrial Performance*		*Total*
	High	*Low*	
Favourable	142 (78.9)	56 (93.3)	198 (82.5)
Unfavourable	38 (21.1)	4 (6.7)	42 (17.5)
Total	180 (100.0)	60 (100.0)	240 (100.0)

X^2= 6.50, DF=1, Significant at 0.01 Level, C= 0.16

Quite logically, a very strong association could be observed between the dispositions and the industrial performance, a finding which could be of applied significance. It is observed that over 90(93.3) percent of the respondents coming from units with high industrial performance are favourably disposed toward WPM whereas the proportion of such respondents among units with low performance is as low as three fourths (78.9 percent). It is however, logical to note that, a favourable disposition toward better practice of PM could as well lead to better performance of the unit which was also supported by the fact that level of productivity was positively associated with the type of disposition as well. It is indeed a finding which supports what is generally assumed to exist in the literature on industrial relations and debated as one of the most desirable implications of PM. However the direction of influence will have to be established to know which one leads to which, that is , whether favourable disposition leads to higher industrial performance or higher industrial performance leads to favourable disposition toward WPM. But it is also significant to note that one goes with other and both happen together, and on this count at least, the favourable disposition toward PM in itself could be considered as a desirable phenomenon having positively associated with the industrial performance . It may also be true that one re-enforces the other as both are complimentary to each other.

It is again rather surprising to note that the favourable disposition is not associated with the nature of personnel relations in the units. As in the case of the climate of industrial relations, personnel relations appear to be having little bearing upon the dispositions the respondents have toward PM. Although the proportion of the respondents with unfavourable disposition among those coming from units with negative personnel relations was higher than the corresponding proportion among those coming from units with positive personnel relations, the association was not statistically significant to arrive at a definite generalization.

As a reversal of the same, again, the favourable dispositions could be stated as having positive implications for productivity.

It is quite interesting to note that the nature of disposition of the workers, trade union leaders and managers is positively influenced by or influences positively the aspects that are related with productivity, performance and operating status and the like but are not influenced by or do not influence aspects relating to industrial relations, personnel relations and so forth. Although it is quite natural to expect that PM being an important area of industrial relations, should in a sense, be influenced by the general milieu of industrial relations and organizational climate, the data presented in the table also indicate to a positive association between the nature of disposition toward WPM and the level of productivity. The attribution that holds good in case of such a relation between disposition and industrial performance as well as operating status also holds good in case of productivity.

TABLE 6.12

Dispositions of the Respondents by Productivity

Dispositions of the Respondents	*Productivity*		*Total*
	High	*Low*	
Favourable	117 (78.0)	81 (90.0)	198 (82.5)
Unfavourable	33 (22.0)	9 (10.0)	42 (17.5)
Total	150 (100.0)	90 (100.0)	240 (100.0)

X^2= 5.61, DF=1, Significant at 0.02 Level, C= 0.15.

Thus, in conclusion with regard to the dispositions it may be stated that, on the whole, an overwhelming majority of the respondents are favourably disposed toward PM and its machineries in operation and such favourable disposition appears to be significantly associated with personal background variables such as age and educational level and surprisingly not with caste, span of career and social origin. Coming to the contextual variables, it is again interesting to note that the dispositions are influenced by the size and age of industry on the one hand and operating status, industrial performance and productivity on the other whereas, sector, climate of industrial relations and personnel relations so widely expected to be significantly associated with dispositions were found to be independent of and from it. On the whole educational level of the participants and size of the organization appear to be holding the key to the understanding of dispositions. Another significant finding is that dispositions are significantly associated with the actual performance of the industry in terms of production, operating status and the overall performance but, quite interestingly seem to be independent of more important variables such as sector, climate of industrial relations as well as personnel relations in the plants which needs to be further probed into.

EXPERIENCES

Operationalization of Concept

Having discussed about the dispositions, an attempt is made here to analyze the experiences of the respondents in WPM and their determinants. As mentioned in the introduction, the composite variable of experience was computed taking into account the combined scores of the respondents on all the constituent variables of the said composite variable, and based on the score, the respondents were classified as those with 'positive experience' and 'negative experience'.

The data pertaining to the experiences so ascertained reveal that, the experiences do not correspond with the dispositions in terms of frequency although two thirds (67.1 percent) of the respondents were found to be with positive experience.

The data presented in the table show that in comparison with the proportion of those with favourable dispositions, the proportion of those with positive experience is considerably low. It was observed that those with favourable dispositions constituted as much as 82 (82.5) percent where as those with positive experience on WPM constituted only 67 (67.1) percent indicating that higher incidence of favourable opinion or disposition need not necessarily coincide with positive experience. It may on the other hand also mean that those who have negative experience about PM need not necessarily be unfavourably disposed toward the PM though it is normally assumed that experiences determine the dispositions and some times dispositions may precondition an individual to experience in a particular way. The findings of the present study seem to negate any such association between the two and indicate to the independence of dispositions from experiences and vice versa.

TABLE 6.13

Respondents' Experience of WPM

Experience of WPM	*Frequency*	*Percentage*
Positive	161	67.08
Negative	79	32.92
Total	240	100.0

It could be observed from the data that surprisingly the proportion of those with negative disposition having positive experience is slightly higher (69.0 percent) than those with favourable dispositions having positive experience (66.7 percent) leading to the conclusion that the dispositions and experiences are two discrete and different things altogether or they have little do with each other as a determinant or a function. Though quite strange, the data indicate to such independence which may be taken up for more structured research in future.

Determinants of Experiences

Coming to the other variables that are assumed to be

associated with the experiences of the respondents, the study focuses on the category of the participants. The data however indicate that the experience of the respondents on the WPM is independent of the category to which they belong. It was observed that the actors belonging to all the three categories, that is, workers, trade union leaders and managerial personnel did not differ significantly with regard to their experiences on the PM. Among workers, those who had positive experiences constituted 64 (64.3) percent, among the trade union leaders they constituted 68 (67.9) percent and almost an equal proportion of the managerial personnel (67.0 percent) had positive experience of PM indicating to the fact that the category of participants did not make much of difference when it comes to the experience on WPM. The non-correspondence between the dispositions and experiences is testified again as the dispositions were found to be varying significantly with the category of the respondents, whereas not such statistically significant association could be observed between the category and the experiences. In the analysis on dispositions and the category of respondents, it was noticed that, managerial personnel had a significantly higher favourable disposition toward WPM whereas in case of experiences, no such statistically significant association could be observed. This may further support the observation that, there is no correspondence between the dispositions and the experiences.

However, age of the respondents was one such variable in respect of which a correspondence could be observed between the dispositions and experience.

It may be observed from the data presented in the table that the positive experience which is not found among respondents coming from young age, increases with age with 67 (67.2) percent of those belonging to middle age and 71(70.8) percent belonging to older age group having positive experience of WPM. The association between experience and

TABLE 6.14

Experience of the Respondents by Age

Experience of the Respondents	*Age*			*Total*
	Young	*Middle Aged*	*Old*	
Favourable	--	127 (67.2)	34 (70.8)	161 (67.1)
Unfavourable	3 (100.0)	62 (32.8)	14 (29.2)	79 (32.9)
Total	3 (100.0)	127 (100.0)	34 (100.0)	240 (100.0)

X^2= 6.42, DF=2, Significant at 0.05 Level, C=0.16

age was statistically significant at .05 level. Such an association could be indicating to the fact that, it needs one to be of more mature out look and approach to experience the WPM in its true perspective. It may also mean that, the younger respondents are yet to be convinced about the advantages and positive implications of PM. However, mere exposure to WPM for a longer duration may not mean much or make much of difference when it comes to their experience because it is testified by the data relating to span of work career. The data on experience viewed in the light of span of career does not yield any definite direction of influence, as it was the case with dispositions also. There appears to be rather very complex relation between experience and age because, age and span of career of the respondents are expected to co-vary and as such the association found between age and experience is expected to be found with span of work career and experience as well, which however, was not found. So it is something which is exclusively concerned with age, that could be making the difference for experience and the changes that come by in attitudes, approaches, perspectives and orientations and even the out look of life with the advancing age that could be of significance in determining the experiences of respondents. Or it may even be the specific events, experiences that are gained in time at different stages of the development of WPM as a movement which differ with age, could be holding the key to this complex association between age and experience of the respondents on WPM.

Further, as in the case of dispositions, even educational level of the respondents was found to be associated with the experience of the respondents of PM, though not as strong as it has been in the case of dispositions.

TABLE 6.15

Experience of the Respondents by Educational Level

Experience of the Respondents	*Educational Level*			*Total*
	Low	*Moderate*	*High*	
Favourable	41 (58.6)	103 (73.0)	17 (58.6)	161 (67.1)
Unfavourable	29 (41.4)	38 (27.0)	12 (41.4)	79 (32.9)
Total	70 (100.0)	141 (100.0)	29 (100.0)	240 (100.0)

X^2= 5.51, DF=2, Significant at 0.05 Level, C= 0.14

The educational level appears to be associated with the experience of the respondents of WPM in a curvilinear fashion with the proportion of those with positive experience rising from 59 (58.6) percent among respondents with low education to 73 percent among those with moderate educational attainments and falls down again to 59 (58.6) percent among those with higher level of education. A linear positive association that was observed in case of educational level and dispositions was not found existing between experience and educational level. It may mean that those with low level of education have less favourable dispositions and less positive experience and among those with moderate levels of education there appears some sort of correspondence between dispositions and experience and when it comes to those with higher levels of educational attainment they appear to have more often favourable dispositions than they have positive experience. It may, thus, be argued that, those with lower levels of education have low expectations and an experience that matches with it and in case of those who are moderately educated they have higher expectations and also matching experience whereas in case of those with higher levels of educational attainments, a higher expectation is not matched by a corresponding type of experience.

Further, it is significant to note that unlike in the case of dispositions, caste background of the respondents was found to be significantly associated with their experience on PM.

TABLE 6.16

Experience of the Respondents by Caste

Experience of the Respondents	*Caste*			*Total*
	Low	*Intermediate*	*High*	
Favourable	57 (64.8)	69 (62.2)	35 (85.4)	161 (67.1)
Unfavourable	31 (35.2)	42 (37.8)	6 (14.6)	79 (32.9)
Total	88 (100.0)	11.1 (100.0)	41 (100.0)	240 (100.0)

X^2= 7.63, DF=2, Significant at 0.02 Level, C= 0.17

The findings indicate that an overwhelming majority (85.4 percent) of those coming from lower castes have positive experiences on WPM and in comparison with corresponding proportion among those coming from intermediate castes (62.2 percent) and the high castes (64.8 percent), the low caste respondents may be taken as being considerably more satisfied with the functioning and practice of WPM in their respective units. The respondents coming from low castes could be having a greater satisfaction with their PM experience because, greater proportion of them as mentioned in the chapter on social profile, come from the category of workers and their expectations could be not as high as those coming from the categories of trade union leaders and the managerial personnel and could be more satisfied with the extent and outcome of PM that they experience in their respective units. This may appear to be more meaningful and logical explanation viewed in the light of the traditional social structure and out look of life in the context of which workers do have a say in the way the industries are managed, even to a moderate extent, could be seen as something more than what they are asking for and feel justified in claiming. However, on the other hand, trade union leaders and management representatives, who more often than not come from intermediate and high castes respectively may not be all that satisfied with the progress achieved by and the manner in which the WPM is practiced and implemented leading to a less positive experience of PM among them. The above argument finds still greater support if the data pertaining to experience are viewed in the light of the respondents' social origin which reveal no statistically significant association. As explained in the section on conceptualization, social origin, as a composite variable is made up of caste, income, occupation and educational background of the family. It was observed that 71 (71.3) percent of those coming from low social origin had positive experience, and as expected, about 61 (61.5) percent of those coming from high social origin had positive experience. Though a similar trend as in case of caste and experience was observed in case of social origin and experience the association between the two are statistically not significant. Thus, non-association of social origin with the experience and significant association of caste, at .02 level, with experience could mean caste with other composite variables may not make much difference for experience but caste in isolation of other social background variables has role to play in shaping the experiences of the respondents, indicating that it is an important variable in the analysis of the respondent's experience on PM. Further even in case of caste, the independence of disposition from experience and visa-versa is evident as caste is significantly associated with experience which is not the case with dispositions indicating again that the dispositions and experiences are, interestingly, independent of each other, which need a further empirical probe.

Coming to the area of participation preferred, the data indicate to a significant association with WPM experience of the respondents .A similar association for that matter, was also observed in case of dispositions.

TABLE 6.17

Experience of the Respondents by Preferred Area for Participation

Experience of the Respondents	*Preferred Area for Participation*			*Total*
	Working Conditions/Wages, Bonus, DA	*Grievance, Welfare, Personnel*	*Production, Development Planning, Technology*	
Favourable	15 (60.0)	60 (58.8)	86 (76.1)	161 (67.1)
Unfavourable	10 (40.0)	42 (41.2)	27 (23.9)	79 (32.9)
Total	25 (100.0)	102 (100.0)	113 (100.0)	240 (100.0)

X^2= 7.88, DF=2, Significant at 0.02 Level, C= 0.17

The data reveal that those preferring areas of participation like productivity and improvement of technology have a greater proportion of those with positive experience (76.1 percent) as compared to the corresponding proportion among those preferring grievances and welfare (58.8 percent) and wages, bonus and working conditions (60.0 percent). A similar association was also found existing in case of dispositions indicating to a closer correspondence between experience and dispositions, which is quite expected. In view of the fact that, such a correspondence was not found in case of other variables, this finding appears to be significant. It may be inferred from the findings that those preferring productivity, discipline and technology as the suitable and ideal areas of participation are found to be more satisfied with the functioning of the machineries of PM. And on the other hand, those considering grievance handling and welfare of workers as the favoured and preferred areas for participation are the least satisfied ones with not much of difference between those who consider that wages, bonus and working conditions as the right areas of PM. Thus in all, it appears that WPM is more effective in areas like production and discipline which are normally viewed as management interests. It is further interesting to note that those issues that are considered as being in the interest of the workers, such as, welfare of the workers, grievance handling and even as crucial issues as wages, bonus and working conditions appear to be not dealt with satisfactorily by the machineries of PM. It may also be recalled here that, even in case of management areas most frequently dealt with by the WPM machineries, as ascertained in chapter V, it is the issues concerning management and those considered as in the interest of the management that figure more frequently than other issues that could be seen as furthering the interests of workers. Thus it may be stated that, both in terms of frequency of dealing with as well as satisfaction with which the issues are dealt with the WPM machineries seem to be furthering the cause of management rather than the workers. This needs a serious rethinking and reorienting the WPM machineries so as to make them focus on issues that concern the workers most so as to elicit active participation of the worker component in these machineries. In the absence of such reorientation, the PM as a positive intervention in the management of firms may loose its relevance and lead to the alienation of worker component from the process and practice of WPM and may lead to further decline in its popularity and subscription.

Having considered the relevance of personal background variables, an attempt is made here to understand the experience of the respondents in the light of contextual and organizational variables as these contextual variables are assumed to be of significance in determining the experiences of the respondents.

Sector is one such contextual variable, which is always assumed to be making difference when it comes to management of industries and particularly the managerial practices. But in terms of the experience of respondents on WPM, the sector appears to be of no significance. It was noted that, the proportion of the respondents having positive experience about PM was almost identical among both the public (66.0 percent) and private (68.9 percent) sector respondents. However, in view of findings with regard to constitution, frequency of meeting, areas of participation and the like which gave a negative profile of the private sector units appears to have little practical or actual impact, as the positive experience of the respondents belonging to private sector is marginally higher than the corresponding proportion among their public sector counterparts.

TABLE 6.18

Experience of the Respondents by Size of Organization

Experience of the Respondents	*Size of Organization*			*Total*
	Small	*Medium*	*Large*	
Favourable	51 (85.0)	35 (58.3)	75 (62.5)	161 (67.1)
Unfavourable	9 (15.0)	25 (41.7)	45 (37.5)	79 (32.9)
Total	60 (100.0)	60 (100.0)	120 (100.0)	240 (100.0)

X^2= 11.94, DF=2, Significant at 0.01 Level, C= 0.21

However, coming to the size of the organization, the findings appear to be in contradiction to the findings on dispositions once again supporting the fact that dispositions and experiences are independent of each other.

It was noted under the discussion on the dispositions that, the respondents coming from organizations with moderate size have highest proportion of those with favourable dispositions, whereas, in case of experience findings seem to indicate to an exactly opposite situation with respondents coming from organizations with moderate size have the lowest proportion of those with positive experience (58.3 percent), whereas, contrary to this, again the proportion of those with positive experiences is highest (85.0 percent) among those coming from small organizations which was exactly opposite of this in case of dispositions. The association between both disposition and size and experience and size being statistically significant in a contradictory manner, the findings might be confirming the independence of dispositions and experiences. Further this may also to the contrary suggest that small organizations provide better or conducive milieu for WPM to be more effectively in operation, though a moderately sized units may foster favourable dispositions better than small units. Thus, different size may be suited for different aspects of PM and a particular size may not be held as conducive for PM at large. However, if it comes to the actual extent and effectiveness, it appears that the smaller size would be more suited which could be discussed in the next chapter.

With regard to the age of industry again, the findings reveal to a somewhat closer correspondence with the type of experience. In case of dispositions, it was observed that the proportion of those with favourable disposition was highest among those coming from older industries, whereas in case of experience, the corresponding proportion was highest among those coming from industries of moderate age.

It may also be noted from the table that the proportion of those having positive experience belonging to young industries is as low as 43 (43.3) percent which could be taken as very low and in a sense alarming as it could be de-motivating the participants to make more sincere efforts in the future to strengthen the PM movement. The curvilinear relationship, significant at .01 level of significance could indicate to the fact that the extent of positive experience increases with the age of industry up to a point but declines thereafter to consolidate at a level which is higher than in the initial stages.

TABLE 6.19

Experience of the Respondents by Age of Industry

Experience of the Respondents	*Age of Industry*			*Total*
	Before 1960	*Between 1960-1980*	*After 1980*	
Favourable	73 (60.8)	75 (83.3)	13 (43.3)	161 (67.1)
Unfavourable	47 (39.2)	15 (16.7)	17 (56.7)	79 (3.29)
Total	120 (100.0)	90 (100.0)	30 (100.0)	240 (100.0)

X^2= 20.54, DF=2, Significant at 0.01 Level, C= 0.28

In view of this, studies that can suggest measures that could keep the positive experience at a higher levels are needed and attempt is made in the subsequent chapters to deal with this issue.

Coming to the operating status of the industry in terms of the PM experience, the findings again indicate to a negatively curvilinear association between the two with highly profitable industries having higher proportion of those with positive experience which decreases with every decreasing stage of productivity up to a stage where the industries just make it even and then the extent of those with positive experience rises again even up to those industries that are incurring heavy loss. It is rather interesting to note that the phenomenon of positive experience is associated with two opposite situations of the same phenomenon, which is rather difficult to explain and attribute. It would thus impel us to infer that there could be two diametrically opposite implications of PM the positive and negative as well. It could it be stated that by giving scope for WPM, there appears slackness in productivity and on the other hand in other cases it motivates the workers and reinforces their commitment and thereby enhances the performance of the industry. Though it is rather difficult to establish and prove such an attribution, it appears that more structured research is warranted.

The climate of industrial relations is another important contextual variable that could be having significant bearing upon the PM experience of the respondents. And accordingly the data analyzed seem to indicate to such an association between the two.

TABLE 6.20

Experience of the Respondents by Climate of Industrial Relations

Experience of the Respondents	*Climate of Industrial Relations*			*Total*
	Peaceful	*Turbulent*	*Mixed*	
Favourable	110 (73.3)	—	51 (56.7)	161 (67.1)
Unfavourable	40 (26.7)	— —	39 (43.3)	79 (32.9)
Total	150 (100.0)	—	90 (100.0)	240 (100.0)

X^2= 7.07, DF=1, Significant at 0.01 Level, C= 0.16

The association between the type of experience and the climate of industrial relations was found to be significant at .01 level indicating to a higher level correlation, which was rather expected. It may be stated based on this significant relationship or association between type of experience and climate of industrial relations that the climate of industrial relations is a very significant contextual component so far as PM is concerned and could as well have an applied significance, to state that, industrial relations must be given due attention to keep the PM more meaningful and active. And even the argument the other way round that, a satisfactory WPM situation could contribute to the improvement of climate of industrial relations, could also be a finding with an applied value for the improvement of the overall performance of the industry. Thus, as frequently cited in the empirical as well as theoretical literature, there appears to be a very close association between the WPM and climate of industrial relations that too of mutually reinforcing nature and one needs to be strengthened in order to achieve better results in the other.

Quite surprisingly, even the industrial performance was found to be independent of the WPM experiences of the respondents. However, does it mean that the working of WPM machineries has nothing to do with the performance of industry altogether is rather a premature question here, which would be taken up in the last chapter on the implications of WPM. Here what is focused is only the individual experiences of the respondents on WPM which may also have some subjective element present in it. However, though very weak, a trend toward correspondence between positive experience and industrial performance was noticed which was as meager as 69.4 percent versus 60.0 percent in respect of high and low industrial performance, with no statistically significant association between the two.

To ascertain it further, the data pertaining to the experiences were analyzed for their relation with the productivity alone.

To ascertain further such a non association between experience and performance, the data pertaining to experience were analyzed for their association with productivity alone assuming that if not with composite variable, at least with a constituent variable the experience on the WPM could be associated. It may be recalled here that the composite variable of industrial performance is made up of several constituent variables out of which productivity was an important one. Even this cross tabulation for that matter did not reveal any statistically significant association between the two with the proportion of those having positive WPM experience being almost identical among the respondents coming from the units with high productivity (67.3 percent) and moderate to low productivity (66.7 percent). This once again indicates to a non correspondence between productivity and experience of the respondents on WPM, which may be interpreted that the experience of the participants of WPM could not necessarily facilitate or retard, elevate or reduce the productivity levels in the work organizations. It is once again interesting to note that productivity was found to be significantly associated with the dispositions of the respondents indicating to again, independence of dispositions and experiences when it comes to their influence on productivity.

In view of a very vague pattern with regard to the association of dispositions and experience with other background and contextual variables, an attempt was made to relate experience with the dispositions . In the foregoing pages it is observed quite frequently that, the association of these two composite variables with other variables not only fail to show a consistency but many a time it is contradictory. In order to ascertain this interesting phenomenon, the data on experience was cross tabulated with data on dispositions and as expected, in view of the trend observed, no association what so ever was found to be existing between the two, negating the common sense argument that experiences determine the attitudes.

Thus with regard to experiences, it may be concluded

that, the experiences of the respondents on WPM is not as positive as favourable are the dispositions. In all about two-third of the respondents have a positive experience which may not be considered as very high. Further, the experience of the respondents on WPM varies significantly with such personal background variables as age, educational level and more importantly caste and social original but it appears that span of career, category of employment of the respondents have nothing to do with their experiences. Coming to the contextual variables, it is further interesting to note that industrial performance and even productivity are independent of the experience and even the sector makes little difference for such experience. But on the other hand, those organizational variables which had little to do with dispositions like climate of industrial relations and personnel relations were found to be significantly influencing the PM experience of the respondents. One important finding of this study is also that there is little, if any, correspondence between the dispositions and experiences, both having different implications for components of industrial process and being differentially influenced by different components of industrial milieu.

Even a substantial difference between the proportion of those with favourable dispositions and positive experience could be a matter of more structured and focused probe. It appears that inspite of an over whelming majority of the respondents having favourable disposition, only about two thirds of the respondents exhibit a positive WPM experience.

It may, thus, be argued that, a majority of those who are the integral part of the process of PM come to it with a favourable attitude and develop a favourable disposition as they participate or are basically those who have been advocating for such a participatory management but their association and involvement in the actual process is not as rewarding, enriching and gratifying as to commensurate with their expectations. There appears to be a lag between expectations and achievements or experiences. As such, it is most important to know whether such a log is decreasing or increasing, to ascertain, measure and predict the future of WPM in Indian context.

Having ascertained the social realities pertaining to the dispositions and experiences on WPM, an attempt is made into the next chapter to probe empirically in to more significant aspects of PM that is the extent and effectiveness of PM and the determinants of extent and effectiveness of PM, which, as stated in the problem statement are the core objectives of the present study along with the implications.

7

PM: Extent and Effectiveness

Having empirically ascertained the dispositions and experiences of the respondents in the last chapter, which would serve as a useful backdrop, an attempt in this chapter is made to ascertain the extent and effectiveness of WPM and the determinants thereof, which constitute the major thrust and represent the prime objectives of the present study.

It is assumed that the extent of WPM and its effectiveness together, for that matter, determine the extent to which the desired implications of WPM are achieved and based on that, we find ample justification for advocating the initiation of this positive intervention in the management of industries. In short, the future of PM in any society and economy, its survival and persistence as a healthy managerial practice would to a considerable extent depend upon the effectiveness with which these machineries function and bring about a creative and constructive social change in the work situation. And to this extent, the present chapter dealing with the extent, effectiveness and their determinants could be viewed as of applied significance and implications for the industrial progress in particular and economic development in general.

As mentioned in the section on conceptualization, the composite variable of extent of WPM is ascertained, measured and classified taking into account the scores of respondents, as representing their respective industries on diverse variables relating to the functioning of WPM machineries particularly, with regard to the areas, frequency, levels and issues of participation, extent of workers' say, incorporation of workers' views in the decision making, influence of workers' views on the final outcome and the like.

It needs to be clarified here that the extent and effectiveness of WPM are viewed as two separate entities here and it is done so justifiably because, extent refers merely to the strength and quantity of participation whereas, effectiveness of WPM emphasizes the qualitative aspect focusing on the influence of WPM on the actual decisions taken and the seriousness with which these decisions are actually implemented. Thus, under this section, an attempt is made to ascertain, identify, measure and classify the quantitative aspects of PM actually in operation and in the next section, attempt will be made to focus on the qualitative aspects of WPM and thereby ascertain the effectiveness of WPM and see whether there is any correspondence between the extent and effectiveness or they are two different phenomena altogether.

Further, since each of the constituent variables of the extent and effectiveness in themselves are important estimates of WPM, before arriving at the analysis of extent and effectiveness, the constituent variables of these two composite variables are explained and analyzed.

EXTENT OF WPM

The Indices and the Concept

The composite variable of extent of WPM was made up of relevant variables such as - nature of WPM, that is formal or informal, number of WPM machineries in operation, frequency and regularity of meetings of JMCs, SFCs and QCs, extent of participation by workers, trade union leaders and managerial personnel's representatives, level at which participation is more meaningful and active, number of areas of management covered under WPM and the like. In all, nine variables were taken to constitute the composite variable of extent of WPM and taking into account the total of the scores of the respondents on all these constituent variables a scale was prepared to classify the extent as high, moderate and low.

One important constituent variable was the extent and nature of the participation of workers' representatives in the machineries of PM which was ascertained on the basis of regularity, seriousness with which the representatives of the workers participated on the PM machineries, the number of issues raised by them, and the extent to which such issues were debated upon and decided in favour of the argument of the workers. Based on this, the participation of workers was classified as 'active' 'somewhat active' and 'inactive'. It is indeed heartening to note that in none of the units, as per the experience of the respondents, the participation of the workers' representatives in the machineries of WPM was inactive.

TABLE 7.1

Extent of Participation of Workers' Representatives by Category

Extent of Participation	*Category*			*Total*
	Managerial Personnel	*Trade Union Leaders*	*Workers*	
Active	42 (75.0)	35 (62.5)	96 (75.0)	173 (72.1)
Somewhat Active	14 (25.0)	21 (37.5)	32 (25.0)	67 (27.9)
Total	56 (100.0)	56 (100.0)	128 (100.0)	240 (100.0)

Although none of the trade union leaders considered the participation of the workers' representatives as totally inactive their conception of the phenomenon was not as positive (62.5 percent) as that of workers and managerial representatives

(75.0 percent). However, if industries are taken as units, represented by the actors in the process of PM, in nearly three fourth of the cases the participation of workers' representatives was active with another one-fourth of the cases representing a somewhat lesser active participation and as such in all, the extent of participation of workers could be considered as reasonably high particularly in view of the speculations and opinions widely held about the apathy of the workers and the presumed incompetence of the workers' representatives to make a meaningful contribution to the process of PM owing to lack of requisite skills, knowledge and aptitude. Thus, the much lamented non-achievement of the desired efficiency in participation and positive outcome of WPM, if true, may be attributed not to the workers' apathy or incompetence, but to other negative components of the industrial milieu. However, as a component of the general extent of WPM, the participation of the workers' representatives may be viewed as reasonably quite high and its influence in determining the general level of WPM extent would be explained in the subsequent section.

TABLE 7.2

Regularity of the Meetings of JMCs, SFCs and QCs

Frequency	*Machinery*			*Average*
	JMC	*SFC*	*QC*	
High	51.9	68.2	66.5	62.2
Moderate	30.1	22.1	23.3	25.2
Low	18.0	9.6	10.2	12.6
Total	100.0	100.0	100.0	100.0

Coming to the regularity of meetings of JMCs, SFCs and QCs, the data seem to indicate that JMCs meetings were less regular than the regularity of the meetings of SFCs and QCs and the regularity of the meetings of SFCs and QCs appeared to be same with SFCs having an edge over QCs. That is, the meetings of the SFCs were most to regular and the JMCs were the least regular.

As mentioned earlier the frequency and regularity of the meetings of the machineries of WPM have been taken as the indices of the extent of WPM.

The frequency of the meetings of WPM machineries were discussed in chapter V focusing on the structural and functional features of the machineries - where it was found that the frequency of the meetings of these machineries varied from moderate to high with SFCs having the highest frequency of the meetings. Similarly even in case of the regularity, the SFCs appear to be having a greater margin over JMCs and a smaller margin over the QCs.

Thus, as mentioned in the chapter V, though JMCs have a wider scope when it comes to the areas of management covered, it is the SFC which could be taken as the real workhorse of the PM, contributing a greater deal to the extent of WPM in terms of frequency and regularity with which the issues are taken up and deliberated upon. If at all the frequency and regularity of deliberations on the issues concerning the management are the true indicators of the extent of WPM, then SFCs could be taken as the machineries that hold greater promise for a better future to the WPM in Indian industries. QCs on the other hand, though found in all the industries studied, functioning actively, they had quite a narrow scope.

Further, coming to the nature of participation of the various actors in the diverse machineries of PM as a measure of extent of PM in general, the data pertaining tc the above seem to indicate that the trade union leaders appear to be more active than are the other actors in the deliberations of the WPM machineries. It may be noted that, it was in case of the trade union leaders that dispositions were relatively less favourable and experience was relatively less positive but interestingly, it is they who are again relatively more active than their worker and managerial counterparts.

TABLE 7.3

Nature of Participation of the Representatives of the Managerial Personnel, Trade Unions and Workers (Estimated by all the Respondents)

Nature of Participation	*Categories*			*Cumulative Total*
	Managerial	*Trade Union Personnel*	*Workers' Leaders*	
Active	123 (51.3)	165 (68.8)	149 (62.1)	437 (60.6)
Somewhat Active	97 (40.4)	61 (25.4)	84 (35.0)	242 (33.6)
Inactive	20 (8.8)	14 (5.8)	07 (2.9)	41 (5.7)
Total	240 (100.0)	240 (100.0)	240 (100.0)	720 (100.0)

It could be seen from the table that the proportion of those who were concerned as active is as high as 69 (68.8) percent among trade union leaders, whereas the corresponding proportion is relatively low among the workers (62.1 percent) and the managerial personnel (51.3 percent). Thus, with regard to the nature of participation, the trade union leaders by and large, appear to be more active and contribute much more than their counterparts to the over all extent of WPM in Indian industries. If at all the trade unions have been viewed as nurseries of industrial democracies, then it could be through such facilitation of PM process that they can be really contributing to the democratization of work place and this could be considered as an important positive aspect of trade unionism.

Further, in ascertaining the extent of WPM, the extent of the participation of the representatives of workers, trade union leaders and managerial personnel in all the three major machineries was taken into consideration. It is logically assumed that, it is the extent of participation of all the parties concerned in all the machineries would provide a more realistic measure of the total PM situation in an industry and the industrial context in general at large. To render it more realistic, the participation in other minor or less important machineries was also taken into consideration by giving weightage to participation in different machineries. Participation in fora like Welfare Committee, Grievance Committee, Wages Committee, Canteen Committee, Discipline Committee, Safety Committee and the like were clubbed together to represent a composite machinery under the title 'Miscellaneous Fora for Participation' and a scale was developed to represent this forum in addition to the three major machineries, that is, JMCs, SFCs and QCs. This measure was developed because, all the major machineries were not found in all the industries studied but one or two and only sometimes all the three machineries were found to be operating in the industries studied in combination with couple of the minor Committees mentioned above. And in order to not to leave out the participation of workers in other machineries from being considered in ascertaining the total extent of participation of workers in the management of the industry, which together in case of a few industries was as significant as that in the major machineries of PM, it was thought that combining the participation in these minor fora with that in the major fora could provide a more realistic measure of PM in a given industry. Thus, in addition to other constituent variables discussed above, the participation and involvement of the workers and other representatives in all these machineries was taken as another major constituent variable in devising the scale employing which, the composite variable of extent of WPM was ascertained. The data pertaining to the same are presented in the following table.

TABLE 7.4

Extent of Participation in JMCs, SFCs, QCs and Miscellaneous Fora

Extent of Participation	*Machineries*				*Cumulative Total*
	JMC	*SFC*	*QC*	*Miscella-neous*	
High	60 (25.0)	150 (62.5)	180 (75.0)	180 (75.0)	570 (59.4)
Moderate	90 (37.5)	30 (12.5)	60 (25.0)	30 (12.5)	210 (21.9)
Low	90 (37.5)	60 (25.0)	—	30 (12.5)	180 (18.8)
Total	240 (100.0)	240 (100.0)	240 (100.0)	240 (100.0)	960 (100.0)

It may be recalled here that, in the chapter on machineries it was found that the participation in QCs was found to be relatively more active than it was in case of JMCs and SFCs, and as such WPM was considered to be focusing more on the immediate concern of managements, that is, quality improvement which was, though in the interest of the workers also in the long run, was not the priority of workers. The analysis presented in the table also reveals that it is the SFCs, which are the real work horse and the main forum for PM in Indian industries by virtue of scope as well as actual participation. QCs, however, though more widely prevalent than any other machinery, for reasons of its narrow scope, could be considered as contributing moderately to the process of PM. It may be stated here for procedural clarification that the category of 'low' in the data pertaining on each machinery also included 'non-existent', in order to give due weightage to all the categories and have equal number of cases in all machineries which would enhance the validity of analysis. Thus, in case of JMCs the category of 'low' includes only the cases of 'non-existent' and as such should not be viewed as the machinery being in operation in all the plants and in 37.5

percent of the cases, the participation in it being 'low'. Hence, wherever JMCs are established they are high to moderately active.

It is also interesting to note that one or the other machineries other than the JMCs, SFCs and QCs, sometimes in multiple numbers were found to be operating in the industries, concurrently with the major machineries mentioned above. And as such, the contribution of these 'miscellaneous' machineries to the general extent of WPM was, by any standard, in no small measure as in 75 percent of the cases, the combined score on this variable was high, with only in 12.5 percent of the cases the participation being low.

The combined score of all the machineries including the 'miscellaneous' was taken as one of the main indices of the extent of WPM in industries along with other variables discussed and a few other variables like the areas of management dealt with and the like which were discussed in the chapter on the structure and functions of machineries of WPM.

Having ascertained the extent of participation, involvement, the nature of participation, the areas and frequency of participation as observed on diverse constituent variables, which served as the indices of the 'extent of WPM', an attempt is made here to focus on the actual extent of WPM so ascertained and its determinants.

The extent of participation identified and measured as explained above, is found to be reasonably high with nearly 90 (87.5) percent of the units exhibiting moderate to high extent of participation. Since the extent of WPM was also viewed as a trait of work organizations, it could as well be stated that, nearly 90 percent of the organizations studied have moderate to high extent of WPM. In an industrial economy with a relatively short history of industrialism, a traditional structural and cultural context, and with an industrial work force that is still considered as traditional in its out look, the extent of WPM observed could be considered by any standard, as reasonably high. As mentioned earlier, the extent may be viewed as a trait distinct from effectiveness as these two dimensions of the WPM process are dealt with separately, obviously because, higher extent may not necessarily be associated with high degree of effectiveness and vice-versa. But it also goes without saying that, a minimum extent of participation is rather indispensable to ensure or achieve a reasonably high degree of effectiveness. On this count, the extent of WPM may be viewed as a necessary pre-condition for effectiveness to be expected, which may be viewed as at least in part, a function of extent. Thus, at least on this count, the extent of participation found to be in practice is of significant implication for democratizing the workplace and the actual extent of WPM observed could be viewed as reflecting a positive situation existing in the Indian work organizations.

Viewed in the light of general opinion held about the situation of WPM in Indian context, which is believed to be not all that encouraging and considered in the backdrop of the WPM milieu painted in the empirical as well as theoretical literature, the observed level of WPM could be considered as quite promising. Even without reference to these negative or poor portrayal of WPM achievements so widely lamented in the journalistic and impressionistic publications, the extent of WPM found to be actually in operation may be viewed as promisingly high. In an era of globalization, liberalization and with the emergence of competitive world markets, where, emphasis is increasingly being placed on quality, adaptability, up-gradation of technology, economic viability of business operations, it appears that humanization and democratization have come to take a back seat and relegated as philanthropic, ideological and utopian issues. But inspite of such developments and irrespective of their natural out come, the study seems to be indicating to a strong commitment to and firm belief in the desirability of WPM in the Indian work organizations. Although it may be viewed as a passing phase, and it is too early to ascertain the implications of the economic trends world over, as it has happened in the West, at this point of time at least, the PM situation in India appears to be far from disappointing. As in the West, where recent trends have come to negate the nostalgia that was associated with the notions of WPM, Co-determination, Syndicalism, Workplace Democracy and the like during late seventies, once Indian business world comes under the true influence of the current trends world over, the enthusiasm apparently prevalent in WPM at present may dissipate. However, it is heartening to note that, at present in about 90 percent of the units where WPM is in operation, the extent of the same is reasonably, or even quite high.

Determinants of Extent

Having ascertained the extent of WPM and the possible antecedents and prospects, the study further seeks to focus on the causal explanatory variables that could be determining its present patterns and levels.

For the purpose of analysis of these determinants, the extent of WPM in general, prevalent in a work organization was attributed to the participants representing each organization, leading to in all 240 observations. This was necessitated to ascertain the influence of personal background variables such as age, educational level, caste, social origin, span of work career and the like on the extent of WPM.

To begin with the personal background variables such as age, education, span of career, caste and social origin are cross tabulated with the data on the extent of WPM to know whether definite pattern could be observed and whether variation in the extent could be attributed to these variables. With regard to the findings concerning age, the data indicate that the extent of WPM significantly associated with age. It was observed that all those belonging to the younger age group were associated with the high extent of WPM and the association was found to be curvilinear in the sense, the proportion of those associated with high extent declined from 100 percent among younger respondents to 44 percent among the middle aged and rose again considerably to 69 (68.8) percent among those belonging to older age groups. It is also interesting to note that none of those belonging to young and old age group were associated with low extent of WPM. The association between age and the extent of WPM was statistically significant with C value being 0.25.

A more significant association was, however, found between the educational level of the respondents and the extent of WPM.

TABLE 7.5

Extent of WPM by the Educational Level of Respondents

Extent of WPM	*Educational Level*			*Total*
	High	*Moderate*	*Low*	
High	42 (60.0)	74 (52.5)	4 (13.8)	120 (50.0)
Moderate	23 (32.9)	48 (34.0)	19 (65.5)	90 (37.5)
Low	5 (7.1)	19 (13.5)	6 (20.7)	30 (12.5)
Total	70 (100.0)	141 (100.0)	29 (100.0)	240 (100.0)

$X^2 = 19.37$, DF= 4, Significant at 0.01 Level, C=0.27

It is observed from the table that the extent of participation increases with the educational level of the respondents. The proportion of those associated with high extent was as low as 4(13.8) percent among respondents with low educational attainments and it increases sharply to 52(52.5) percent among those with moderate levels of education reaching a still higher level of 60 percent among those with high levels of educational attainment indicating that higher levels of educational attainment facilitate and enable the participants to involve themselves with greater facility and frequency. The relationship between the extent of WPM and educational level was statistically significant at 0.01 level with 'C' value being as high as 0.27. It may also be recalled here that those with higher levels of education were more favourably disposed toward WPM and had more positive experience on it and as such, a higher extent of WPM being associated with higher level of educational attainment could be viewed as quite logical. It may thus, be assumed that, a higher level of education is desirable and rather necessary to enable the participants to contribute more constructively to the process of PM. It may be due to this reason that the respondents belonging to managerial personnel, who are relatively better educated, are found to be contributing more to the extent of WPM. If at all this finding is taken as having any applied implication for the process of WPM, then it may be stated that, it is in the interest of the WPM movement in general that the workers need to be better educated and a higher premium needs to be placed on the training and educational programmes for the workers, and particularly for those associated with the WPM process in the work organizations and further higher educational level per se may be viewed as a positive trait of the working class in general.

It is further interesting to note that, much against what could be expected in view of the association found between extent and education, a negative association was found between the caste status of the respondents and the extent of WPM associated with them. About 68(68.3) percent of those coming from lower castes were associated with higher extent of WPM and the corresponding proportion was nearly half of this (38.7 percent) among those belonging to intermediate castes. However it was found to be much higher than this proportion (55.7 percent) among those coming from the higher castes. Thus, no linear association was found to be existing between caste and extent of WPM. The extent varied significantly with the caste of the respondents (association was statistically significant at 0.01 level with 'C' value being 0.24). Though there is some measure of in-congruence between the association of WPM with education and social origin on the one hand and the caste background of the respondents on the other, the association of the extent of WPM with the latter may be thought of as existing owing to the lower caste respondents finding a forum to share responsibility with those of higher occupational status in the work organizations in managing the affairs of the industry and those belonging to intermediate castes finding it as a situation of dilemma, in the sense they have a status neither as high as to match that of managers nor as low as workers who take it as an unprecedented opportunity and press hard to make the best out of it. This may be further supported by the fact that, the proportion of those associated with high extent of WPM rises again sharply among the respondents belonging to higher castes.

A similar curvilinear association was also observed between the extent of WPM and the span of career of those associated with the process of WPM. The extent was found to be higher (54.2 percent) among those with short span of career which declines quite much among those with a moderate span of career (37.6 percent) and rises again sharply among those with long span of career (58.5 percent). However on the whole, those with long span of career were found to be associated with a relatively higher extent of WPM and the relation between the extent and span of career was significant at 0.05 level. It may be assumed that, those with short span of career find it quite prestigious and rather even thrilling experience to be associated with the decision making process and tend to be actively associated with it and thereby contribute to the extent of WPM. Those in the intermediate stages of their career tend develop some sort of apathy, possibly due to the meager results and poor outcome of it. However, as they progress in their career, may be, they tend to reconcile with the situation and come to realize that, WPM is rather the only hope and an avenue for workers to establish control over their working lives and tend take the machineries of PM rather seriously. As such, a longer association with professional life could be considered as having a positive impact on the extent of WPM in industries coupled with those who have just entered into the professional career. If this finding is taken as having any suggestive value, then it may be stated that it is rather advantageous to have those who have longer stint at their professional career or those who have just made beginning on the machineries of WPM in order to improve the functioning of these machineries.

Lastly, with regard to the social origin of the respondents as a an explanatory variable, the data seem to be indicating a rather weak positive association between the two.

TABLE 7.6

Extent of WPM by Social Origin of the Respondents

Extent	*Social Origin*		*Total*
	High	*Low*	
High	59 (56.7)	61 (44.9)	120 (50.0)
Moderate	38 (36.5)	52 (38.2)	90 (37.5)
Low	07 (6.8)	23 (16.9)	30 (12.5)
Total	104 (100.0)	136 (100.0)	240 (100.0)

$X^2 = 6.59$, DF = 2, Significant at 0.05 Level, C=0.16

The data seem to indicate that higher level of participation in terms of extent for that matter is higher with those coming from higher social origin. It may be observed from the data presented in the table that an overwhelming majority of the respondents (93.2 percent) coming from higher social origin are associated with moderate to high and on the other hand the proportion of those with low participation among the respondents coming from low social origin is as high as about 17(16.9) percent which is nearly three times higher (6.8 percent) than the corresponding proportion among those with high social origin. The association between the extent of WPM and the social origin of the respondents was found to be statistically significant at 0.05 level with 'C' value being 0.16. The observed relation could be suggesting that those coming from lower social origin owing to lower caste status and lower educational level in particular might be finding it rather difficult to cope up with the demands of skill, know how and expertise that is called for to participate actively in the machineries of PM. They might be, as speculated in the literature on industrial relations in Indian context, finding themselves in a disadvantageous position vis-a-vis their counterparts from the high social origin in dealing with, bargaining and sharing the responsibility of managing the enterprise which, more often than not is huge, technically advanced and complex in its structure and functioning. It may, on the other hand, be also attributed to the fact that WPM in more cases than not being management interest oriented as demonstrated in the chapter on the structure and functioning of the machineries, elicits a greater participation by the management representatives who again come preponderantly from the high social origin.

But what is normally expected in view of workers' representatives having a highly favourable disposition toward the PM is that, the workers having got an opportunity to have a say in the taking of decisions that could have important bearing on their lives would participate with greater zeal and enthusiasm and contribute to the overall extent of WPM in industry and since most of the workers' representatives emanate from lower social origins, it is the lower social origin which would have been a strong fort, vehement advocate and practitioner of WPM which in fact is not found to be so. On the other hand it may also be viewed as a positive sign as those coming from higher social origin contribute significantly to the process of WPM, particularly in a stage where their counterparts from lower social origins are not yet in a position to come up to the expectations owing to the disadvantages they could be affected with being from low social origin.

Thus, with regard to the personal background variables, the findings seem to state that educational level of the participants makes much more positive difference for the extent of WPM than the span of career and even the social origin, though age and caste may be also of moderate relevance. Hence, care needs to be taken to see that, relatively more educated members are drawn from among workers, trade union leaders as well as the managerial personnel to officiate and operate the machineries of WPM.

Apart from the personal traits and background of the actors in the machineries of PM, the organizational and contextual variables are assumed to be determining the extent of WPM in the work organizations. In the literature on PM, these variables are considered as important as, if not more than, the personal traits of those who represent various sections of industry on the WPM machineries. It is but natural to assume that the variables like size, age, sector and technology could be the organizational and contextual variables that could have important bearing on the extent of WPM as it is in this context the patterns of management develop and manifest themselves. The ideologies, practices, priorities and philosophies are assumed to be varying with these organizational variables and WPM could be just one of those practices. An attempt is, hence, made in this section to analyze the implications of these variables for the extent of WPM.

Sector is one such important variable when it comes to the study of industrial practices. Sector, as it refers to ownership of the industry, should be considered as an important variable in the study of management and managerial practices in industry - and the data analyzed in this study also support this assumption with public sector industries exhibiting considerably higher degree of WPM than it is found in the private sector industries.

TABLE 7.7

Extent of WPM by Sector

Extent of WPM	*Sector*		*Total*
	Public	*Private*	
High	120 (80.0)	—	120 (50.0)
Moderate	30 (20.0)	60 (66.7)	90 (37.5)
Low	—	30 (33.3)	30 (12.5)
Total	150 (100.0)	90 (100.0)	240 (100.0)

X^2=154.67, DF=2, Significant at 0.01 Level, C = 0.62

It is significant to note that in none of the private sector units, the extent of WPM was found to be high whereas the corresponding proportion in the public sector industries was as high as 80 percent. In private sector the extent of participation was mostly moderate and even low but in none of the public sector units the WPM extent was found to be low.

It may be recalled here, even the analysis of other aspects of WPM in the previous chapters indicated to a more positive disposition and more favourable climate of opinion for WPM in public sector industries than they were in case of the private sector units and the finding indicating to a similar pattern in case of the extent of WPM is quite expected. The reasons why the public sector units exhibit higher extent of WPM may not be far to seek, in the sense, it is in the public sector industries that statutory obligations on the part of management are more readily met with than it is in case of privately owned units and the profit motive not being the sole purpose of existence of the enterprise in public sector, the managerial practices that may some times amount to forfeiture of some of the managerial prerogatives could be conceded, even though it might possibly affect the performance and profitability of the industry adversely. On the other hand, the private sector units where the viability depends on profitability of operation and those that always operate under pressure from the equity holder to operate profitably may be less inclined to leave important decisions to be taken with consultation and approval of the workers. It is again in the private sector that we find closer identification and commitment of management with the ownership whereas in the public sector, there is a clearer segregation and demarcation between management and ownership as in public sector units even the management is employed by the owner. Thus, except for status in organizational hierarchy, the employment status of both workers and the management is not much different and as such, the workers having say in the running or management of industry may not amount to a breach of privilege for the management and such a welcome or favourable outlook or attitude coupled with the statutory obligations imposed by their owners themselves may pave the way for a better or more conducive climate for PM resulting in its higher incidence practice than it is found in the private sector units. The variance of extent of WPM with sector was found to be statistically highly significant with 'C' value being as considerably high as 0.62.

An equally significant (C=0.61) association was also found between the extent and size of the organization. Size has universally been considered as a very important trait of organizations in the empirical and the theoretical literature on sociology of organizations, management, industrial psychology and so forth. In the administration or management of industries or work organizations, in general size plays an important role which determines other organizational traits such as formalization, centralization, specialization, departmentalization, bureaucratization and even organizational climate and organizational culture are viewed as the functions of the size. And in view of this, the PM coming to be influenced by the size is quite expected.

It is quite significant to note that in the analysis of dispositions and experiences, a moderate size was associated with favourable disposition and positive experience whereas in case of the extent of participation, the large organizations appear to be better placed.

TABLE 7.8

Extent of WPM by the Size of Organization

Extent of WPM	*Size of Organization*			*Total*
	Small	*Moderate*	*Large*	
High	—	30 (50.0)	90 (75.0)	120 (50.0)
Moderate	30 (50.0)	30 (50.0)	30 (25.0)	90 (37.5)
Low	30 (50.0)	—	—	30 (12.5)
Total	60 (100.0)	60 (100.0)	120 (100.0)	240 (100.0)

X^2 = 145.00, DF= 4, Significant at 0.01 Level, C=0.61

Three-fourths of those belonging to large work organizations are associated with high extent of WPM whereas the corresponding proportion among those associated with small organizations is nil and conversely, half of those coming from small organizations have been associated with low extent of WPM, supporting the argument that large organizations facilitate greater WPM. This is further supported by the fact that all the organizations that are associated with low extent are the small organizations. As mentioned in the methodology, size was taken as an important criterion based on which the sample of organizations was drawn and even the very selection of universe of organizations was based on size, stating that certain minimum size of organizations may be viewed as the necessary pre-condition for PM to be practically, feasibly and meaningfully in operation and it appears that such an assumption is empirically justified in view of the findings of the present study which indicate to a positive association between extent of WPM and the size of organization, that is, with increase in the size of the organization the extent of WPM increased and such an increase was rather quite significant. It was argued in the previous chapter that, too large organizations could be unwieldy for workers representatives to comprehend and be confident with regard to skills, know-how and expertise to make a meaningful contribution to the process of decision making and administration and it is because of this, the experiences of the respondents may not be all that positive with regard to WPM and so with the dispositions. However, in case of actual participation, such an explanation appears to be untenable and on the contrary, the larger organizations appear to be providing a better forum and more conducive climate for WPM. Based on this, it may also be argued that the formalization, impersonalization, bureaucratization so commonly associated with large organizations do not appear to be of any negative implications for the extent of WPM and on the other hand provide a more conducive milieu for the functioning of PM machineries. On the other hand, informality, face to face contact and personal intimacy so often conspicuously found associated with the smaller work organizations may not be holding a very big promise for WPM process.

Similarly a positive association was also found between the age of the industry and the extent of WPM.

TABLE 7.9

Extent of WPM by the Age of Industry

Extent of WPM	*Age of Industry*			*Total*
	Before 1960	*Between 1960-1980*	*After 1980*	
High	90 (75.0)	30 (33.3)	—	120 (50.0)
Moderate	30 (25.0)	30 (33.3)	30 (100.0)	90 (37.5)
Low	—	30 (33.3)	—	30 (12.5)
Total	120 (100.0)	90 (100.0)	30 (100.0)	240 (100.0)

X^2 = 121.67, DF= 4, Significant at 0.01 Level, C=0.58

It may be noted from the table that 75 percent of those industries established before 1960 are associated with high extent of WPM and the corresponding proportion among these having been established after 1980 is nil and on the other hand in those industries established in between, the proportion of 'high' 'moderate' and 'low' is exactly one-third each. Thus, the data seem to indicate that the extent of WPM increased definitely and steadily with the age of the industry. A similar association for that matter, was also observed between dispositions, experience and age and in this case there appears to be a complimentarity between dispositions, experiences and the actual operation. As attributed in the case of dispositions and experiences, it may be stated that the older units tend to have better established structures, traditions and well established trade unions and above all a mature industrial subculture with workers, managements and the trade union as its participants, which may be a pre-condition for WPM to work. It may also be stated that it is in the older industries that the parties to the production could have come to realize the advantages as well as inevitability of peaceful co-existence in bringing about mutual benefits and as such managements and unions and workers tend to explore the possibilities as well as the avenues of collaboration, coordination and codetermination to achieve the best for both the parties and tend to end up in having better results on WPM front. Thus, age could be another organizational variables to be watching for when it comes to achievement in the area of WPM. Although age of an industry is a trait or property which can not be controlled or manipulated, it may at least give us an idea as to organization with what kind of traits could be more suitable for introduction of PM as an innovative positive intervention in the organizational management.

Further, an attempt is made here to ascertain the influence of other organizational traits for the extent of WPM. Sector, size and age are understood to be universal features of industrial organizations that are focused upon, but there could be other organizational features which could also be of relevance in ascertaining the extent of WPM such as the degree of complexity and bureaucratization as organizational variables and degree of unionization and affiliation pattern as contextual variables.

In terms of complexity of organizational structure, the findings seem to indicate to a very strong positive association between the degree of structural complexity of organizations and the extent of WPM. Although strangely enough, more complex organizations appear to be fostering better WPM than are those characterized by low degree of organizational complexity. The data reveal that all those organizations associated with high extent of participation have moderate to high structural complexity. It is further interesting to note that none of the organization with low complexity had a high extent of WPM. In fact, what is assumed is the complexity of organizational structure would rather be a factor retarding WPM owing to workers' representatives not being able to respond effectively in such organizations. However, it appears that the degree of complexity that goes with organizational size renders organizations more amenable for introduction of PM. It may also mean that units with no formally established internal structure and procedures may not offer a favourable organizational milieu for experimenting PM. This could be stated on the basis of a statistically very strong association between the degree of organizational complexity and the extent of WPM (C=0.71).

Since the degree of complexity and the resultant degree of formalization are assumed to be contributing to the degree of bureaucratization, instead of focusing on individual traits of bureaucratization an attempt is made here to ascertain the implications of the degree of bureaucratization as a trait of organizational climate for the extent of WPM and the analysis, as in case of complexity, reveals a positive association between the two. It was observed that all the industries which stood at 'high' in the scale of bureaucratization were associated with high extent of WPM. Thus, bureaucratization which is so often viewed as synonymous to formalism, impersonalism, rationalism, ritualism, red-tapism and the like is assumed to be less suited for an innovative intervention in the tradition of human relations approach but such an assumption is rather not supported by the data in this study and on the contrary it may suggest that the bureaucratic rationalism, accountability and rational co-ordination as organizational traits that could enhance the organization's suitability for the PM practices. It may be explained so that, the bureaucratic structures which emphasise formal rules of business and procedure, develop well defined divisions and subdivisions with well defined authority and systems of communication, may be found suitable in facilitating the functioning of WPM machineries.

Equally important were the factors relating to industrial relations scene in determining the extent of WPM.

TABLE 7.10

Extent of WPM by the Extent of Unionization

Extent of WPM	*Extent of Unionization in the Plant*		*Total*
	High	*Moderate*	
High	90 (60.0)	30 (33.3)	120 (50.0)
Moderate	60 (40.0)	30 (33.3)	90 (37.5)
Low	—	30 (33.3)	30 (12.5)
Total	150 (100.0)	90 (100.0)	240 (100.0)

x^2=58.66, DF=2, Significant at 0.01 Level, C = 0.44

It was observed that extent of WPM and extent of unionization co-vary positively. The degree or extent of unionization was classified as low (less than 50 percent), moderate (50 to 75 percent) and high (more than 75 percent) and it was noticed that none of the units studied had less than 50 percent unionization, a little over one-third (37.5 percent) of the units moderately unionized and about two-thirds (62.5 percent) of the units were on the higher side of unionization with more than 75 percent of the workforce being unionized. Further a very strong association was found to be existing between the two indicating that a strong union movement is complimentary to the extent of WPM. The literature on industrial relations has come to repeatedly indicate that the nature of working conditions, the bargaining position and reward structures do vary with the strength of unionism which is achieved through an enhanced awareness, consciousness of class interests and collective representation. It may also appear rather logical that workers need to be represented by a strong and mature unionism to exercise and enjoy their rights and all pervasive unionism may be thought of as giving rise to a union subculture in the plant wherein industrialism becomes a dominant way of life with its norms, beliefs, values, customs, rituals, folkways and fads. Such a mature industrial way of life is believed as an ideal setting for any kind of a positive experiment and WPM could be just one among them.

However, it may be noted that it is not mere unionism but unionism with no extreme ideology that really makes difference. It is observed that all those associated with leftist unionism exhibit a very low level of WPM. It is observed from the data that all the units with independent unionism that is, with no political and ideological affiliations are associated with high extent of WPM. All those with rightist and other moderate unionism tend to be represented by a moderate extent of WPM and quite interestingly all the units with leftist unionism are associated with low extent of WPM. It may, thus be argued that, unionism without any political overtones is best suited for WPM and in a way it acts as complimentary to the process of PM and may promote its extent. On the other hand, affiliation to extreme leftist ideology tends to have a dampening effect on the spirit of WPM, may be because collaborating with the management is against the communist ideology which seeks to bring about ownership, or in the extreme cases, even the dictatorship of working class. As such to collaborate with the management may be viewed as a compromise with the ultimate goal of communism. Similarly, unionism of moderate nature and even to some extent the rightist ideology are found to be with moderate extent of WPM. Thus, it is not only the extent of unionism but also the union's ideological affiliations appear to be of some consequence to the general extent of WPM.

Further, the extent was also found significantly associated with the dispositions and experiences of the respondents. It is quite logical to assume that units where the dispositions of the parties to the process of WPM is favourable, the actual extent of WPM is expected to be high. The data seem to indicate to such an association when it is observed that among those with favourable disposition, over 50(52.5) percent of the respondents are associated with high extent of WPM whereas the corresponding proportion among these with unfavourable disposition is as low as 38(38.1) percent. Conversely among those with unfavourable disposition, respondents associated with low extent of WPM constitute almost one-fourth (23.8 percent) with corresponding proportion among the favourably disposed is as low as 10(10.1) percent indicating to the fact that dispositions of the parties to the WPM might play an important role in determining the extent of WPM in the plants.

Still more significant association was found between the extent of WPM and the experience. It was observed from the data that over 50(53.4) percent of those having positive experience were associated with high extent of WPM whereas the corresponding proportion among those having negative experience was around 40(43.0) percent. The positive association between the two was statistically significant at 0.01 level with 'C' value being 0.27.

Thus, with regard to the extent of WPM analysed in the light of dispositions and experiences of the respondents, it may be stated that a climate of favourable disposition and pleasant or meaningfully positive experience could be considered as necessary preconditions for WPM to attain higher levels of activation and deal with more areas of management.

Thus, the extent of WPM, which was one of the main thrusts of the present study could be stated as reasonably high and varying significantly with personal background variables such as age, educational level and social origin, dispositions and experiences on the one hand and organizational variables such as sector, size, age, degrees of bureaucratization, unionization and the union affiliations on the other.

EFFECTIVENESS OF WPM

The Indices and the Concept

Having empirically ascertained the extent and constituents of the extent of WPM and the determinants, an attempt is made in this section to focus on the degree of effectiveness and its determinants. Just as in case of the composite variable of extent, the composite variable of effectiveness of WPM was made up of several discrete variables focusing on the diverse aspects of effectiveness, which were taken as the indices of effectiveness.

TABLE 7.11

Workers' Say in the Machineries of PM

Workers' Say	*Machineries*			*Cumulative Total*
	JMCs	*SFCs*	*QCs*	
Much	120 (50.0)	150 (62.5)	120 (50.0)	390 (54.2)
Somewhat	30 (12.5)	60 (25.0)	60 (25.0)	150 (20.8)
Less	90 (37.5)	30 (12.5)	60 (25.0)	180 (25.0)
Total	240 (100.0)	240 (100.0)	240 (100.0)	720 (100.0)

The composite variable of effectiveness was made up of the respondents' scores on workers' say in JMCs, SFCs and QCs, effectiveness of JMCs, SFCs and QCs in dealing with the issues, extent of implementation of decisions of WPM machineries, impact of workers' participation on the outcome, overall control exercised by the WPM machinereis on the administration, relevance of issues raised in the WPM machineries to the needs and aspirations of the workers.

Coming to the workers' say in the machineries of JMCs, SFCs and QCs, the data seem to indicate that workers have a more than moderate say in the proceedings of these WPM machineries.

The total score of the respondents on all the three major machineries of WPM, as stated above, indicates to a rather gratifying situation, wherein 75 percent of the respondents have score high enough to be considered as having much to somewhat, that is, high to moderate say in the machineries of PM. And even the remaining 25 percent representing 'little' say includes cases where the machineries were non-existent indicating that if participation or say in only the machineries in existence is taken into consideration, then the proportion of those having greater say would have been still higher. For example in case of JMCs, wherever they are in operation, the workers' say is either much or somewhat and in case of 90 respondents the JMCs were not in operation. But since a scale of 'say' in WPM machinereis was being attempted, as one of the indices of effectiveness, equal weightage had to be given to all the machineries, scoring non-existence of machineries as having little say. In view of this, it may be stated that the extent of workers' say in the machineries of PM in reality is much higher than what is depicted in the table indicating to the fact that workers do, in fact, have a considerable say in the functioning of WPM machineries wherever they are found in operation.

Coming to the effectiveness of these machineries in dealing with the issues raised in them, somewhat a similar picture was found, indicating that they are more than moderately effective in dealing with issues as and when they come up or raised before them. Just as in case of workers' say in these machineries, the SFCs were found to be relatively more effective in dealing with issues than were either JMCs or QCs.

TABLE 7.12

Extent of Effectiveness of PM Machineries in Dealing with Issues

Effectiveness of WPM Machineries	*Machineries*			*Cumulative Total*
	JMCs	*SFCs*	*QCs*	
High	150 (62.5)	150 (62.5)	120 (50.0)	420 (58.3)
Moderate	—	90 (37.5)	60 (25.0)	150 (20.8)
Low	90 (37.5)	—	60 (25.0)	150 (20.8)
Total	240 (100.0)	240 (100.0)	240 (100.0)	720 (100.0)

It is evident from the data presented in the table that the effectiveness of dealing with issues raised is relatively higher with SFCs than it is with JMCs and QCs. It may appear rather logical that having a say is one thing and influencing the decisions in an effective manner appears to be different from this. But, it is rather gratifying to note that the effectiveness in dealing with the issues is much higher than having a say in the decision making process. Although both of them appear to be mutually complimentary and two dimensions of the same entity, it is significant to note that effectiveness in dealing with issues raised could be stated as contributing more significantly to the effectiveness than mere having say in the deliberations of these machineries and as such may be considered as a more important index of the effectiveness of WPM machineries than the former. Further, even taken independently, it is interesting to note that QCs, though found more universally than any other machinery, are less effective in dealing with issues raised in them. It may be noted here that, QCs deal principally with issues relating to quality and other than quality there is nothing much which these machineries deal with and naturally, quality is rather a difficult issue to deal with as it depends not only on will and wish but more on the expertise, competence, skill, co-operation, co-ordination and know-how. As such, the QCs could be lagging behind other machineries in their effectiveness in dealing with issues raised in them. However, all the machineries taken together, the effectiveness appears to be quite high.

Coming to the extent of implementation of decisions taken in PM machineries as an index of effectiveness of WPM, the data reveal that, in comparison with workers' having a say in the machineries as well as the effectiveness in dealing with issues raised in the machineries, the implementation of decisions taken in WPM machineries appears to be contributing less to the effectiveness of WPM.

TABLE 7.13

Extent of Implementation of Decisions Taken in PM Machineries

Extent of Implementation	*Frequency*	*Percentage*
High	94	39.2
Moderate	130	54.2
Low	16	6.7
Total	240	100.0

Inspite of workers' say in the machineries of PM being relatively high and the effectiveness with which the issues raised in these machineries being still higher, the implementation of the decisions taken in the machineries appears to be relatively low. Although the proportion of respondents associated with low extent of implementation is quite low at about 7(6.6) percent, the frequency with which higher extent of implementation of decisions takes place in WPM machineries is also quite low at 39(39.2) percent.

Participating in the decision making process, having a say in the decisions taken and dealing effectively with issues raised in the WPM machineries may be taken as, at the most, the preparatory tasks but what is more important and of applied significance is the extent to which the decisions taken in the PM machineries are actually implemented and as such this may be taken as an important index of the effectiveness of WPM. Arriving at a consensus opinion and a unanimous decision is always a less difficult task and as the experience shows, the managements lack the will and commitment to put these decisions in action in right earnest and many a time the decisions are kept in cold storage leading to stalemate on important issues. On the other hand, the decisions taken under pressure many a time later on prove to be not feasible in view of their implications for the industry at large. In view of this, there could be a lag between decisions taken and their implementation. The lower proportion of units with high incidence of implementation of decisions taken, as observed from the data, may not be an unexpected or unforeseen phenomenon in the operation of PM.

The impact of workers' participation on the outcome of WPM machineries, which is a measure of how much of the outcome is in commensuration with the workers' point of view, could also be an index of effectiveness of WPM. The data pertaining to the same reveal that such an impact is to a considerable extent.

TABLE 7.14

Impact of Deliberations on the Outcome of the Machineries

Impact on Outcome	*Frequency*	*Percentage*
High	165	68.8
Moderate	61	25.4
Low	14	05.8
Total	240	100.0

In terms of impact of the deliberations on the outcome of the machineries, the data indicate to a very promising situation, as in nearly 70(68.8) percent of the cases, the impact is high which is followed by another one fourth (25.4 percent) of the cases where the impact is moderate with only about 6 (5.8) percent of the cases having low impact. In fact, to what extent the final outcome of the deliberations bear the stamp of WPM machineries and to what extent the issues being dealt with are in tune with the discussions undertaken in the meetings can be taken as an important index of the effectiveness of the WPM process, which is found to be quite high particularly in view of what is generally opined in the literature as very positive.

In addition to these variables discussed, two more variables, namely the control of WPM machineries over the administration of the industry and the relevance of issues raised in the machineries of WPM to the wishes and aspirations of the workers were also taken to calculate the score of each respondent to have scale of effectiveness and using suitable scaling techniques, the respondents were classified as belonging to three categories of effectiveness as 'high', 'moderate' and 'low'. The data pertaining to the level of effectiveness so ascertained are presented in the following table.

TABLE 7.15

Level of Effectiveness of WPM

Level of Effectiveness	*Frequency*	*Percentage*
High	90	37.5
Moderate	90	37.5
Low	60	25.0
Total	240	100.0

It may be observed from the table that the effectiveness of WPM, when considered as a very important criterion as an estimate of success of WPM is reasonably high with 75 percent of the respondents being associated with high to moderate level of effectiveness. Again, viewed in the light of general opinion held regarding the functioning of WPM machineries, which is not all that favourable, the perceived or observed level of effectiveness could be considered as more than reasonably high. For a developing economy with traditional workforce operating in a still traditional social structure, the level of effectiveness with which the WPM machineries operate may be considered as quite promising and gratifying though there is still scope for improvement.

Determinants of Effectiveness

Thus, having ascertained the level of effectiveness with which the PM machineries function, an attempt is made here to focus on the determinants of the level of effectiveness. Just as in case of extent of WPM, the causative variables are divided into two for all categories as personal background variables and organization and contextual variables with a view to ascertain the relative importance of these causative variables.

TABLE 7.16

Level of Effectiveness of WPM by Caste of Respondents

Level of Effectiveness	*Caste*			*Total*
	High	*Intermediate*	*Low*	
High	37 (42.0)	30 (27.0)	23 (56.1)	90 (37.5)
Moderate	37 (42.0)	42 (37.8)	11 (26.8)	90 (37.5)
Low	14 (15.9)	39 (35.1)	7 (17.1)	60 (25.0)
Total	88 (100.0)	111 (100.0)	41 (100.0)	240 (100.0)

X^2=17.74, DF=4, Significant at 0.01 Level, C=0.26

Age is one such personal background variable which might be important from the point of view of participation in any institution for that matter. However, no such significant association was found between the level of effectiveness and the age of the respondents. Least effective in participation were those in the middle age group with all the young respondents, though very few were associated with high level of effectiveness.

However, in terms of caste, a significant association was observed which was, as in the case of extent of WPM, curvilinear in nature with those coming from intermediate castes being associated with low effectiveness.

The findings seem to indicate that, the lower caste respondents are relatively the most effective ones in the WPM machineries (56.1 percent) as compared to those coming from intermediate (27.0 percent) and high caste (42.0 percent) respondents, negating the assumption that effective participation in and management of any institution and organization goes with caste, with high caste people being endowed with better skills, aptitude, expertise as well as status required for such tasks. On the contrary, the low caste respondents are found to be not only with requisite skills, expertise and aptitude but are also found to be operating more effectively availing the opportunities for such tasks, which may be viewed as a positive development. What is also rather unexpected revelation is that, the intermediate castes not being enterprising and active as they are normally or generally thought of. The intermediate castes are viewed as the Indian counterpart of the so called enterprising, upwardly mobile, dynamic middle classes everywhere. But it appears that there is rather low correspondence between the middle classes and intermediate castes when it comes to effectiveness in matters relating to their occupational life, management of work situations and bargaining for better rewards, compensations and working conditions. This could be a matter for further probe.

Coming to the span of career as a causal variable determining the level of effectiveness, further, findings indicate to no definite pattern and no statistically significant association between them. It was, observed, none the less, that it is again those with short span of career who had the highest proportion (50.0 percent) of those associated with high level of effectiveness as against the ones with medium (29.0 percent) and long span of career (41.5 percent). This finding, however, is in commensuration with the finding on the age, as age and span of career must be positively associated. This may lead to a conclusion that it is the young and those who have entered the professional life relatively recently are the ones who contribute to a greater extent and effectiveness of WPM.

However a significantly high positive association was found between the level of effectiveness and the level of educational attainments of the respondents, although quite expectedly.

TABLE 7.17

Level of Effectiveness of WPM by the Level of Education

Level of Effectiveness of WPM	*Level of Education*			*Total*
	High	*Moderate*	*Low*	
High	32 (45.7)	54 (38.3)	4 (13.8)	90 (37.5)
Moderate	29 (41.4)	56 (39.7)	5 (17.2)	90 (37.5)
Low	9 (12.9)	31 (22.0)	20 (69.0)	60 (25.0)
Total	70 (100.0)	141 (100.0)	29 (100.0)	240 (100.0)

X^2= 36.34, DF=4, Significant at 0.01 Level, C=0.36

The data presented in the table reveal that the level of effectiveness increases with the level of educational attainment with high level of effectiveness constituting just 13(13.8) percent among those with low educational level, rising to a considerably higher extent (45.7 percent) among those with higher level of education. Similarly the proportion of those associated with low effectiveness among those with low level of education is as high as 70(69.0) percent and the corresponding proportion among those with high education is as low as 13(12.9) percent indicating to a very strong association between the level of effectiveness of WPM and the educational level of the participants.

Educational level, as viewed in the analysis throughout, appears to one of the most important explanatory variables in the functioning of the PM machineries. It is found significantly associated with the dispositions, experiences, extent and effectiveness and as such may be viewed as the most important causative factor in the functioning of PM. It may also be argued that it is the educational level which enables an individual to participate in a process which calls for awareness, capacity to comprehend and conceptualize and at the same time, it is education which makes an individual confident of self and secularizes the outlook which may be the best solution for countering the dampening effect and constraining influence of traditional order and outlook. Education may also be viewed as contributing to the development of positive disposition toward values like liberty, equality, humanity, human dignity and human rights as well as equity which may in turn contribute in rendering a participant in WPM to perform more actively and effectively.

Coming to the last personal background variable, that is, the composite variable of social origin, the association was in a way different from the one found with caste indicating that though caste is one of the components of social origin, the curvilinear association found between effectiveness and caste was not found with social origin. In case of caste, the lower castes were found to more effective than those coming from intermediate and high castes, whereas in case of social origin it is those coming from high social origin are relatively more effective in WPM machineries than are those coming from low social origin. This may mean that other components of social origin such as, education, income and occupational status could be of a more determinate role to play in determining the level of effectiveness than is caste. In support of this it was noticed that, in all 85 (84.6) percent of those coming from high social origin were associated with high to moderate level of effectiveness whereas, the corresponding proportion among those coming from low social origin is as low as 67(67.4) percent. The association between the same was statistically significant at 0.01 level with 'C' value being 0.19.

Thus, with regard to the personal background variables in the analysis of the level of effectiveness of WPM, it may be concluded that age and span of career were found to be of little relevance whereas caste, social origin and particularly educational level was found to be of significance in determining the level of effectiveness, which was in general found to be reasonably high.

More important than the personal background variables, it is assumed, are the organisational and contextual variables in determining the effectiveness of WPM. Personal background variables would take into consideration the individual capabilities, skills, aptitudes, cultural background and mental make up but the organisational and contextual variables represent the climate of opinion, organisational climate, structural and functional features and general socio-economic milieu as factors determining the level of effectiveness and as such may be considered as more important collective phenomenon than the individual background of persons. As such, the following section deals with one of the most important concerns of the present study.

A very strong statistically significant association was

found between the effectiveness and sector. It is interesting to note that none from the public sector units is associated with the low effectiveness and none from the private sector is associated with high level of effectiveness with the proportion of those associated with moderate level of effectiveness being almost equal among both. 67 (66.7) percent of those from private sector were associated with low effectiveness with the corresponding proportion among those from public sector being nil. The association was significant at 0.01 level with 'C' value being as high as 0.62.

This finding is consistent with the earlier findings wherein public sector units were found to be considerably more favourable toward, more active in and more committed to WPM ascertained in terms of their composition, frequency of meeting, in terms of attitudes and experiences and even the extent of WPM. Although the positive implications of WPM for the productivity, climate of industrial relations and the industrial performance in general would be analyzed and discussed in the next chapter, it is significant to note here that the level of effectiveness which could be holding key to the positive aspects WPM and as such viewed as important index of WPM in operation, is considerably higher in public sector units. Thus, the public sector may be viewed as not only being more favourable to the PM experiment, as a statutory requirement but also being more efficient in running these machineries. Being higher on the scale of extent and effectiveness of WPM, even if this is not leading to or resulting in concrete benefits to the parties concerned, at least in terms of democratizing and humanizing the work place, the public sector is found to be ahead of or leading the private sector.

An equally strong association was observed between the level of effectiveness and the size of the organization. Just as in case of sector, none of the small units were associated with high level of effectiveness and none of the large units were associated with low level of effectiveness.

TABLE 7.18

Level of Effectiveness of WPM by Size of Organization

Level of Effectiveness of WPM	*Size of Organization*			*Totai*
	Small	*Medium*	*Large*	
High	—	30 (50.0)	60 (50.0)	90 (37.5)
Moderate	30 (50.0)	—	60 (50.0)	90 (37.5)
Low	30 (50.0)	30 (50.0)	—	60 (25.0)
Total	60 (100.0)	60 (100.0)	120 (100.0)	240 (100.0)

X^2=120.00, DF=4, Significant at 0.01 Level, C=0.57

The size of organization, it may be recal'ed here that, was also positively associated with the extent of participation and here it is found equally more significantly associated with the level of effectiveness indicating that larger organizations have in-built traits or properties that make them considerably more suited for PM. It is further interesting to note that among moderate sized organizations half were associated with high level of effectiveness and the other half were associated with low level of effectiveness. Thus, it may stated with confidence that the level of effectiveness of WPM increases with the size of the organization and it also proves the assumption that for PM to be meaningfully in operation, the organizations have to be of considerable size. It may thus be argued that WPM can be implemented effectively only in such organizations that have a high degree of formalization, bureaucratisation and structural complexity. In short, the WPM is viable and can be put effectively into practice in such prototype industrial organizations that represent the industrial era rather than pre-industrial or post industrial.

Similarly, the nature of relationship that was observed

between the extent of WPM and the age of industry was also observed between the effectiveness and the age of industry. The older industries with larger size in public sector, then, could be taken as an ideal breeding ground for WPM culture to thrive and be perpetuated. The data pertaining to the level of effectiveness viewed in the light of the age of the work organization reveal that half (50.0 percent) of the units established between 1960 and 1980 come to be associated with high level of effectiveness with none of the organizations coming into being after 1980 have been associated with the high level of effectiveness, suggesting that the level of effectiveness increases with the age of organization. The relationship between the level of effectiveness and age of the organization was statistically significant at 0.01 level with 'C' value being as high as 0.45.

Further, the findings seem to suggest that, the organizations with moderate degree of complexity exhibit higher degree (66.7 percent) of effectiveness as compared with work organizations characterized by high degree of complexity (25.0 percent) or those with low degree of organizational complexity among which none were associated with high degree of effectiveness. Further, all the organizations with high degree of bureaucratization were associated with high degree of effectiveness with none of the organizations with low degree of bureaucratization being high on effectiveness of WPM. As such, coming to the structural features of the organization it was noticed that organizations with large size, moderate degree of complexity and high degree of bureaucratization, as ascertained based on the degree of centralization, formalization, division of labour, specialization and so forth were found to be the most suitable or hospitable organizations for adopting the practice of PM. The findings of the study seem to indicate that, for WPM machineries to be established, and these machineries to be functioning in a reasonably active manner and to be effective in realizing their objectives, the organizations have to be with the traits mentioned above, that is small organizations with simple informal structures and procedures of administration, run on the pattern of family business are unsuited for the WPM machineries to be functioning at their full potential and in an effective manner.

Further, quite interestingly, the level of effectiveness in WPM was independent of the dispositions and experiences of the parties to the WPM process, negating the argument that, a favourable disposition toward and positive experience on WPM are pre-conditions for WPM process to be effective. However, it may be noted that dispositions of the participants were overwhelmingly favourable, and experiences were equally positive and as such, the implications of strong negative experience or strong unfavourable dispositions could not be ascertained.

Lastly, coming to the climate of industrial relations as a determinant of the level of effectiveness, it was noted that, the union management relations being overwhelmingly peaceful, the implications of hostile industrial relations could not be ascertained. Further, no statistically significant association could be found between the level of effectiveness and the degree of unionization in the plant. Although the extent of WPM was found to be positively associated with the degree of unionization, it appears that the effectiveness is independent of the degree of unionization.

However, it is interesting to note that though level of effectiveness is independent of the degree of unionization in the plant, the affiliation patterns of unions has something to do with the level of effectiveness as, a statistically significant association was found between the two at 0.01 level with 'C' value being very high at 0.73. A very significant association was also observed between the extent and affiliation pattern with independent unions having the highest extent whereas the leftist unions were found to be associated with the least extent. A similar, but much stronger association was found between the level of effectiveness and the affiliation status and pattern of the unions operating in the plants. The data indicate that the level of effectiveness was highest (66.7 percent) among those units associated with independent unions without affiliation to any federation or with political ideologies and overtones. In case of units associated with independent unions, another one-third (33.3 percent) were associated with moderate level of effectiveness with none being rated as low on effectiveness. Contrary to this, all the units having unions with leftist affiliations were exclusively associated with low level of effectiveness with none representing even moderate level of effectiveness. Units associated with unions having rightist leanings were all found to be having moderate levels of effectiveness with moderates being divided equally with moderate and low levels of effectiveness. As explained in case of extent, the leftist unions are fundamentally against sharing of power or responsibility with the management as it is against their ideology of working class dictatorship and the extent being considerably low, it is quite expected that the effectiveness could be low as well. Further, the very high level of effectiveness among units associated with independent unions could be attributed to such unions having no ideological constraints, political overtones and federating controls which can interfere in their involvement in the process of WPM. The politicization of union movement which is considered as a bane of Indian trade union movement along with outside leadership is again found to be having yet another negative implication for the system of industrial relations and as such needs to be warded-off or at least kept to its minimum.

It was stated at the beginning of this chapter that the extent and effectiveness are viewed as two exclusive entities different from each other as mere extent of WPM cannot guarantee its being effectively practiced. In some units the extent may be low and effectiveness may be high and other way argument may also hold good. The extent was viewed as a quantitative measure and the effectiveness was viewed as a qualitative measure and between these two dimensions of PM, correspondence or complimentarity was not viewed as natural, inevitable or invariable. This was, however, a hypothetical argument, stated for the purpose only of analysis and interpretation of the two most important dimensions of the WPM and it was also, at the same time, assumed that, a positive association could be found between the two which was supported by the data rather emphatically. The data pertaining to effectiveness cross tabulated with the extent reveal that 75 percent of those units with high extent of WPM were also found to be associated with high level of effectiveness and remaining 25 percent were moderately effective with none being in low category of effectiveness. On the contrary, none of the units associated with low extent of WPM were found to be with high level of effectiveness nor even with moderate level of effectiveness with all belonging to this (100 percent) category having low level of effectiveness.

Thus, with regard to the level of effectiveness viewed in terms of extent it may be stated that there is a very strong positive association between the two, though both are not synonymous as conceived in the literature mistakenly. It may further be stated, based on the findings, that some minimum extent of WPM is absolutely necessary for the extent of effectiveness to be on the higher side, that is some minimum quantity is essential to ensure the quality and the quality for that matter improves with increase in quantity as well. It may also mean that for effectiveness to be on the higher side, the extent of WPM has got to be reasonably high. Put in other words, with extent of WPM being low, the effectiveness can not be high as the analysis indicates to a very strong positive association between the two at 0.01 level with 'C' value being as high as 0.69. Thus, when it comes to WPM, the extent and effectiveness, the two most important aspects could be considered as mutually complimentary, particularly, the impact of extent on effectiveness can not be underestimated, in view of which wherever there is a need to enhance the effectiveness of WPM, efforts should be made to increase the extent of participation in the first instance.

Thus, with regard to effectiveness of WPM in Indian industries, by way of conclusion, it may be stated that though not as high as extent of WPM, the level of effectiveness is reasonably high for a developing economy with a workforce of mainly traditional out look on life operating in a traditional social order. Further, the level of effectiveness is found to be significantly varying with educational level of the respondents and to some extent with caste and social origin. However it was the organizational and contextual variables which were found to be more significantly influencing the level of effectiveness. The analysis of data pertaining to effectiveness in the light of these contextual and organizational variables reveals that it is the public sector units of larger size established quite some time back have such a higher level of effectiveness which is incomparable with their small private sector units of recent origin. Further, a moderate level of complexity coupled with high degree of bureaucratization could be taken as the right mix of milieu for PM operation and practice to be more effective. In terms of climate of industrial relations, it is significant to note that their implications for effectiveness could not be ascertained owing to an overwhelmingly majority of the units having cordial industrial relations. However, in terms of extent and nature of unionism as components of climate of industrial relations, the findings indicate that it is not the extent of unionization that matters when it comes to the level of effectiveness but it is the type of nature of affiliation that has a considerable say in determining the level of effectiveness, that is, it is the politically and ideologically neutral unionism that contributes a great deal to the effectiveness of WPM with leftist unions having a negative impact on the same. Lastly, a very high positive association was found between the effectiveness and the extent of WPM which could be indicating to an internal consistency between two positive and most important dimensions of WPM with higher level of effectiveness being closely associated with high extent of participation.

Having empirically ascertained the extent of WPM and its determinants on the one hand and the levels of effectiveness of WPM and its determinants on the other, an attempt is made in the next chapter to probe into or ascertain the implications of the extent and effectiveness for the productivity, climate of industrial relations and for the industrial performance in general.

8

PM: Impact and Implications

This chapter deals with the implications of WPM for diverse components of industrial milieu both individual and collective, that is, for the workers and management as individual beings on the one hand and for the organization, industry and economy at large on the other. It is always assumed that the PM enhances job satisfaction, morale, commitment, identification, improves climate of industrial relations, organizational climate and enhances productivity and thereby contributes to the overall performance of the industry. This is in turn assumed to be associated with the extent and effectiveness of WPM in the plants.

Having found the extent and level of effectiveness quite reasonably high, an attempt is made in this chapter to identify, analyze, measure and interpret the implication of the extent and level of effectiveness of WPM for the structure and functioning of the work organizations. As such, this is an important core chapter dealing empirically with the impact and hence the desirability of WPM in Indian context and to that extent can be considered as of applied significance.

In the previous chapter it was noted that, the extent and effectiveness as aspects of WPM vary significantly with several variables representing the industrial milieu and in a way, these components in themselves could be taken as significant areas of the implications of PM. As such, an attempt is made in this chapter to ascertain empirically the implications of the extent and effectiveness of WPM for all those aspects constituting core of what is conceived as the industrial performance per se. However, for the purpose of analysis, the implications of WPM are ascertained under three broad categories, that is, climate of industrial relations, productivity and lastly, industrial performance and implications of extent and effectiveness of WPM for these variables are ascertained in this chapter.

EXTENT AND IMPLICATIONS

Climate of Industrial Relations

This composite variable was ascertained on the basis of number of strikes, lockouts and other work stoppages during the last five years, the man days lost, the outstanding grievances, union-management relations and the like. The total of the scores of respondents on all the above variables was taken to classify the type of industry represented by these respondents as cordial and neutral.

It was noted that the incidence of number of strikes, lock-outs and closure for other reasons were far in between and infrequent and the duration of these work stoppages were of not much serious nature and had not resulted in the loss of too many man days, particularly because, the strikes were not of long duration. Union-management relations were found to be quite cordial, rather, very cordial (93.0 percent) and only in a few cases it could be viewed as neutral (7.0 percent). The ratio of grievances pending to grievances solved was 1:3.5 and represented a rather happy state, particularly in view of the sluggish way in which the grievances get redressed and disposed.

Extent of unionization was another component taken to ascertain the climate of industrial relations which was found to be rather high with two thirds (62.5 percent) of the cases being associated with high degree of unionization and about one third (37.5 percent) of the respondents belonging to moderately unionized plants. However, extent of WPM was found to be associated with the degree of unionization. A statistically significant association was indicative of a trend toward increasing positive association between the extent of WPM and the degree of unionization. However, in case of effectiveness no such association was found.

Based on these scores, the data pertaining to the composite variable of industrial relations was ascertained and the finding reveal that about two thirds of the plants (62.5 percent) had cordial industrial relations and the remaining 37 (37.5) percent of the respondents belonged to the units in which the industrial relations could at best be described as neutral.

Having thus ascertained the climate of industrial relations, an attempt was made to know whether the extent of WPM has any implications for the same or to see whether the climate of industrial relations was the function of the extent of WPM.

TABLE 8.1

Climate of Industrial Relations by Extent of WPM

Climate of Industrial Relations	*Extent of WPM*			*Total*
	High	*Moderate*	*Low*	
Peaceful	90 (75.0)	30 (33.3)	30 (100.0)	150 (62.5)
Neutral	30 (25.0)	60 (66.7)	—	90 (37.5)
Total	120 (100.0)	90 (100.0)	30 (100.0)	240 (100.0)

X^2= 58.66, DF=2, Significant at 0.01 Level, C=0.44

As expected, the climate of industrial relations appears to be a function of the extent of WPM or stated other way round, the cordial climate of industrial relations promote the extent of WPM. It appears and it is quite logical to argue also that high extent of WPM breeds better industrial relations climate through better understanding between the parties, better interaction leading to the establishment of more cordial relationships between the managements, workers or unions. On the other hand, such a cordial climate of industrial relations as well could be considered as a precondition for a more active and meaningful operation of the machineries of WPM.

The table reveals that three-fourths (75 percent) of those having high extent of WPM are associated with cordial industrial relations. The corresponding proportion among those with moderate extent of participation comes down to 33 (33.3) percent. But it is rather surprising to note that again in case of those with low extent of WPM, all are associated with cordial climate of industrial relations which is rather difficult or complex to explain. It may be attributed to the fact that some small organizations with extremely cordial industrial relations hardly emphasize such formal avenues of participation and for them it may not be all that necessary to participate as their needs and aspirations could be met with through informal networks of relations and obligations. This could be a situation where, the cordial industrial relations system is substituting for the development of and active participation in the machineries of PM. The argument, further, is supported by a statistically significant relationship between the climate of industrial relations and the extent of WPM with 'C' value being as high as 0.44. In all, it may be stated that the extent of WPM has a positive implication for the climate of industrial relations and it could as well be vice-versa.

Further, this cordial climate of industrial relations in turn is responsible for other positive gains for industry, which may also be taken as indirect benefits of PM. For instance, the cordial climate of industrial relation could be taken as a causal factor in determining the extent of positive impact on outcome of WPM. The association between the climate of industrial relations and positive impact on the outcome of WPM was found to be statistically significant at 0.02 level with 'C' value being 0.18. It is but natural that the impact of the outcome of WPM is positive when the relationship between the parties to WPM are cordial. However, the findings of the present study provide empirical proof for this positive impact based on empirical facts.

Similarly, it was noticed that, the extent of implementation of the decisions of WPM was much higher in those units where the climate of industrial relations was cordial. The association was statistically significant at 0.01 level, stating that naturally where there is mutual trust, good will and confidence between the managements and the workers, there is also will to implement the decisions taken jointly in the WPM machineries.

However, the positive climate did not ensure a positive impact of WPM on the administration in general. Another most important implication of cordial climate of industrial relations on the WPM was a greater participation of workers' representatives in WPM machineries. The data indicates a very strong positive association ('C'=0.44) between the climate of industrial relations and the extent of participation of workers' representatives in the machineries of WPM and greater say of workers' representatives in the JMCs (C=0.44), effectiveness of SFCs (C=0.25) and even the personnel relations (C=0.28). Thus the climate of industrial relations which is assumed to be a function of high extent of WPM, in turn is associated with several important aspects of WPM and as such these two could be considered as mutually reinforcing and to this extent it may be stated that efforts need to be put in this direction to promote both in the interest of both.

Productivity

Further, the study seeks to focus on the implications of

WPM for productivity and other related aspects, such as morale, job satisfaction, commitment, capacity utilization and the like.

One of the most widely discussed, debated and accepted fact is the positive implications of PM for the productivity. The literature on PM, as evident from the review presented in the earlier portion of this book, is replete with studies and findings supporting the nexus between these two variables, particularly in such a direction as to state that higher extent of WPM induces higher level of productivity. Many studies have taken this association itself as the true touchstone of the effectiveness of WPM. The findings of the present study also support this assumption and duplicate the finding.

TABLE 8.2

Productivity and Extent of WPM

Productivity	*Extent*			*Total*
	High	*Moderate*	*Low*	
High	90 (75.0)	60 (66.7)	—	150 (62.5)
Low	30 (25.0)	30 (33.3)	30 (100.0)	90 (37.5)
Total	120 (100.0)	90 (100.0)	30 (100.0)	240 (100.0)

X^2=26.66, DF=2, Significant at 0.01 Level, C=0.31

The findings of the present study, in tune with logic and expectation, tend to confirm the positive implications of PM for productivity. It is observed from the table that, the proportion those with high productivity is as high as 75 percent among those associated with high extent and declines to two-thirds (66.7 percent) among those with moderate extent of WPM with none having high productivity among those with low extent of WPM. Similarly the proportion of those with low productivity goes on from 25 percent among those with high extent to one-third (33.3 percent) among those with moderate extent and reaching 100 percent among those with low extent. The association being significant at 0.01 level with 'C' value being 0.31, the association between the two appears to be strong. It is in this context again that, the study has proved that PM could be a very strong positive force in the development of industry and economy at large through motivating higher level of productivity. It is understood that PM induces higher level of productivity through greater job satisfaction that the employees derive in a work situation they have been able to create by their own decisions, through higher levels of morale that naturally come by owing to the confidence the workers come to have in themselves, through the powers of decision making that come to be vested in them and the control they would exercise on the conditions affecting their working lives, through greater commitment and identification they develop toward the firm by coming to be the integral part of organization at every level and through increase in the extent of capacity utilization owing to all the above. Thus, the extent of WPM is viewed as setting a chain reaction in operation to influence several phenomena associated with productivity and thereby productivity itself.

The above argument is supported by the fact that, job satisfaction is significantly associated with extent of WPM as its function and further productivity is significantly associated with job satisfaction as its function. Extent of WPM and level of job satisfaction were found to be significantly associated at 0.01 level with 'C' value being as high as 0.44, supporting the statement that the extent of WPM induces greater level of job satisfaction and further job satisfaction was found to be positively associated with productivity.

TABLE 8.3

Job Satisfaction and Productivity

Productivity	*Overall Job Satisfaction*		*Total*
	High	*Moderate*	
High	90 (100.0)	60 (40.0)	150 (62.5)
Low	—	90 (60.0)	90 (37.5)
Total	90 (100.0)	150 (100.0)	240 (100.0)

X^2=86.40, DF=1, Significant at 0.01 Level, C=0.51

The literature in Industrial Sociology and Organizational Behaviour has equivocally evidenced the positive impact of job satisfaction on productivity level in work organizations and the findings of the present study are in conformity with this pattern. The data reveal that all the units characterized by high degree of job satisfaction are associated with high degree of productivity and 60 percent of those having moderate job satisfaction are associated with low productivity. The association between the two is quite strong with 'C' value being as high as 0.51. This could be taken as another positive implication of the PM practices found in the work organizations.

Industrial Performance

Industrial performance was another composite variable which was analyzed for its relation with the WPM. Since it was found that PM as a positive innovative intervention in the management of work organization has different implications for different aspects of work organization, a composite variable incorporating several structural and functional aspects of work organization was attempted to be developed which can provide a more realistic index and measure of the performance of industry. Accordingly, a composite variable identified as "industrial performance" was developed based on such diverse variables like capacity utilization, operating status, climate of industrial relations and level of productivity. It was taken as a more realistic measure of the functioning and performance of a work organization than any other constituent variable taken in isolation and individually. The data pertaining to the composite variable of industrial performance so ascertained reveals that 75 percent of units under study exhibited a high industrial performance and in the case of remaining 25 percent of the cases the industrial performance was low.

TABLE 8.4

Industrial Performance by Extent of WPM

Industrial Performance	*Extent of WPM*			*Total*
	High	*Moderate*	*Low*	
High	120 (100.0)	60 (66.7)	—	180 (75.0)
Low	—	30 (33.3)	30 (100.0)	60 (25.0)
Total	120 (100.0)	90 (100.0)	30 (100.0)	240 (100.0)

X^2=13.33, DF=2, Significant at 0.01 Level, C=0.22

For a developing economy like India, which is lamented to be plagued with diverse teething problems and especially problems relating to requisite kind of workforce, to have 75 percent of the industrial units performing at a higher level, as ascertained on the basis of diverse indices can be looked upon as much higher than what could be reasonably expected. However to what extent this level of performance could be attributed to the WPM as a managerial intervention is rather a more pertinent question sought to be answered. Although there could be other factors contributing to this level of industrial performance, an attempt is made here to analyze the level of industrial performance in the light of extent of WPM.

The analysis, quite logically, indicates to a positive association between the two.

The data presented in the table 8.4 indicates to a positive association between the extent of WPM and the level of industrial performance. All the units with high extent of WPM are associated with high industrial performance and contrary to this all the units associated with low extent of WPM are found associated with low level of industrial performance and the association between the two was found to be statistically significant at 0.01 level with 'C' value being 0.22. As such, the overall industrial performance, which is made up of diverse indices, could be viewed as a function of the extent of WPM. This could put an end to an ongoing debate as to whether WPM is practicable in Indian context and if practised, whether it could be of any positive implications for the industry and economy at large. Thus, if the findings of this study are taken as being of some suggestive value, then, it may be stated that efforts need to be put in rendering WPM as a living and vibrant institution or practice that could in the ultimate analysis can contribute to the emergence of a more sound and viable economy.

Coming to the other constituents of the composite variable of industrial performance, it may be noted that productivity has already been found to be positively varying with the extent of WPM and so is the climate of industrial relations. As such only two other variables such as operating status and capacity utilization have to be probed into. Further, since capacity utilization has been quite high uniformly in all the units, the question of cross tabulation of the data pertaining to capacity utilization does not arise at all.

Operating Status

Coming to the operating status viewed as a function of

the extent of WPM, the data indicate to a very strong association between the two.

TABLE 8.5

Operating Status by Extent of WPM

Extent of WPM	*Operating Status*					*Total*
	Incurring Heavy Loss	*Incurring Loss*	*Making it Even*	*Profit Making*	*Highly Profit Making*	
High	7 (33.3)	37 (61.7)	—	53 (88.3)	23 (33.3)	120 (50.0)
Moderate	7 (33.3)	23 (38.3)	30 (100.0)	7 (11.7)	23 (33.3)	90 (37.5)
Low	7 (33.3)	—	—	— (33.3)	23 (12.5)	30
Total	21 (100.0)	60 (100.0)	30 (100.0)	60 (100.0)	69 (100.0)	240 (100.0)

X^2=131.62, DF=8, Significant at 0.01 Level, C=0.59

Although the relationship between operating status and the extent of WPM was not linear or not in a definite pattern, it is indicative of a curvilinear association between the two. The data seem to indicate that the operating status of the firm improves with the extent of WPM up to a point with highly profit making firms again coming to be associated with units of all levels of WPM. It is significant to note that all the firms making it even have moderate extent of WPM and nearly 90 (88.3) percent of the profit making units are associated with high extent of WPM. Having reached this high level of operating status in units with high extent of WPM, the proportion comes down to one third (33.3 percent) among those with highly profit making units suggesting a curvilinear association between the two. This may suggest that WPM promotes operating status up to a point and beyond that it comes to be of not much practical value. Or otherwise, it may be stated that in such organizations that are very high in operational status, other causative variables might be in operation. However, the relationship being statistically significant at 0.01 level with 'C' value being as high as 0.59, it may as well be stated that the extent of WPM has a definite positive implication for operating status.

Operating status was further analyzed in terms of sector to know whether sector has anything to say about the operating status, particularly in view of the fact that sector was significantly associated with the extent of WPM.

TABLE 8.6

Operating Status by Sector

Sector	*Operating Status*					*Total*
	Incurring Heavy Loss	*Incurring Loss*	*Making it Even*	*Profit Making*	*Highly Profit Making*	
Public	7 (33.3)	37 (61.7)	30 (100.0)	53 (88.3)	23 (33.3)	150 (62.5)
Private	14 (66.7)	23 (38.3)	—	7 (11.7)	46 (66.7)	90 (37.5)
Total	21 (100.0)	60 (100.0)	30 (100.0)	60 (100.0)	69 (100.0)	240 (100.0)

X^2=67.78, DF=4, Significant at 0.01 Level, C=0.48

The analysis of operating status by sector reveals quite significant pattern of association with public sector units being associated with better operating status with highly profitable operation again coming to be associated with private sector.

It is interesting to note that all the industries making it just even are public sector units with nearly 90 (88.3) percent of the profit making industries also being from public sector. However, 67(66.7) percent of all the highly profitable units and similar proportion of units incurring heavy loss are from private sector. It may, thus, be stated that owing to high extent and more effective WPM, the public sector industries have been able to keep losses to minimum and making reasonably high profits, whereas, the private sector units due to their poor track record on the extent and effectiveness of WPM end up either incurring too heavy losses or earn very high profits.

Even the dispositions and experiences of the respondents on WPM were found to be significantly associated with the operating status (both at 0.01 level with 'C' value being 0.21 and 0.35 respectively) indicating that the favourable dispositions toward and positive experiences on WPM could improve operating status of an industry and thereby the industrial performance in general.

Thus, with regard to implications of WPM on industry, as ascertained through the extent of WPM, it may be concluded on the basis of findings that, as has been frequently speculated, the extent of WPM has been found to be of positive implications for the climate of industrial relations even for the individual constituent components of this composite variable. Even more important aspect of industrial operation that comes under the positive influence of extent of WPM is the productivity, which is also related with other aspects relevant to the extent of WPM. Further, the industrial performance, a variable which was formulated by taking into account all the important parameters of positive industrial operation, and as such the most important index of the health of work organization was also found to be a significant function of the extent of WPM though in case of operating status, its impact was not totally positive but curvilinear. Thus, it appears that, there should be no doubt whatsoever as to whether deliberate attempt should be made to increase the extent of WPM, which is a measure of areas of management dealt with, the level at which participation takes place, the frequency with which such participation takes place and the extent of say and involvement the parties to the process of WPM have.

Coming to the last phase of the study, an attempt is made to focus on the implications of the effectiveness of WPM for the industrial operation in general. As stated earlier, the effectiveness refers to the qualitative aspect of the process of WPM and such could be having, sometimes more important implications for the performance of industrial organization than the quantitative dimension represented by the extent of WPM. It is assumed that, though extent and effectiveness of WPM were found to be mutually reinforcing, its contextual implications for various components of industrial milieu could be different.

The implications of the effectiveness of WPM are ascertained again for three major concerns of industrial management in the order of importance as ascertained in the case of the extent of WPM, that is, the climate of industrial relations, productivity and the industrial performance.

EFFECTIVENESS AND IMPLICATIONS

Climate of Industrial Relations

Surprisingly enough, the level of effectiveness of WPM was not as significantly associated with the climate of industrial relations as was the extent of WPM.

TABLE 8.7

Climate of Industrial Relations by the Effectiveness of WPM

Climate of Industrial Relations	*Effectiveness of WPM*			*Total*
	High	*Moderate*	*Low*	
Peaceful	60 (66.7)	60 (66.7)	30 (50.0)	150 (62.5)
Neutral	30 (33.3)	30 (33.3)	30 (50.0)	90 (37.5)
Total	90 (100.0)	90 (100.0)	60 (100.0)	240 (100.0)

X^2=5.33, DF=2, Significant at 0.05 Level, C=0.14

The proportion of those associated with peaceful industrial relations among those associated with high and moderate effectiveness is same (66.7 percent) which comes down to a half (50.0) percent among those associated with low level of effectiveness, indicating to a rather weak impact of the effectiveness of WPM on the climate of industrial relations. It may thus mean, though rather strange, that, when it comes to the climate of industrial relations, it is the extent of WPM which matters more than the effectiveness of it. Here, the extent may refer to the number of contacts, frequency of interaction, participation in the deliberations - which are expected to breed confidence, good will, harmony and mutual trust leading to better understanding. Whereas, the effectiveness measured in terms of the extent to which the decisions taken are implemented and how far these decisions reflect the wishes and aspirations of the workers and the like may be of greater implications for productivity and industrial performance which would be probed into next, but these aspects may not mean very much so far as building cordial and better relations among the workers and management and as such may not be of as considerable significance in shaping the industrial relations as is the extent of WPM.

As mentioned earlier, the climate of industrial relations was based not only on the number, duration of strike, lock out, closure, man days lost and so forth, but also on the general personnel relations and personnel practices in the units as such. Personnel relations as one of the constituents is considered here for its implications on issues related to the effectiveness of participation. Since effectiveness of WPM was found to be associated with climate of industrial relations, an attempt is made here to ascertain the impact of personnel relations for the level of productivity.

The analysis of data pertaining to the above variable reveals that favourable personnel relations do mean a lot for the productivity and to some extent the productivity could be viewed as a function of healthy and cordial personnel relations which may in turn be affected by the effective WPM. It is observed that over 70 (71.4) percent of those having high productivity are associated with the favourable personnel relations. The corresponding proportion among those associated with unfavourable personnel relations is altogether nil. The findings thus, could suggest that in order to keep the level of productivity high, personnel relations need to be carefully handled.

TABLE 8.8

Personnel Relations and Productivity

Productivity	*Personnel Relations*		*Total*
	Favourable	*Unfavourable*	
High	150 (71.4)	—	150 (62.5)
Low	60 (28.6)	3090 (100.0)	(37.5)
Total	210 (100.0)	30 (100.0)	240 (100.0)

X^2=57.14, DF=1, Significant at 0.01 Level, C = 0.43

Thus, with regard to the implications of the effectiveness of WPM for the climate of industrial relations, the findings seem to be suggesting to a positive association between the two, though not as strong as the one found with extent of WPM.

Productivity

Further, focusing on the implication of effectiveness for the issues concerning productivity, the data surprisingly suggest that there is no statistically significant association between the two indicating again that, the level of effectiveness is not as important as is the extent in determining the productivity.

TABLE 8.9

Productivity by Level of Effectiveness

Productivity	*Effectiveness of WPM*			*Total*
	High	*Moderate*	*Low*	
High	60 (66.7)	60 (66.7)	30 (50.0)	150 (62.5)
Low	30 (33.3)	30 (33.3)	3090 (50.0)	(37.5)
Total	90 (100.0)	90 (100.0)	60 (100.0)	240 (100.0)

X^2=5.33, DF=2, Significant at 0.05 Level, C=0.14

It is rather quite logical to expect the level of effectiveness with which the PM machineries operate to be of significant implications for the level of productivity in the plant. Although the analysis of the data pertaining to these two variables indicated to a similar trend as could be observed from the table, it appears that the association between the two is not as strong or as close as could be expected with association being statistically significant barely at 0.05 level. On this count the significance of WPM can receive a set back. It may also be noted that even in the case of climate of industrial relations, the relationship was almost of similar strength.

Hence, even in case of productivity, the level of effectiveness is found to be of less functional significance and functional consequence, than is the extent of WPM as found also in the case of climate of industrial relations.

However, it may still be assumed that though not as significant as the extent of WPM, the effectiveness may be of functional consequence for issues of more general nature than are the climate of industrial relations and productivity that are discussed in the next section. It may also be noted here incidentally that, a comparative look at the findings relating to perceived levels of extent and effectiveness is in favour of extent wherein the units with high extent constitute 50 percent, moderate extent represent 37.5 percent with low extent being only 12.5 percent. Whereas in case of effectiveness, proportion of those with high level of effectiveness is 37.5 percent, moderate level of effectiveness also is 37.5 percent and the proportion of those with low level of effectiveness is as high as 25 percent. Thus, the general level of effectiveness being low, the impact of it might also be low owing to which, it is found to be less significant in relation to the climate of industrial relations as well as productivity. As stated earlier, however, the effectiveness may be of important functional consequences to the issues of more general nature which is probed into next.

Industrial Performance

The industrial performance, as stated earlier is a more general or a broader concept, incorporating all the indices of performance of an industry like production, personnel, industrial relations, operating status, capacity utilization and the like and as such is taken as more comprehensive index of the performance or health of an industry. An attempt is made here to ascertain the implications of the effectiveness of WPM for this composite variable.

TABLE 8.10

Industrial Performance by Level of Effectiveness

Industrial Performance	*Effectiveness*			*Total*
	High	*Moderate*	*Low*	
High	90 (100.0)	60 (66.7)	30 (50.0)	180 (75.0)
Low	—	30 (33.3)	30 (50.0)	60 (25.0)
Total	90 (100.0)	90 (100.0)	60 (100.0)	240 (100.0)

X^2=53.33, DF=2, Significant at 0.01 Level, C=0.42

Accordingly, the data pertaining to the industrial performance were viewed in the light of the level of effectiveness and the findings suggest to a highly significant association between the two.

It was assumed earlier, that the effectiveness being a more important aspect of PM, could be having more important implications for more general and important issues relating to the functioning of a work organization and the findings of the present study seem to say exactly what was assumed. It may be observed from the table that of those industries that are high on WPM effectiveness, all (100 percent) are associated with high level of industrial performance. On the other hand units with moderate effectiveness are less likely (66.7 percent) to have high performance and those with low level of effectiveness are still less likely (50 percent) to have higher levels of industrial performance. This could be one of the most important implications of WPM for the industry. It is further significant to note that, the impact of effectiveness on industrial performance is much greater than that of the extent of WPM in case of which, the association with industrial performance was significant with 'C' value being 0.23. This in comparison with association between effectiveness and industrial performance which is as high as nearly twice the score, that is, 0.42, may clearly indicate that mere higher extent of WPM may not be of as much a positive implications for the general well being of the industrial organization as is that of higher level of effectiveness of WPM. Based on the findings, it may as well be suggested that while stressing the greater implementation and bringing more and more areas of management under the scope of WPM, emphasis or premium should also be placed on rendering the process of PM more meaningful and effective.

Further, analysis of relationship between effectiveness and the operating status indicates as to why the association between effectiveness and operating status is significant inspite of its weak association with climate of industrial relations as well as productivity. It may be noted here that the climate of industrial relations in the industries studied was in general quite cordial and as such the relationship was classified only as cordial and neutral, with none of the industries having explicitly hostile industrial relations. In case of productivity also, the general situation was quite adequate. This is testified by the fact that in all the industries studied the capacity utilization was in excess of 90 percent which was classified as high and as such, no industry was found with moderate or low extent of capacity utilization.

In view of this, that is, the capacity utilization in all the industries (100 percent) being high, the impact of the extent of WPM and its level of effectiveness was not analyzed. Thus, non-association or a very weak association between level of effectiveness and climate of industrial relations on the one hand and productivity on the other could be misleading in the absence of such an explanation and the effectiveness of WPM observed could as well have had its influence on both, the climate of industrial relations as well as the productivity which could be proved through analysis.

Operating Status

In support of the above argument, the analysis of operating status in the light of effectiveness indicates to a very strong association between the two. The operating status which is ascertained on the basis of final outcome of the operations in terms of extent of profit and loss could, infact, be taken as a more important index of industrial performance than the climate of industrial relations, productivity, personnel relations and the like, although earning profit at any cost, particularly at the cost of human factor or element of the process of production may not be taken as desirable. However, profits earned within the limits of human rights and dignity could be considered as the most welcome outcome of industrial activity.

Hence, the association between the effectiveness and operating status analyzed is presented in the table.

TABLE 8.11

Operating Status by Level of Effectiveness

Effectiveness of WPM	*Operating Status*					*Total*
	Incurring Heavy Loss	*Incurring Loss*	*Making it Even*	*Profit Making*	*Highly Profit Making*	
High	7 (33.3)	14 (23.3)	—	46 (76.7)	23 (33.3)	90 (37.5)
Moderate	7 (33.3)	23 (38.3)	30 (100.0)	7 (11.7)	23 (33.3)	90 (37.5)
Low	7 (33.3)	23 (38.3)	—	7 (11.7)	23 (33.3)	60 (25.0)
Total	21 (100.0)	60 (100.0)	30 (100.0)	60 (100.0)	69 (100.0)	240 (100.0)

X^2=100.31, DF=8, Significant at 0.01 Level, C=0.54

A very high positive association may be observed between operating status and the level of effectiveness from the data presented in the table. This could be a finding that might appeal to the managements most, as many a time they seem to be reluctant to experiment WPM on the grounds that it might erode into their profits, particularly in view of the conflicting interests of workers and management owing to which their participation in decision making is feared to influence the decisions in favour of workers' interests. It may also be on the count that, the worker component in the PM machineries is not skilled and competent enough to make the process really work in the larger interest of the firm. But all these assumptions appear to be baseless, unfounded and are without empirical evidence. On the contrary, the empirical evidence is in support of WPM in so far as operating status of the industry is concerned. It may be observed from the table that only one third of those incurring loss are associated with the high level of effectiveness whereas, the corresponding proportion among those earning profit is as high as 77 (76.7) percent. It is also significant to note that all those units that are making it even have moderately effective WPM in operation.

In top, with regard to effectiveness, it may be stated that, though not as significantly influencing the climate of industrial relations and productivity positively as the extent of WPM, the level of effectiveness is rather more important than the WPM extent in determining the industrial performance which counts more in the final analysis.

Thus, with regard to the implications of PM for the industry and the issues relating to them, the study bifurcates the total process as representing extent and effectiveness, that is the quantitative and qualitative dimensions of the process of PM and attempt was made to ascertain the implications of these two dimensions of PM on diverse aspects of industrial milieu separately. It is interesting to note that the extent and effectiveness though found to be mutually reinforcing and complimentary in the previous chapter, are found to be having differential implications for different aspects of industrial process. The quantitative aspect, that is extent of WPM is found to be significantly influencing the quantitative aspects like productivity, climate of industrial relations and operating status of industry whereas the qualitative dimensions of WPM, that is, effectiveness is found to be influencing more significantly the qualitative aspects of industrial operation represented by the total industrial performance which was a more comprehensive and more integrated measure of the functioning of the industries studied. In fact, both the dimensions together were, for that matter, found to be influencing rather every aspect of industrial operation and management in a positive manner. And as such PM in general, the findings indicate that, is a positive practice which is in the interest of the industry in particular and the economy in general. Moreover, it is also found to be having a soothing effect, and as such dampens the climate of industrial relations and improves the personnel milieu.

As such, the study appears to be studded with findings that could be of long range and long term applied significance and policy implications based upon empirical inquiry.

Hence, an attempt is made in the next chapter to summarize the major findings of the study and to propose a few suggestions and recommendations based thereon which could be of significant applied implications and provide invaluable academic and intellectual insights and inputs for a more realistic and effective policy on industrial relations.

9

Conclusions and Suggestions

The present work entitled "Participative Management, Productivity and Industrial Performance" seeks to probe empirically into the social realities of WPM in Indian context. The need for this work has been more than justified as discussed in the review of literature, in view of the applied significance the findings of the study could have for the operating status of the industry, climate of industrial relations, productivity and in general the industrial performance and economic development on the one hand and important academic and intellectual insights from Sociological perspective this work can provide for industrial administration and formulation of more realistic policy on industrial relations on the other. The study is also significant in view of its being academically warranted and called for owing to this area of Sociological specialization lacking in empirical studies resulting in unwarranted and unfounded generalizations.

CONCLUSIONS

The study, as stated in the statement of problem, seeks to probe empirically into the indices, in order to identify and ascertain the extent and effectiveness of WPM in practice and their determinants and lastly to examine the implications of PM for diverse vital components of industrial milieu and operation. In doing so, before coming to these core chapters focusing on the main thrust of the present study, an attempt is made to provide a requisite backdrop in the form of socio-economic portrait or profile of the respondents who actually participate in the machineries of WPM representing managerial personnel, trade union leaders and workers and an attempt is also made to provide an account of their dispositions and experiences and a detailed analysis of the structural and functional features or dimensions of the machineries of WPM in operation in the selected industries. It is assumed that an empirical account of these background variables representing the socio-economic background, attitudinal and experience aspects of respondents toward various aspects of PM and the structural and functional features of the machineries would serve as a base from which one can develop and operationalize the explanatory variables which can in turn account for the extent and effectiveness of WPM and help identify the determinants of the extent and the effectiveness. As such, the study makes provision for three separate chapters one each on social profile, structural and functional profile of PM machineries and disposition and experience of respondents on PM. These three chapters provide a necessary prelude for the two core chapters on extent, effectiveness and their determinants and the implications of WPM to follow as the seventh and eighth chapter.

With regard to the socio-economic background of the respondents, the findings indicate that, the workers represent relatively higher age group as compared to the trade union leaders, with managers representing the wider age group as being represented in all the age groups. With regard to the sex composition, it may be stated based on the data that, the WPM is an exclusively male domain, with no single respondent being a female. An overwhelming majority (93 percent) of the worker respondents were Hindus followed by Christians (6.3 percent) and Muslims (0.8 percent), whereas in case of trade union leaders about 2(1.8) percent were Christians. The caste composition states that the proportion of respondents coming from high castes is highest among the managerial respondents (55.4 percent) and as such in view of the general extent of urbanization in India which is less than 30 percent (1991 Census), the urban background of the respondents engaged in industrial employment appears rather conspicuous.

With regard to family occupation, the respondents come mainly from intermediate type of occupational background, neither high nor low and among them the managerial respondents have a slightly upper hand in terms of higher occupations. An overwhelming majority of the respondents (95 percent) are married. It was observed, as expected, the income varies significantly with the categories of the respondents. Coming to the career patterns, the findings reveal that 90 percent of the workers are operatives and so were 69 percent of the trade union leaders at one time or the other and with other categories of occupations they come to associate themselves with, nearly 90 percent of the union leaders have or had a paid job negating much lamented high incidence or extent of outside leadership in Indian unionism. It was also noticed that not many of the managerial respondents are from high ranking managerial positions indicating that managements take representation on WPM machineries not all that seriously and do not place it higher in their priorities.

Even in terms of span of career, it appears that only about one half of the managerial respondents are with long span of career, say, a career spanning over two decades. But other categories fielded their senior members, suggesting that PM is an area of managing industrial relations that calls for professional exposure and maturity. These respondents were further, upwardly mobile and more so were the managerial respondents. Lastly about social origin, which was a composite variable representing the socio-economic background of the respondents, the findings reveal that there is almost a perfect complimentarity between their official status and social origin with over 85 percent of the managerial respondents coming from high social origin followed by trade union leaders (48 percent) and workers (22 percent). This finding may indicate that status on job is in commensuration with status off the job, which is tested for its implications for WPM in subsequent chapters.

The next chapter on PM machineries deals with the structural and functional dimensions of the machineries in operation and it is noted that a wide varieties of machineries are found existing in the industries and are named mainly after the functions they perform like, Welfare Committee, Grievance Committee, Canteen Committee and Works' Committee. But more frequently and universally found machineries are JMCs, SFCs and QCs, out of which again, the QCs are the most frequently found machineries in Indian industries. By nature, JMCs have a greater scope of operation in terms of areas of management they come to deal with and they are also viewed as the highest fora where at WPM can be visualized, leaving out Board Room participation or Worker Director experiments which are not in vogue yet and are still not realized and widely practiced. SFCs are the real workhorse of WPM schemes in terms of issues dealt with, frequency of interaction and also in terms of impact of deliberation on the final outcome in the form of a policy for practice. The QCs were, by nature, were of limited scope of activity as they were confined largely to quality control, maintenance, waste reduction, pilferage proofing, time scheduling, standardization of work procedures and the like and their level of operation was much below JMCs. In terms of the nature of their membership composition, the findings indicate that the JMCs are union-worker biased, SFCs are management biased and the QCs, though taken as representing management interest, that is quality improvement, are more balanced than the rest. The system of communication was found to be rather informal in nature more so in case of SFCs and most in case of QCs. The functioning of these machineries is not all that bureaucratic, except in case of a few industries with not all that cordial industrial relations, which in turn dilute the seriousness and sanctity of the institution of WPM.

With regard to the areas of management the machineries deal with, which were classified as management interests and worker interests, the study reveals that, the JMCs had an agenda which was management biased whereas, in case of SFCs, it was worker biased. Since PM is an innovative intervention introduced to bring about tangible, concrete and positive changes in the working lives of operatives, and thereby, as long range goal, bring about industrial development, can not loose sight of workers' interests and as such, it is not enough if the concerns of these machineries are balanced but at least at the beginning they need to be in favour of workers. Even with regard to the frequency of the meetings, the findings indicate to a situation which is not very gratifying as the periodicity of the meetings appears only in the books but the actual meetings are held only as and when they are inevitably warranted.

With regard to the extent and effectiveness of participation the study reveals that the extent is reasonably high in all the machineries and it was relatively higher in SFCs. The extent of workers' participation in these machineries is found to be varying with sector, size and age of the industries. Even in terms of effectiveness, measured in terms of the extent of 'workers' say' in the functioning and outcome of these machineries and the extent of impact of deliberations on the administration of the firm, the findings reveal that the effectiveness is much higher than what is assumed and the lower levels of effectiveness of WPM machineries which is so often lamented, for that matter, is rather unwarranted. Further, as in the case of extent, the degree of effectiveness of participation of workers in these machineries varies significantly with sector and size of the work organizations. Another important finding is that, the public sector units are more positively associated with all the aspects of WPM, like frequency of meetings, extent of participation and effectiveness. Even in case of QCs, the assumption that private sector is more quality conscious and the public sector as complacent about the same finds no empirical support or evidence. On the contrary, it is in the public sector units that the QCs are operating more actively and effectively.

The next chapter deals with the respondents' disposition toward and experiences of PM process and practices. The dispositions of the respondents are ascertained on the basis of respondents' responses to a series of questions relating to and their opinion regarding the need for PM, its assumed implications for industry and workers, climate of industrial relations, importance of workers' say in the decision making process and the like. Findings of the study on each of these constituent variables of the composite variable of dispositions are discussed in chapter six. Based on the analysis, several conclusions could be arrived at on various aspects of WPM. The analysis of the responses seems to indicate that the WPM in Indian context is geared to the needs and aspirations of the workers and the managements, but not catering to the ideological needs of the trade unionism. Even with regard to the respondents' conception about the skills and aptitude of workers to enable them to participate effectively in the WPM process, the findings reveal that the workers and managerial respondents have a positive estimate of the above. But the trade union leaders are a bit apprehensive about endorsing this opinion.

With regard to disposition as a composite variable it was found that an overwhelming majority of them (83 percent) had favourable disposition toward WPM which may be viewed as considerably high particularly in view of the socio-cultural context in which the Indian industrial worker operates today. It was also significant as well as gratifying to note that managerial personnel were more favourably disposed toward WPM than are their counterparts among trade union leaders and workers.

The dispositions were further found to be positively varying with size, age and educational level. The data pertaining to disposition analyzed in terms of contextual and organizational variables reveal that organizations with moderate size established much earlier, that is, the older industries with relatively better record of performance tend to display a favourable disposition toward WPM. A finding of applied implications pertaining to the dispositions is that the favourable dispositions are found to be influencing productivity, operating status and industrial performance positively, though not climate of industrial relations.

Coming to the experience of the respondents with WPM, it is gratifying to note that irrespective of category, two thirds of the respondents have a positive experience. Though in comparison with favourable disposition (83 percent), the proportion of those with positive experience was low (67.1 percent), it may still be considered as high as it refers not merely to the opinion but to the concrete experiences the respondents had of WPM in the machineries. Just as in the case of dispositions, age and particularly educational level of the respondents were the important explanatory variables in determining the experiences of the participants in WPM machineries. It is significant to note that the experiences of the respondents viewed in terms of areas and issues and their frequency and satisfaction reveals that the WPM could be furthering the cause or interests of the managements rather than working class warranting rethinking about and reorientation of the WPM machineries to ward-off possible alienation of working class from WPM practices on account of its being not relevant and responsive to their needs and aspirations.

In terms of organizational variables the findings indicate that size and age of the organization do influence the experience on WPM and similarly, the climate of industrial relations could be viewed as a function of the experience on WPM. It is quite interesting to note that, the disposition as an attitudinal variable significantly influences productivity, operating status and industrial performance with no impact on climate of industrial and personnel relations whereas experience as a cognitive variable influences the climate of industrial relations but not productivity, operating status and industrial performance. This necessitated the cross tabulation of data on dispositions and experiences. Such an analysis negates the commonsense argument, with no significant association being found between the two. In view of this, it may be stated that dispositions are not conditioned by experiences and experiences are not influenced by dispositions in the context of WPM as both could be seen as two discrete, independent and mutually exclusive aspects of WPM process.

It is also significant to note that the experiences on WPM are not as positive, as favourable are the dispositions and there is little correspondence between the two as well as between their implications for various aspects of industrial operations. Thus, inspite of the climate of opinion and attitudes being overwhelmingly favourable, the experiences are not equally rewarding, enriching and gratifying which may decide the future of WPM in Indian context.

The next chapter deals with the main thrust of the present study that is, the extent and effectiveness, that is the quantitative and qualitative aspects of WPM and their determinants. As stated in the statement of the problem, this aspect of WPM is shrouded with controversies and beset with numerous speculations and unfounded and premature hypotheses. As such, the findings of this study coming under this chapter can be viewed as representing the core of this work and being as of short term and long term applied implications.

The extent of WPM, ascertained as discussed in the chapter, is reasonably high with nearly 90 percent of the units exhibiting moderate to high extent of WPM. Viewed in Indian context with its traits being considered as not as conducive as found in the West for WPM, particularly with regard to the recent origin of industrial subculture and traditional social structure as well as traditional outlook of life, the perceived level could be taken as more than reasonably high and testifying to a positive situation existing in Indian work organizations for WPM to be meaningfully in operation. Thus, the situation appears to be more positive and promising than it is portrayed or painted in the literature on industrial relations scene in India.

Further, a curvilinear association was found to be existing between the extent of WPM and age and a very strong positive association was found between the educational level of the respondents and the extent of WPM. It is also interesting and significant to note that owing to a negative association between caste status and extent, the respondents coming from lower castes were found to be significantly contributing to the extent of WPM. However, irrespective of the association of caste, WPM was found to be positively varying with the social origin, indicating that caste is not the sole factor influencing the extent of WPM when it comes to the social background of the respondents.

With regard to the organizational and contextual variables, the study finds that the public sector industries of relatively large size established quite some time back with complex and formal bureaucratic structure exhibit a high extent of WPM. Quite interestingly, although unions in general, owing to ideological considerations, are opposed to the idea of WPM, the extent of unionization in the plant was positively associated with extent of WPM. It is still more significant to note that, a strong independent union movement with no ideological or political overtones facilitates a higher extent of WPM. The leftist orientations or allegiance of the unionism, which is ideologically against codetermination or collaboration with the management or employers represents the least conducive context for the extent of WPM.

However, more significant determinants of the extent of

WPM are the dispositions and experiences, of those who participate in the WPM machineries, toward the philosophy and practice of WPM. The extent of WPM can be viewed as a function of dispositions and experiences of the respondents.

The level of effectiveness and its determinants constituted a more important and primary focus of the study than the extent because extent was viewed as quantitative dimension and the effectiveness was viewed as a qualitative dimension of PM and when it comes to the positive implications of PM, the qualitative measure is considered, logically, as more important than the quantitative measure. And the level of effectiveness identified and measured as explained in the chapter appears to be not in commensuration with the extent of WPM observed, with 75 percent of the respondents operating with moderate to high level of effectiveness. But though not as high as the extent, the level of effectiveness in the absence of above comparison could be stated as reasonably high, although there is scope for further improvement.

Further, it was found that as in the case of extent, a curvilinear relationship was found between caste and level of effectiveness with respondents from intermediate castes being least effective. A very strong positive association was also found between the educational level of the respondents and the level of effectiveness. Although age and span of career were surprisingly not important in explaining the level of effectiveness, social origin was found to be so. It may be recalled here that the extent was independent of the social origin which may indicate that in terms of extent or quantity of WPM, social origin may not be all that important but when it comes to effectiveness or quality of WPM, the social origin, made up of caste, income, occupation and education of the respondent, makes the difference.

With regard to contextual variables a very significant association was found between the effectiveness of WPM and sector of industry which was overwhelmingly in favour of public sector units, as was in the case of extent of WPM too. Though the public sector is not considered as profit making one, at least in terms of democratizing and humanizing the work places the public sector units are way ahead of their private sector counterparts. In terms of size, the findings indicate that larger organizations have in built traits, properties and milieu that make them considerably more suited for effective WPM. Further, with age of the industry also found to be significantly influencing the level of effectiveness, in terms of organizational variables it may be stated that, large and old public sector industries represent the ideal breeding ground for WPM culture to thrive and perpetuate.

Coming to the industrial relations situation in the plant, it is found that unlike in case of the extent, degree of unionization did not have a say in determining the level of effectiveness. But however, as in the case of extent, the affiliation pattern of unions very strongly influenced the level of effectiveness, with independent unions being most hospitable and facilitating and the leftist unions being least so. Thus, ideological orientations, federational allegiance and political affiliation and overtones of the unions in operation, particularly of leftist nature are detrimental to the practice and effectiveness of WPM. The study more significantly found that the extent and effectiveness are mutually complimentary with a very strong positive association between the two. The extent and effectiveness being the two most important aspects of WPM, the finding that the relationship between the two is so strong as to be even thought of a mutually reinforcing, could be of significant applied implications.

An attempt is made in the next chapter to focus empirically upon the implications of WPM for the various components of industrial milieu to find justification or otherwise for its being advocated as a positive managerial intervention and pursued as a healthy managerial practice. The chapter, in fact, analyses the implications of the extent and level of effectiveness of WPM for various indices of industrial situation and performance, and to that extent may be viewed as an extension of the previous chapter. Impact of WPM is ascertained in all on four parameters, namely, climate of industrial relations, productivity, operating status and industrial performance.

Climate of industrial relations is a composite variable reflecting the overall situation, as explained in the chapter. The findings indicate that owing to a strong association between the two, the climate of industrial relations could be viewed as a function of the extent of WPM and may not be equally that of effectiveness that is, the quantity, measured in terms of frequency, areas of management, the scope and level of participation, has a greater impact on the climate of industrial relations as these lead to greater scope, frequency, the depth of interaction leading to confidence, good will, trust and understanding. Thus, if climate of industrial relations is the target to be focused, then increasing the extent could be the means of achieving this. In turn, the climate of industrial relations was found to be significantly associated with the positive impact of WPM and greater participation of workers' representatives.

Coming to the productivity as an area of implication of PM, the findings testify to the fact that both extent and the level of effectiveness have a positive impact on productivity but, extent has a more determinate role to play than the level of effectiveness. It is in this context again the study has proved that PM could be a very strong positive force in the development of industry and economy at large through motivating and facilitating the achievement of higher levels of productivity through high levels of job satisfaction, morale, more cordial industrial relations and the like. This argument was supported by the fact that, job satisfaction and morale co-vary with the extent of WPM and job satisfaction and morale in turn, co-vary with productivity.

Coming to more direct and tangible implication of WPM for the industry, that is, operating status, classified in terms of extent of profit earned or loss incurred, the findings suggest that both the aspects of PM, that is, extent and level of effectiveness have a considerable influence on the same. The impact of extent and effectiveness of WPM on operating status was found to be statistically very significant. This could be a finding that might appeal to the managements most as the general misconception among the management about WPM is that it could erode into their profits owing to contrasting and conflicting interests.

Finally coming to the implications of PM for industrial performance, a more general index of industrial operations and health, ascertained by taking into consideration such diverse variables like capacity utilization, operating status, climate of industrial relations and level of productivity, the study clearly indicates to a very strong positive influence of WPM on the general performance of the industry. Both the extent (C=0.22) and particularly the level of effectiveness (C=0.42) could be taken as the factors significantly influencing the industrial performance in general. This finding may put an end to an ongoing debate as to whether WPM is practicable and if practised whether it brings about concrete and tangible benefits to the parties to production in particular and industry and economy in general. That is to state again, the qualitative aspects of WPM are more important than quantitative aspects in bringing about far reaching, long range, more desirable improvement in industrial operations and through these in the economy and society at large. However, extent and effectiveness together can foster a still better industrial situation.

SUGGESTIONS

Keeping in view these findings of considerable applied significance and policy implications, a few suggestions are attempted here which are assumed to be of utility in not only rendering the process of WPM more meaningful and effective but also in rendering industrial operations more smooth and profitable.

In doing so it is endeavoured to focus on the strong points and lacunae of the process of WPM in operation at present and also the explanatory variables found to be complimentary and contradictory to the process and practice of WPM. However, quite a few suggestions can be deduced and derived from the findings discussed in the chapters themselves. The study having found and proved the positive and desirable implications of WPM, this section would confine itself to suggest how to render this process more universal and effective.

In view of its positive impact on the workers, industry, management and economy, efforts need to be made to extend the PM practice to more and more industries through persuasion or education or through statutory provisions. And in order to see that, the nostalgic infatuation with WPM in the beginning will not peter away to be reduced to an aborted and abandoned scheme, as it is almost about to be viewed as in the West, particularly in view of the impact of economic trends of liberalization and globalization world over. Since the challenges being faced by WPM in Indian context are more complex and far more formidable than the ones faced elsewhere due to lack of emergence of a well developed, streamlined and subscribed industrial subculture, owing to traditional social order, traditional out look of the working class and recent origin of industrialism, efforts need to be made to counter the dampening effect and constraining influence of these factors on the scheme, spirit and practice of WPM.

Coming to the findings of the present study, having found the disposition, experiences, extent and effectiveness reasonably positive and high, efforts need to be made to focus on the factors that have facilitated this favourable situation and to maintain these levels and then to enhance and reinforce them through manipulating these factors.

With regard to the background variables determining the extent and effectiveness of WPM on the one hand and dispositions and experiences on the other, educational level of the respondents stands out as distinctly more important variable. The managerial respondents by necessity have high educational levels, as such, it is desirable to have such representatives from the workers and the trade union leaders who have higher levels of educational attainments to ensure more favourable dispositions among them toward WPM and requisite expertise and skill to participate more meaningfully and effectively. Further, in view of the extent and nature of participation being dependent on the age and exposure to the machineries of WPM in particular and to the world of trade, industry and business in general, senior and more mature representatives from among the respective categories need to be nominated to the machineries of WPM. Further in case of managerial representatives, care needs to be taken to see that they are endowed with enough responsibility, requisite authority and autonomy to enable them to take important decisions on behalf of management in the machineries on the spot.

The machineries were found to be differentially active, differentially effective with focus on different areas of management in the same industry. As such, the patterns, procedures followed by more active and effective machineries could be adopted by all the machineries to have uniformly higher levels of achievements. Further, Board Room Participation or Worker Director Schemes appear to be on paper only with no sincere efforts by both the parties to realize such a level of participation which, otherwise would have given a new impetus and better thrust to the WPM scheme. The composition of the membership of the machineries too needs to be more balanced.

The functioning of the machineries appeared to be too informal and casual which breed complacency and lead to lack of accountability. As such, rules of business and standardized procedures need to be evolved and followed in the functioning of the machineries. Even in terms of areas of management dealt with by the machineries there appears to be differential emphasis on worker and management interests and many a time managerial interests superseding those of workers, undermining the very spirit and philosophy of WPM. The machineries need to approach workers' needs as the immediate or short term goals and take industrial development as the long term goal in dealing with diverse issues.

In view of the extent of WPM being positively associated with the extent of unionism, unionism needs to be not looked down upon as detrimental to workplace discipline and democracy, and on the contrary needs to be encouraged, so as to have workers' interests better represented on diverse WPM fora. However, such unionism should be independent and free from ideological affiliations and political overtones particularly of the leftist allegiance and orientations.

Further, in view of productivity and climate of industrial relations and operating status coming to be significantly associated with favourable opinion or disposition among the participants, efforts need to be made in orienting the participants to the benefits of WPM and thereby bring about perceptual and attitudinal changes in them to peruse WPM as a desired practice. Need for such an orientation is more among the workers as they are found to be relatively less favourably disposed toward WPM than their managerial and union counterparts. The experiences on WPM are not in commensuration with the dispositions, that is lagging behind dispositions. Thus, a match between the two could be an ideal situation to strive for. Thus, to harness and exploit such a favourable climate of opinion and to have it matched by the concrete experiences should constitute the prime aim of the parties concerned and policy endeavours.

Similarly, the effectiveness, that is the quality of WPM is found to be lagging behind the extent or the quantitative aspect of WPM. Such perceived lagging in effectiveness is attributed to lack of education among participants, leftist and politicized unionism, lack of procedural specificity and casual approach. Attempts should be made to ward-off or minimise the incidence of these constraining factors to enhance the extent and increase effectiveness which are found to be mutually reinforcing forces.

This desired state can be achieved with high degree of confidence, as the study has indicated that the higher extent and higher level of effectiveness of WPM together can boost productivity through increased job satisfaction and morale, can bring about a cordial or harmonious climate of industrial relations, bring an improvement in the operating status and foster an overall better industrial performance, which should be welcome by workers, unions, managements and society at large.

Finally, it may be stated here that several important aspects of WPM which are of functional consequence to the industrial management and operation are mutually complementary and reinforcing and one aspect can not improve or thrive at the cost of others. This being the organic network of interdependence and inter-relationships, an improvement in this system requires or calls for an integrated approach rather than piecemeal. Thus, the success of PM as a positive managerial intervention and a healthy management practice in pursuit of industrial excellence and eventually the future of WPM in Indian context could depend on how meaningfully, sincerely and with what degree of genuine concern parties to PM nurture and participate in this system.

The above suggestions are made in the light of the findings of the present study with its inherent limitations. However, more than methodological sophistication, it is the commitment to values and spirit of empirical tradition and ethics of scientific objectivism that has been the guiding force and as such, the methodological short-comings, if any, are believed to have been more than overcome by this commitment, and the suggestions that are the outcome of this commitment are strongly believed to be of applied implications on this count. Albeit, nothing is ultimate in pursuit of knowledge and scientific excellence, the present study may represent an advanced stage in it for subsequent studies to improve upon, and help bring a better system of industrial relations and elevate Sociology to the status of scientific enterprise.

Bibliography

Abegglen, J.C., 1958, *The Japanese Factory*, Bombay, Asia Publishing House.

Agarwal, R.D., 1984, "Model Scheme For Workers' Participation In Management - A Point of View", in R.S. Dwivedi (Ed.) *Manpower Management-An Integrated Approach To Personnel Management and Labour Relations*, New Delhi, Prentice Hall of India, pp. 301-307.

Aggarwal, Pratap C., 1973, "Cultural Milieu In India And Participative Management", in C.P. Thakur and K.C. Sethi (Eds.) *Industrial Democracy: Some Issues and Experiences*, New Delhi, Sri Ram Centre, pp. 1-10.

Albrecht, Sandra L., 1983, "Forms of Industrial and Economic Democracy: A Comparison of Prevailing Approaches", *Mid American Review of Sociology*, 8:2, pp. 43-66.

Alexander, K.C., 1972, *Participative Management - The Indian Experience*, New Delhi, Sri Ram Centre.

_____ 1973, "Workers' Participation in Management", in C.P. Thakur and K.C. Sethi (Eds.) *Industrial Democracy: Some Issues and Experiences*, New Delhi, Sri Ram Centre, pp. 159-171.

Alter, Norbert., 1986, "Concerning Participatory Management", *Futuribles*, 99, pp. 75-77.

Anantaraman, V., 1980, *Human Relations in Industry*, New Delhi, S. Chand & Co. Ltd.

Anderson, Carl R., 1984, *Management Skills, Functions and Organization Performance*, Dubuque, Lowa, Brown Publishers.

Anthony, William P., 1978, *Participative Management*, California, Addison- Wesley Publishing Company.

Argyle, M. et al., 1958, "Supervisory methods related to productivity, absenteeism and labour turnover", *Human Relations*, 11, pp. 23-40.

Argyris, Chris, 1964, *Integrating the Individual and the Organization*, New York, John Wiley.

______ 1967, "Organizational Leadership And Participative Management", in S.G. Huneryager and I.L. Heckman (Eds.) *Human Relations In Management*, Bombay, D.B. Taraporevala Sons & Co. Ltd., pp. 606-614.

Armstrong, Michael., 1988, *A Handbook of Personnel Management Practice*, London, Kogan Page.

Arora, Balwinder., 1992, "Participative Management or Managed Participation - The Case of India", *Economic and Industrial Democracy*, 13:2, pp. 263-272.

Arya, P.P., 1983, *Labour Management Relations In Public Sector Undertaking*, New Delhi, Deep & Deep Publications.

Athreya, Mrityunjay., 1973, "Organizational Determinants of Participation", in C.P.Thakur and K.C. Sethi (Eds.) *Industrial Democracy: Some Issues and Experiences*, New Delhi, Sri Ram Center, pp. 67-92.

Aziz, Abdul., 1980, *Workers' Participation In Management*, New Delhi, Ashish Publishing House.

Balfour, Campbell., 1973, (Ed.) *Participation In Industry*, London, Croom Helm, pp. 1-20.

Balundgi, L.R. and M.M. Bagali.,1994, "Worker Participation In Management - A Conceptual Framework", *Management & Labour Studies*, 19:2, pp. 91-98.

Batchelor, A.H., 1984, "Human Relations or Human Resources?", in R.S. Dwivedi (Ed.) *Manpower Management - An Integrated Approach To Personnel Management And Labour Relations*, New Delhi, Prentice Hall of India, pp. 261-264.

Beach, Dale S., 1965, *Personnel - The Management of People at Work*, London, Collier McMillan.

Bendix, Reinhard., 1956, *Work and Authority in Industry: Ideologies of Management in the Course of Industrialization*, New York, John Wiley.

Berglind, Hans., 1978, "From Industrial to "Service" Society:

Mobility & Participation in the Swedish Labor Force", *International Journal of Contemporary Sociology*, 15:1-2, pp. 91-114.

Bertsch, Gary K. and Josip Obradovic., 1979, "Participation and Influence in Yugoslav Self - Management", *Industrial Relations*, 18:3, pp. 322-329.

Beynon, H. and R.M. Blackburn., 1972, *Perception of Work*, Cambridge, Cambridge University Press.

Bhagoliwal, T.N., 1989, *Economics of Labour and Industrial Relations*, Agra, Sahitya Bhawan.

Bhatia, S.K., 1988, *Personnel Management And Industrial Relations*, New Delhi, Deep & Deep Publications.

Bhatnagar, Deepti., 1991, "Workers' Participation in BHEL, Tiruchi: Structure and Reality", *Vikalpa - The Journal For Decision Makers*, 16:4, pp. 65-67.

_____ 1990, "Participatory Desire and Deprivation Among Employees in two Indian Organizations", in M.K. Singh and A. Bhattacharya (Eds.) *Participatory Management And Corporate Growth*, New Delhi, Discovery Publishing House, pp. 282-308.

Bhattacharya, A.M., 1990, "Participatory Management and Labour Commitment", in M.K.Singh and A. Bhattacharya (Eds.) *Participatory Management And Corporate Growth*, New Delhi, Discovery Publishing House, pp. 1-62.

Bhattacharya, Dipak Kumar., 1993, "Workers' Participation In Management", in Ruddar Dutt (Ed.) *Workers' Participation And Workers' Ownership*, Delhi, Pragati Publications, pp. 288-298.

Bhattacharya, J.B., 1993(a) "Statutory Workers' Participation", in Ruddar Dutt (Ed.) *Workers' Participation And Workers' Ownership*, Delhi, Pragati Publications, pp. 113-122.

_____ 1993(b), "Worker Ownership and Management of Industry", in Ruddar Dutt (Ed.) *Workers' Participation And Workers' Ownership*, Delhi, Pragati Publications, pp. 334-340.

Bhowmik, Sharit K., 1994, *Worker Cooperatives: An Alternative Strategy For Industrial Growth*, Pondichery, French Institute.

Bhuyan, S.K. and P.C. Nath., 1989, "Quality Circle For Continuous Quality Improvement", in *Excellence Through Participation:*

Quality the Only Way, Proceedings of the International Convention on Quality Control Circles, New Delhi, India, Dec. 6-9, 1989, Organized by Quality Circle Forum of India, pp. 57-62.

Biswas, S.K., 1993, "Japanese Model of Workers' Involvement: A Succor For India", in Ruddar Dutt (Ed.) *Workers' Participation And Workers' Ownership*, Delhi, Pragati Publications, pp. 170-182.

Blake, R.B. and J.S. Mountan., 1964, *The Managerial Grid: Key Orientation for Achieving Production through People*, Texas, Gulf Publishing Co.

Blumberg, Paul., 1968, *Industrial Democracy: The Sociology of Participation*, London, Constable.

Blyton, Paul., 1985, "Workplace Democracy, Unemployment and the Reduction of Working Time", *Economic and Industrial Democracy*, 6:1, pp. 113-120.

Bohle, Fritz., 1985, "Managerial Information Policies and Worker Representation", *Soziale Welt*, 36:2, pp. 242-260.

Brag, J.E. and R.I. Andrews., 1973, "Participative decision making: An experimental study in a hospital", *Journal of Applied Behavioral Science*, 9:6, pp. 727-735.

Brannen, Peter et al., 1976, *The Worker Directors: A Sociology of Participation*, London, Hutchinson.

Broad, Geoffrey and John Beishon., 1977, *Participation, Management And Control*, Unit 15, Keynes, Open University Press, pp. 3-52.

Brown, Leslie H., 1985, "Democracy in Organizations: Membership Participation & Organizational Characteristics in U.S. Retail Co-operatives", *Organization Studies*, 6:4, pp. 313-334.

Burns, T. and G. Stalker., 1961, *The Management of Innovation*, London, Tavistock Publications.

Butteriss, Margaret., 1971, *Job Enrichment and Employee Participation - A Study*, Lodnon, Institute of Personnel Management.

Carey, Alex., 1979, "The Norwegian Experiments in Democracy at Work", *The Australian and Newzealand Journal of Sociology*, 15:2, pp. 89-95.

Cauter, J. and J. Downham., 1954, *The Communication of Ideas*, London, Chatto and Windus.

Chamberlain, N.W., 1951, *Collective Bargaining*, New York, McGraw Hill.

Chaney, Frederick B. and Kenneth S. Teel., 1969, "Participative Management - A Practical Experience", in Keith Davis (Ed.) *Organizational Behaviour - A Book of Readings*, New York, McGraw Hill Series in Management, pp. 166-175.

Chase, William., 1986, "Workers' Control and Socialist Democracy", *UM Science and Society*, 50:2, pp. 226-238.

Chaudhuri, K.K., 1990, "In Search of a Framework for Employee Participation", in C. Lakshmanna et al. (Eds.) *Workers' Participation And Industrial Democracy: Global Perspective*, New Delhi, Ajanta Publications, pp. 257-270.

Chhabra, T.N. et al., 1977, *Managing People at Work: Management Principles, Personnel Management and Organization Behaviour*, Delhi, Dhanpat Rai & Sons.

Cherns, A.B., 1973, "Conditions For An Effective Management Philosophy of Participation", in C.P. Thakur and K.C. Sethi (Eds.) *Industrial Democracy: Some Issues and Experiences*, New Delhi, Sri Ram Centre, pp. 93-99.

Cherunilam, Francis., 1989, *Industrial Economics: Indian Perspective*, Bombay, Himalaya Publishing House.

Clarke, R.O. et. al., 1972, *Workers' Participation in Management in Britain*, London, Heineman Educational Books.

Clegg, Stewart., 1979, "Employee Participation in Australia: The New Legitimacy", *Social Alternatives*, 1:4, pp. 59-65.

Coch, Lester and J.R.P. Jr. French., 1948, "Overcoming Resistance to Change", *Human Relations*, 1, pp. 512-532.

Cole, G.D.H., 1957, *The Case for Industrial Partnership*, London, McMillan.

Confederation of British Industry., 1976, *Involving People, CBI Proposals for Employee Participation*, London, Saffron Press.

Cordova, E., 1982, "Workers' participation in decisions within enterprises: recent trends and problems", *International Labour Review*, 121:2, pp. 125-140.

Cornfield, Daniel B., 1994-95, "Labour and the Participative

Potential of the New Technologies and Syndicalism", *Sociologia-del-Trabajo*, 23, pp. 27-53.

Creighton, W.B., 1977, "The Bullock Report - The Coming of the Age of Democracy", *British Journal of Law and Society*, 4:1, pp. 1-17.

Dachler, Peter H. and Bernard Wilpert., 1978, "Conceptual Dimensions and Boundaries of Participation in Organization: A Critical Evaluation", *Administrative Science Quarterly*, 23, pp. 1-39.

Dahlstrom, Edmund., 1977, "Efficiency, Satisfaction & Democracy in Work: Conception of Industrial Relations in Post-War Sweden", *Acta-Sociologica*, 20:1, pp. 25-53.

Dahrendorf, Ralf., 1959 , *Class and Class Conflict in Industrial Society*, London, Routledge & Kegan Paul.

Dale, Earnest., 1949, *Greater Productivity through Labour Management Co-operation*, New York, Management Association.

Dandekar, V.M., 1993 , "Let the Workers Own and Manage", in Ruddar Dutt (Ed.) *Workers' Participation And Workers' Ownership*, Delhi, Pragati Publications, pp. 49-66.

Daniel, W.W. and Neil McIntosh., 1972 , *The Right to Manage ? A study of leadership & reform in employee relations*, London, MacDonald & James.

Danitch, Leo., 1977, "The Importance of Workers' Control for Revolutionary Change", Monthly *Review*, 29:10, pp. 37-48.

Das, Naba Gopal., 1964, *Experiments in Industrial Democracy*, Bombay, Asia Publishing House.

Davar, Rustom S., 1976, *Personnel Management and Industrial Relations in India*, Delhi, Vikas Publishing House.

_______, 1974, "Employee Participation in Management - A Fad or a Spur for Higher Productivity? ", in S.A. Sapre (Ed.) *Labour Participation In Management*, Bombay, Joint Management Council: Government Central Press, pp. 1-10.

Davis, Keith., 1969(a), "Participative Management", in Keith Davis (Ed.) *Organizational Behaviour - A Book of Readings*, New York, McGraw - Hill Series in Management, pp. 165-166.

________, 1967(b),"The Case For Participative Management", in S.G. Huneryager and I.L. Heckman (Eds.) *Human Relations In Management*, Bombay, D.B. Taraporevala Sons & Co. Ltd., pp. 615-621.

________, 1976(c) , "The Case For Participative Management", in Herbert, J. Chruden and Arthur, W. Sherman, Jr (Eds.) *Readings in Personnel Management*, Cincinnati, West Chicago, South-Western Publishing Co., pp. 280-286.

Derber, Milton., 1969 , "Cross Currents in Workers' Participation", *Industrial Relations*, 9, pp. 123-136.

Desai, S.S.M., 1988, *Industrial Economy of India*, Bombay, Himalaya Publishing House.

Deutsch, Steven., 1981,"Work Environment Reform and Industrial Democracy", *Sociology of Work & Occupations*, 8:2, pp. 180-194.

Dey, B.R., 1988, *Quality Circles: Concepts and Practices*, Pune, Tata Management Training Centre.

Dhingra, O.P., 1972, "Participative Predisposition of Managers In The Indian Public Sector Industry", in C.P. Thakur and K.C. Sethi (Eds.) *Industrial Democracy: Some Issues and Experiences*, New Delhi, Sri Ram Centre, pp. 100-117.

Drago, Robert and Mark Wooden., 1990, "The Determinants of Participatory Management", *British Journal of Industrial Relations*, 29:2, pp. 177-204.

Drucker, Peter F., 1964, *The New Society - The Anatomy of the Industrial Order*, London Heinman.

Dubin, Robert., 1967, "Power and Union-Management Relations", in William, A. Faunçe (Ed.) *Reading in Industrial Sociology*, Englewood Cliffs, Prentice Hall, pp. 465-481.

Dwivedi, R.S., (Ed.), 1984, *Manpower Management: An Integrated Approach To Personnel Management And Labour Relations*, New Delhi, Prentice Hall of India, pp. 257-260.

Eaton, Adrienne E., 1988 , "Local Union Control of Worker Participation & Labour Management Co-operation Programmes", *Dissertation Abstracts International A: The Humanities & Social Sciences*, 49:5, P. 1283-A.

________, 1988, "The Survival of Employee Participation

Programs In Unionized Setting", *Industrial and Labor Relations Review*, 47:3, pp. 371-389.

Edelstein, J. et al., 1976, "Research Areas in National Union Democracy", *Industrial Relations*, 16:2, pp. 186-198.

Emery, F.E. and E.L. Trist., 1959, *Socio-Technical Systems in Management Sciences: Models and Techniques*, London, Pergamon Press.

__________, 1959, "The Causal Texture of Organizational Environments", in F.E. Emery (Ed.) *Systems Thinking*, Harmondsworth, Penguin Books, pp. 241-260.

Etzioni, A., 1959 , *A Comparative Analysis of Complex Organizations*, New York, The Free Press.

Fantasia et al., 1988, "A Critical View of the Worker Participation in American Industry", *UM Work and Occupations*, 15:4, pp. 468-488.

Farnham, David., 1987, "Employee involvement, representation and participation", in Sally Harper (Ed.) *Personnel Management Handbook*, Hampshire, U.K., Gower Publications, pp. 569-586.

Foy, Nancy and Gadon Herman. 1976, "Worker Participation: Contrasts in Three Countries", *Harvard Business Review*, 54:3, pp. 71-83.

Francis, James G. and Gene Milbourn Jr., 1980, *Human Behaviour In The Work Environment: A Managerial Perspective*, Santa Monica, California, Good Year Publishing Company.

French, John et al., 1960, "An experiment on participation in a Norwegian factory", *Human Relations*, 13:1, pp. 3-19.

Gardner, G., 1977, "Workers' participation: A critical evaluation of Coch and French", *Human Relations*, 30, pp. 1071-1078.

Gaudier, Maryse., 1988, "Workers' Participation within the New Industrial Order: A Review of Literature", *Labour and Society*, 13:3, pp. 313-332.

Gherardi, Silvia et al., 1990, "Industrial Democracy and Organizational Symbolism", in C. Lakshmanna et al (Eds.) *Workers' Participation And Industrial Democracy: Global Perspectives*, New Delhi, Ajanta Publications, pp. 39-52.

Ghiya, D.P., 1993, "Workers' Participation in Management in Indian Railways", in Ruddar Dutt (Ed.) *Workers' Participation And Workers' Ownership*, Delhi, Pragati Publications, pp. 265-275.

Giobbio, Aldo., 1978, "Worker Participation and Industrial Democracy", *Sociologia*, 12:2, pp. 3-40.

Giri, D.V. and S.C. Panda., 1993, "Workers' Participation and Industrial Relations in the Indian Coal Industry", in Ruddar Dutt (Ed.) *Workers' Participation And Workers' Ownership*, Delhi, Pragati Publications, pp. 276-287.

Giri, V.V., 1962, *Labour Problems in Indian Industry*, Bombay, Asia Publishing House.

Goldthorpe, J.H. et al., 1968, *The Affluent Worker: Industrial Attitudes and Behaviour*, Cambridge, Cambridge University Press.

Goode, William J. and Paul K. Hatt., 1952, *Methods In Social Research*, New York, McGraw-Hill Book Company.

Goodman, P., 1979, *Assessing Organizational Change: The Rushton Quality of Work Experiment*, New York, Wiley - Interscience.

Government of India., 1931, *Report of Royal Commission on Labour in India*, New Delhi, Government of India.

________, 1947, *Industrial Disputes Act*, Section 3.

________, 1951-1979, *Five Year Plans*, Planning Commission, Delhi, Manager Publication.

________, 1956, *Industrial Policy Resolution*.

________, 1957, 1959, *Indian Labour Conference*.

________, 1958, 1960, *Recommendations of the Seminar on Labour Management Cooperation*, New Delhi, Government of India.

________, 1965, *Report of the Working of Joint Management Councils*, New Delhi, Ministry of Labour and Employment.

________, 1969, *Report of the National Commission on Labour*, New Delhi, Government of India.

________, 1975, *20 Point Economic Programme*.

________, 1975, 1976(a), *Annual Report*, Ministry of Labour, Government of India, Vol. 1.

________, 1975, 1976 (b), *Indian Labour Year Books*, New Delhi, Publications Division.

__________, 1977, *Recommendations of the Committee on Workers' Participation in Management.*

__________, 1978, Report of the Tripartite Committee on the Functions of WCs, Ministry of Labour, Government of India, 25th Nov. 1978.

Greenberg, Edward S., 1980, "Participation in Industrial Decision Making & Work Satisfaction: The Case of Producer Co-operatives", *Social Science Quarterly*, 60:4, 551-569.

Guest, David and Derek Fatchett., 1974, *Worker Participation: Individual Control And Performance*, London, Institute of Personnel Management.

Gupta, Sushma., 1989, "Quality Circles - Impact On Organizational Culture", in *Excellence Through Participation: Quality the Only Way*, Proceedings of the International Convention on Quality Control Circles, New Delhi, India, Dec. 6-9, 1989, Organized by Quality Circle Forum of India, pp. 121-123.

Gyanchand, 1993, "Industrial Democracy", in Ruddar Dutt (Ed.) *Workers' Participation And Workers' Ownership*, Delhi, Pragati Publications, pp. 1-30.

Haire, M. et al., 1996, *Managerial Thinking: An International Analysis*, New York, John Wiley & Sons.

Hameed, Syed, 1973, "Participative Management And Industrial Relations Setting", in C.P. Thakur and K.C. Sethi (Eds.) *Industrial Democracy: Some Issues and Experiences*, New Delhi, Sri Ram Centre, pp. 34-48.

Hammer, Tove H. and Robert N. Stern., 1986, "A Yo-Yo Model of Cooperation: Union Participation in Management at the Rath Packing Company", *Industrial and Labor Relations Review*, 30:3, pp. 337-349.

Hammer, Tove H. et al., 1991, "Worker Representation On Boards of Directors: A Study of Competing Roles", *Industrial and Labor Relations Review*, 44:4, pp. 661-670.

Harbinson, P. and C.A. Myers., 1959, *Management in the Industrial World: An International Analysis*, New York, McGraw Hill.

Hebden, John E. and Graham H. Shaw., 1977, *Pathways to participation*, London, Associated Business Programmes.

Heckscher, C., 1988, *The New Unionism*, New York, Basic Books.

Helm, Jutta A., 1986, "Codetermination in West Germany: What Difference Has it Made?", *West European Politics*, 9:1, pp. 32-53.

Herzberg, Frederick et al., 1959, *The motivation to work*, New York, Wiley.

Hildebrandt, Eckart., 1990, "Demands of Systematic Rationalization - A Plea for Restructuring in the Policies and Practices of Industrial Democracy", in C. Lakshmanna et al (Eds.) *Workers' Participation And Industrial Democracy: Global Perspective*, New Delhi, Ajanta Publications, pp. 285-300.

Hill, Stephen., 1991(a), "Why Quality Circles Failed but Total Quality Management Might Succeed", *British Journal of Industrial Relations*, 29:4, pp. 541-568.

__________, 1991(b), "How do you manage a flexible firm? The total quality model", *Work, Employment and Society*, 5, pp. 397-415.

Hirschman, Albert., 1970, *Exit, Voice and Loyalty*, Harvard, Cambridge Mass.

Holmstrom, Mark., 1985, "How the Managed Manage the Managers : Workers' Co-ops in Italy", *Anthropology Today*, 1:6, pp. 7-12.

__________, 1994, *Flexible Specialization in a Labour Surplus Economy*, Pondichery, French Institute.

Holter, Horriet., 1965, "Attitude towards employees' participation in company's decision making process - A study of non-supervisory employees in some Norwegian firms", *Human Relations*, 18:4, pp. 297-319.

Hull, Frank and Azumi Koya., 1988, "Technology and Participation in Japanese Factories: The Consequences for Morale and Productivity", *UM Work and Occupations*, 15:4, pp. 423-448.

Huneryager, S.G. and I.L. Heckmann., (Eds.), 1967, *Human Relations In Management*, Bombay, D.B. Taraporevala Sons. & Co. Ltd., pp. 580-591.

Huss, Carol., 1973, "Experiment In Participation", in C.P. Thakur and K.C. Sethi (Eds.) *Industrial Democracy - Some Issues and Experiences*, New Delhi, Sri Ram Centre, pp. 186-204.

IDE International Research Group., 1979, "Participation: formal rules, influence and environment", *Industrial Relations*, 18, pp. 273-294.

IDE International Research Group., 1981, *Industrial Democracy in Europe*, Oxford, Clarendon Press.

Institute of Economic Growth., 1962, *Participation in Management: The Indian Experiment*, Delhi, Delhi University.

Ishikawa, Akihiro., 1984, "Japanese Trade - Unionism in a Changing Environment", *International Social Science Journal*, 36:2, pp. 271-283.

__________, 1990, "Frontiers of Sociological Studies in Industrial Democracy", in C. Lakshmanna et al. (Eds.) *Workers' Participation And Industrial Democracy: Global Perspective*, New Delhi, Ajanta Publications, pp. 13-19.

Ivancevich, J.M., 1976, "Effects of goal setting on performance and job satisfaction", *Journal of Applied Psychology*, 61:5, pp. 605-612.

Ivanova, Slavka., 1989, "Brigades in Bulgaria & Participation", *UM Sociologie du Travail*, 31:3,pp. 301-313.

Jacobson, E., 1951, *Foreman - Steward Participation Practices and Worker Attitudes in a Unionized Factory*, Unpublished doctoral dissertation, University of Michigan.

Jacques, Elliot., 1968, *Employer Participation and Managerial Authority*, London, Brunel University.

Jain, Hem C., 1990, "Workers' Participation in Canada: Current Developments and Challenges", in C. Lakshmanna et al. *Workers' Participation And Industrial Democracy: Global Perspective*, New Delhi, Ajanta Publications, pp. 71-82.

Jecchinis, Chris., 1985, "Lower Level Workers' Participation in Management: Cross National Experience & New Trends", *Crossroads*, 18, pp. 23-32.

Johannesen, Janette Eadon., 1979, "VAG - A Need For Education", *Industrial Relations*, 18:3, pp. 364-369.

Joshi, Arun., 1972, "Foreword", in K.C. Alexander's Participative

Management: The Indian Experience, New Delhi, Sri Ram Centre, pp. v-vi.

Joshi, Rameshchandra, D., 1974, "Workers' Participation in Management", in S.A. Sapre (Ed.) *Labour Participation In Management*, Bombay, Joint Management Council: Government Central Press, pp. 25-40.

Kar, Biman., 1993, "Labour Participation in Railway Management", in Ruddar Dutt (Ed.) *Workers' Participation And Workers' Ownership*, Delhi, Pragati Publications, pp. 259-264.

Karnik, V.B., 1974, "Foreward", in S.A. Sapre (Ed.) *Labour Participation In Management*, Bombay, Joint Management Council: Government Central Press, pp. V-VII.

Katz, D. et al., 1950, *Productivity, Supervision and Morale in an Office Situation*, Ann Arbor, University of Michigan Institute for Social Research.

Keller, Berndt K., 1995, "Rapporteur's Report: Emerging Models of Worker Participation and Representation", *British Journal of Industrial Relations*, 33:3, pp. 317-327.

Kennedy, V.D., 1966, *Unions, Employees and Government*, Bombay, Manaktalas and Sons.

Khanna, S. et al., 1981, *Workers' participation and Development: The Indian Experience*, Hague, ISS.

Kher, Manik., 1988, *Alienation From Work and Organization - Revisiting The Theory*, New Delhi, Indus Publishing Co.

________, 1990, "Effective Industrial Democracy: Alternatives in the Indian Context", in C. Lakshmanna et al (Eds.) *Workers' Participation And Industrial Democracy: Global Perspective*, New Delhi, Ajanta Publications, pp. 247-256.

Komozin et al., 1989, "Self - Administration on the Shop - Floor Level", *Sotsiologicheskie Issledovaniya*, 16:4, pp. 74-81.

Koopman, Ivema et al., 1977, "Participation, Motivation and Power Situation", *Mens en Onderneming*, 31:5, pp. 263-284.

Koziara, Edward C., 1979, "Workers' Participation in Malta", *Industrial Relations*, 18:3, pp. 381-384.

Krech, D. and R.S. Crutchfield., 1948, *Theory and Problems of Social Psychology*, New York, McGraw Hill.

Kumar, R., 1992, *Labour Participation In Management- A Case Study of Two Organizations in U.P.*, Delhi, Ajanta Publications.

________, 1990, "Participative Management in India: Problems and Prospects", in C. Lakshmanna et al (Eds.) *Workers' Participation And Industrial Democracy: Global Perspective*, New Delhi, Ajanta Publications, pp. 199-211.

Laaksonen, Oiva., 1990, "Workers' Participation in Chinese Enterprises After Mao", in C. Lakshmanna et al (Eds.) *Workers' Participation And Industrial Democracy: Global Perspective*, New Delhi, Ajanta Publications, pp. 55-70.

Laflamme, Gilles et al., 1987, "Workers' participation and personnel policies in Canada: Some hopeful signs", *International Labour Review*, 126:2, pp. 219-228.

Laidlaw, Karen A., 1977, "The Industrial Community in Peru: An Experiment in Worker Participation", *International Review of Modern Sociology*, 7:1, pp. 1-11.

Lakshmanna C., 1988, Proceedings of the International Workshop on "Experiments and Experiences of Workers' Participation for Effective Industrial Democracy," Hyderabad, India, Dec. 28-30, 1988, Organized by the Indian Chapter of Research Committee 10 of International Sociological Association.

__________, 1990, "Workers' Participation in Management: Formulation, Shifts and Current Situation in Policy Perspective in India", in C. Lakshmanna et al (Eds.) *Workers' Participation And Industrial Democracy: Global Perspective*, New Delhi, Ajanta Publications, pp. 163-169.

Lakshmanna, Mamta., 1990, "Workers' Participation in Management - Indian Trade Union Perspective", in C. Lakshmanna et al (Eds.) *Workers' participation And Industrial Democracy: Global Perspective*, New Delhi, Ajanta Publications, pp. 171-175.

Lal, Meera., 1993, "Workers' Participation in Management in Banking Sector", in Ruddar Dutt (Ed.) *Workers'*

Participation And Workers' Ownership, Delhi, Pragati Publications, pp. 132-142.

Lambert, Richard D., 1963, *Workers, Factories and Social Change in India*, Princeton, New Jersey, Princeton University Press.

Lammers, C.J., 1967, "Power and participation in decision - making in formal organization", *American Journal of Sociology*, 173:2, pp 201-210.

Lawler, Edward A. and J. Richard Hackman., 1969, "Impact of employees participation in the development of pay incentive plans", *Journal of Applied Psychology*, 53:6, pp. 467-471.

Lawrence, Lois C. and Patricia Cain Smith, 1955, "Group Decision and Employee Participation", *Journal of Applied Psychology*, 39, pp. 334-337.

Lewin, K. et al., 1939, "Patterns of aggressive behaviour in experimentally created climates", *Journal of Psychology*, 10, pp. 229-271.

Likert, Rensis., 1961 *New Patterns of Management*, New York, McGraw Hill.

__________, 1967(a) The Human Organization: Its Management and Value, New York, McGraw Hill.

__________, 1967(b), "Group Processes And Organizational Performance", in S.G. Huneryager and I.L. Heckman (Eds.) *Human Relations In Management*, Bombay, D.B. Tarporevala Sons & Co. Ltd., pp. 622-641.

Locke, E.A. and D.M. Schweiger., 1979, "Participation in decision making: One more look", in B.M. Staw and L.L. Cummings (Eds.) *Research in Organizational Behaviour*, Greenwich, Conn., JAI Press, Vol. 1, pp. 265-339.

Long, Richard J., 1978, "The Effects of Employee Ownership on Organizational Identification, Employee Job Attitudes and Organizational Performance: A Tentative Framework and Empirical Findings", *Human Relations*, 31:1, pp. 29-47.

Macbeath, Innis., 1976, "Workers' Participation in Decision Making", in John Melling et al (Eds.) *Workers' Participation*, Keynes, Open University Press, Paper 8, pp. 7-45.

Macy, B.A, 1982, "The Boliver quality of work program: success or failure", in R. Zager and M. Rosow (Eds.) *The innovative organization: productivity programs in action*, New York, Pergamon, pp. 184-221.

Macy, B.A. and P.H. Mirvis, 1982 "Organizational effectiveness and program costs benefits", *Evaluation Review*, 6:3, pp. 301-372.

Macy, B.A. et al., 1989, "A Test of Participation Theory in a Work Re-design Field Setting: Degree of Participation and Comparison Site Contrasts", *Human Relations*, 42:12, pp. 1095-1165.

Madaiah, M. and R. Ramapriya, 1989, *Karnataka Economy: Growth, Issues and Lines of Development*, Bombay, Himalaya Publishing House.

Madhusudhana Rao, M, 1986, *Labour Management Relations And Trade Union Leadership*, New Delhi, Deep & Deep Publications.

Maier, N.R.F, 1952, *Principles of Human Relations*, New York, Wiley.

Mamoria, C.B, 1971, *Organization And Financing of Industries In India*, Allahabad, Kitab Mahal.

Mamoria, C.B. and Satish Mamoria, 1988, *Dynamics of Industrial Relations*, Bombay, Himalaya Publishing House.

Mankidy, Jacob, 1995, "Changing Perspectives of Worker Participation in India with Particular Reference to the Banking Industry", *British Journal of Industrial Relations*, 33:3, pp. 443-458.

Mann, F.C. and J.K. Dent, 1954, *Appraisal of Supervisors and the Attitudes of their Employees in an Electric Power Company*, Ann Arbor: Survey Research Centre, University of Michigan.

Marchington, Mick, 1987, "Employee Participation", in Brain Towers (Ed.) *A Hand Book of Industrial Relations Practice*, London, Kogan Page, pp. 162-182.

Marchington, Mick and Ray Loveridge, 1983, "Management Decision-making and Shopfloor Participation", in Keith Thurley and Stephen Wood (Eds.) *Industrial Relations and Management Strategy*, Cambridge, Cambridge University Press, pp. 73-82.

Maslow, Abraham, 1943, "A theory of human motivation", *Psychological Review*, 50, pp. 370-396.

Matejko, Alexander, 1977, "Management Participation", *Revue Internationale de Sociologie*, 13:3, pp. 159-210.

Mayo, Elton, 1941, *Management and Morale*, Cambridge, Harvard University Press.

McClelland, David C, 1965, "Achievement motivation can be developed", *Harvard Business Review*, 43, pp. 7-15.

McGregor, Douglas M, 1960, *The Human Side of Enterprise*, New York, McGraw-Hill.

Mehtras, V.G, 1966, *Labour Participation in Management*, Bombay, Manaktalas.

Melling, John et al., 1976, "Decision making in Britain", in John Melling et al (Eds.) *Workers' Participation*, Keynes, Open University Press, Paper 9, pp. 49-60.

Michael, V.P, 1979, *Industrial Relations in India and Workers' Involvement in Management*, Bombay, Himalaya Publishing House.

Miller, Douglas, 1979, "The Industrial Representation of Labour Unions in the Federal Republic of Germany", *Soziale Welt*, 30:3, pp. 328-353.

Miller, Jon, 1980, "Decision - Making and Organizational Effectiveness: Participation and Perceptions", *Sociology of Work and Occupations*, 7:1, pp. 55-79.

Misir, Prem, 1993 , *Workers' Participation In Management*, New Delhi, Reliance Publishing House.

Monappa, Arun and Mirza Saiyadain, 1996, *Personnel Management*, New Delhi, Tata McGraw - Hill Publishing Co. Ltd.

Mongia, J.N, 1980, *Readings In Indian Labour and Social Welfare*, Delhi, Atma Ram & Sons.

Morse, N.C, 1953, *Satisfactions in the White-Collar Job*, Ann Arbor: Survey Research Centre, University of Michigan.

Morse, N.C. and E. Reimer, 1956, "The experimental change of a major organizational variable", *Journal of Abnormal and Social Psychology*, 52, pp. 120-129.

Nadkarni, Lakshmi, 1990, "The Practice of Participative Management - Experiences of Pune Factories", in C. Lakshmanna et al (Eds.) *Workers' Participation and Industrial Democracy: Global Perspective*, New Delhi, Ajanta Publications, pp. 301-308.

Nadler, D.A. et al., 1980, "Factors Influencing the Success of Labour Management Quality of Work Life Projects", *Journal of Occupational Behaviour*, 1:1, pp. 53-67.

Nagaraju, S, 1981, *Industrial Relations System in India*, Allahabad, Chugh Publications.

Nair, M.N.K, 1970, "Joint Consultation", *Indian Manager*, 1, pp. 40-55.

Nandi, S.N, 1985, "A Conceptual Model of Effective Working of QCC in Indian Context", *Lok Udyog*, 19:1, pp. 3-11.

Nanjundappa, D.M, 1993, "Employee Ownership for a Stable Industrial Base", in Ruddar Dutt (Ed.) *Workers' Participation And Workers' Ownership*,Delhi, Pragati Publications, pp. 31-48.

Narayana, B.L. and M.V. Moorthy, 1970, *Participation of Workers in Welfare Work, Research Programme Committee*, Planning Commission, Government of India.

Nightingale,Donald V, 1979, "The Formally Participative Organization", *Industrial Relations*, 18:3, pp. 310-321.

__________, 1982, *Work Place Democracy: An Inquiry into Employee Participation in Canadian Work Organizations*, Toronto, University of Toronto Press.

Obradovic, Josip, 1979, "Branch of Industry and Industrial Behaviour in the Process of Decision Making", *Sociologiju*, 21:4, pp. 369-395.

Odaka, K, 1975, *Toward Industrial Democracy - Management and Workers in Modern Japan, Cambridge, Harvard University Press.*

Ojha, N.K, 1993, "Workers' Participation in Management", in Ruddar Dutt (Ed.) *Workers' Participation And Workers' Ownership*, Delhi, Pragati Publications, pp. 152-169.

Optner, S.L, 1965, *Systems Analysis for Business and Industrial Problem Solving*, New Jersey, Prentice - Hall.

Oranti, Oscar A, 1955, *Jobs and Workers in India*, New York, Ithaka.

Ozaki, Muneto, 1996, "Labour Relations and Work Organization in Industrialized Countries", *International Labour Review*, 135:1, pp. 37-57.

Pace, David and John Hunter, 1978, *Direct participation in action: the new bureaucracy*, Norman, Saxon House.

Panakal, J.A. et al., 1979, "Training for Effective Participative Management", *Industrial Relations*, 31:5, pp. 21-23.

Pandey, S.N, 1986, "Towards Successful Participative Management", *Workers' Education*, 3, pp. 23-27.

Patchen, Martin, 1970, *Participation, Achievement and Involvement on the Job*, Englewood Cliffs, Prentice - Hall.

Patel, S.K. and R.C. Talati, 1993, "Workers' Participation in Management", in Ruddar Dutt (Ed.) *Workers' Participation And Workers' Ownership*, Delhi, Pragati Publications, pp. 307-319.

Peretiatkowicz, Anatol, 1990, "Democracy in Selected Polish State Enterprises", in C. Lakshmanna et al. (Ed.) *Workers' Participation And Industrial Democracy: Global Perspective*, New Delhi, Ajanta Publications, pp. 333-343.

Perumal, Velayudha S,1993, "Workers' Ownership of Industries - The Yugoslav Model and a Perspective for India", in Ruddar Dutt (Ed.) *Workers' Participation And Workers' Ownership*, Delhi, Pragati Publications, pp. 327-333.

Pillai, Krishna, P.N, 1984, "Collective Bargaining - Preparation, Negotiation And Administration", in N. Krishnaswamy and S. Sampangiramaiah (Eds.) *Management Development Programme On Issues and Trends in Industrial Relations* (Conference Proceedings), Bangalore, IIM, pp. 1-25.

Pimentel, Duarte et al., 1977, "The Simoes Factory: Self-Determination or Delegation of Power? A Case Study of Entrepreneurial Intervention", *Analise-Social*, 13:2, pp. 355-418.

Poole, Michael, 1975, *Workers' Participation in Industry*, London, Routledge & Kegan Paul.

_________, 1979, "Industrial Democracy: A Comparative Analysis", *Industrial Relations*, 18:3, pp. 262-272.

Prasad, Allan, 1973, *Personnel Management And Industrial Relations In The Public Sector*, Bombay, Progressive Corporation Private Ltd.

Prasad, Maya, 1993, "Workers' Participation in Management: The Experience of the Public Sector Units in India", in Ruddar Dutt (Ed.) *Workers' Participation And Workers' Ownership*, Delhi, Pragati Publications, pp. 227-237.

Punekar, S.D., 1977, "Worker Participation in Management", *The Indian Journal of Social Work*, 38:2, pp. 157-163.

Pylee, M.V, 1975, *Worker Participation In Management Myth And Reality*, New Delhi, N.V. Publications.

Ramsay, Harvie, 1976, "Participation: The Shop-floor View", *British Journal of Industrial Relations*, 44:2, pp. 128-141.

_________, 1977, "Cycles of control: Worker Participation in Sociological and Historical Perspective", *Sociology*, 11, pp. 481-506.

Ramaswamy, E.A, 1988, *Worker Consciousness And Trade Union Response*, Delhi, Oxford University Press.

Ranade, V.V, 1974, "Labour Participation in Management", in S.A. Sapre (Ed.) *Labour Participation In Management*, Bombay, Joint Management Council: Government Central Press, pp. 20-24.

Ray, Pranabesh, 1995, "In Search of Participation", *Indian Journal of Industrial Relations*, 31:2, pp. 246-261.

Reindrop, Julian, 1971, *Leaders and Leadership in the Trade Unions in Bangalore*, Madras, The Christian Literature Society.

Roberts, Erine, 1973, *Workers' Control*, London, George Allen & Unwin Ltd.

Roethlisberger, F.J, 1941, *Management And Morale*, Cambridge, Harvard University Press.

Rojek, Chris and C. Wilson David, 1987, "Workers' Self - Management in the World System: The Yugoslav Case", *Organization Studies*, 8:4, pp. 297-308.

Rosenberg, Richard D. and Rosenstrin Eliezer, 1980, "Participation and Productivity: An Empirical Study", *Industrial and Labor Relations Review*, 33:3, pp. 355-367.

Ronney, Patrick Michael, 1988, "Worker Participation in Employee - Owned Firms", *UM Journal of Economic Issues*, 22:2, pp. 451-458.

Roy, S.K, 1973, "Participative Management In Public Industry: Organizational Ground Work Necessary", in C.P. Thakur and K.C. Sethi (Eds.) *Industrial Democracy: Some Issues and Experiences*; New Delhi, Sri Ram Centre, pp. 49-66.

Russell, Raymond, 1988, "Forms and Extent of Employee Participation in the Contemporary United States", *UM Work and Occupations*, 15:4, pp. 374-395.

Russell, Raymond et al., 1979, "Participation, Influence & Worker Ownership", *Industrial Relations*, 18:3, pp. 330-341.

Sahai, Jugendra and Minoo Mishra, 1990, "Workers' Participation in Management - A Sociological Study with Special Reference to Bhilai Steel Plant: a Public Sector Undertaking", in C. Lakshmanna et al. (Eds.) *Workers' Participation And Industrial Democracy: Global Perspective*, New Delhi, Ajanta Publications, pp. 177-183.

Sahu, Bhabatosh, 1985, *Dynamics of Participative Management: Indian Experience*, Bombay, Himalaya Publishing House.

Saibaba, G. et al., 1990, "Quality Control Circles Policies And Implementation In India: An Expositionary Analysis", *The Indian Journal of Labour Economics*, 33:4, pp. 296-302.

Salamon, Michael, 1987, *Industrial Relations: Theory and Practice*, Englewood Cliffs, Prentice Hall.

Sandberg, Ake, 1990, "Participation and Democratization in Working Life: Some Swedish Experiences", in C. Lakshmanna et al (Eds.) *Workers' Participation And Industrial Democracy: Global Perspective*, New Delhi, Ajanta Publications, pp. 21-38.

Sandkull, Bengt, 1984, "Managing the Democratization Process in Worker Cooperatives", *Economic and Industrial Democarcy*, 5:3, pp. 359-389

Sarikwal, R.C, 1990, "Workers' Participation as a Form of Industrial Democracy in India: The Experience of a Private

Sector Undertaking", in C. Lakshmanna et al (Eds.) *Workers' Participation And Industrial Democracy: Global Perspective*, New Delhi, Ajanta Publications, pp. 185-197.

Sarma, A.M, 1990(a), "Workers' Participation, Self Management and Workers' Control", Indian *Journal of Social Work*, 51:2, pp. 279-290.

__________, 1990(b), "Workers' Participation, Self Management and Workers' Control", in C. Lakshmanna et al. (Eds.) *Workers' Participation And Industrial Democracy: Global Perspective*, New Delhi, Ajanta Publications, pp. 309-325.

Satya Raju, R, 1993, "Employee Participation in Management: The Indian Experience", in Ruddar Dutt (Ed.) *Workers' Participation and Workers' Ownership*, Delhi, Pragati Publications, pp. 216-226.

Saxena, A.N, 1979, "Workers' Participation For Industrial Democracy", *Industrial Relations*, 31:4, pp. 13-17.

Schaake, Bert, 1979, "Work - Councils and Management Consultants", *Mens en onderneming*, 33:6, pp. 519-531.

Schregle, Johannes, 1976, "Workers' participation in decisions within undertakings", *International Labour Review*, 113:1, pp. 1-15.

Scoville, J.G, 1980, "Organizing Our Thoughts about Workers' Participation", *Labour and Society*, 5:3, pp. 255-265.

__________, 1987, "Workers' Participation in the Federal Republic of Germany in an International Perspective", *International Labour Review*, 126:3, pp. 317-327.

Seashore, et al., 1963, *Changing the Structure and Functioning of an Organization: Report on a field experiment*, Ann Arbor, Michigan: Survey Research Centre, University of Michigan.

Sen, Ratna, 1995, "Workers' Industrial Cooperatives And Workers' Management", *Indian Journal of Industrial Relations*, 30:3, pp. 320-326.

Sethi, K.C, 1973, "Participative Management: Lessons From Yugoslav Experience", in C.P. Thakur and K.C. Sethi (Eds.) *Industrial Democracy: Some Issues and Experiences*", New Delhi, Sri Ram Centre, pp. 118-139.

Sharma, B.R, 1974, *The Indian Industrial Worker*, Delhi, Vikas Publishing House.

Sharma, N.K, 1976, "Workers' Participation in India", *Indian Finance*, 98, pp. 488-492.

Sharma, R.C. and Anil Kumar, 1993, "Workers' Participation in Management in Public Enterprises", in Ruddar Dutt (Ed.) *Workers' Participation And Workers' Ownership*, Delhi, Pragati Publications, pp. 83-91.

Sharma, R.C. and P.J. Philip, 1993, "Workers' Participation In Management in Haryana", in Ruddar Dutt (Ed.) *Workers' Participation and Workers' Ownership*, Delhi, Pragati Publications, pp. 249-258.

Sharma, Tulsi Ram and S.D. Singh Chauhan, 1989, *Industrial Economics*, Agra, Educational Publishers.

Sherlekar et al., 1986, *Industrial Organization And Management*, Bombay, Himalaya Publishing House.

Sheth, N.R, 1972(a), "Hazards of Industrial Democracy", *Economic and Political Weekly*, 7:35, pp. 119-122.

__________, 1972(b), *The Joint Management Council: Problems and Prospects*, New Delhi, Sri Ram Centre For Industrial Relations.

__________, 1991, "At Tiruchi: They Are On Firm Ground and Lucky", *Vikalpa - The Journal For Decision Makers*, 16:4, pp. 63-64.

__________, 1973, "The Ends And Means In Joint Consultation", in C.P. Thakur and K.C. Sethi (Eds.) *Industrial Democracy: Some Issues And Experiences*, New Delhi, Sri Ram Centre, pp. 140-157.

Shlapentokh, Vladimir, 1988, "Workers' Involvement in the Soviet Union: From Lenin to Gorbachev", *UM Work and Occupations*, 15:4, pp. 449-467.

Shuchman, A, 1957, *Co-determination, Labor's Middle Way in Germany*, Washington, Public Affairs Press.

Shukla, B.N. and Bimla Shukla, 1993(a), "Workers' Participation in Management: Statutory or Non-Statutory", in Ruddar Dutt (Ed.) *Workers' Participation And Workers' Ownership*, Delhi, Pragati Publications, pp. 123-131.

_________, 1993(b), "Workers' Ownership and Management of Industry", in Ruddar Dutt (Ed.) *Workers' Participation And Workers' Ownership*, Delhi, Pragati Publications, pp. 341-353.

Shukla, M.C, 1970, *Business Organization And Management*, New Delhi, S. Chand & Co.

Shumachar, E.F,1975, *Small is Beautiful*, New York, Harper & Row.

Siegal, A.L. and R.A. Ruh, 1973, "Job Involvement, Participation in Decision Making, Personal Background and Job Behaviour", *Organization Behaviour and Human Performance*, 9, pp. 318-327.

Singh, Amarjit and A.N. Sadhu, 1988, *Industrial Economics*, Bombay, Himalaya Publishing House.

Singh, Balendrakumar, 1988, "Relationship of Participation And Alienation With Job Involvement", *Indian Journal of Industrial Relations*, 23:4, pp. 498-507.

Singh, Bhagwan Prasad, 1993, "Workers' Participation in Management", in Ruddar Dutt (Ed.) *Workers' Participation And Workers' Ownership*, Delhi, Pragati Publications, pp. 106-112.

Singh, Bikrama, 1993, "Participative Management in Public Undertakings: Some Experiences", in Ruddar Dutt (Ed.) *Workers' Participation And Workers' Ownership*, Delhi, Pragati Publications, pp. 143-151.

Singh, Biswa Nath and Mamata Singh, 1993, "Participative Management in Principle and Practice" in Ruddar Dutt (Ed.) *Workers' Participation And Workers' Ownership*, Delhi, Pragati Publications, pp. 197-207.

Singh, Harendra Narain and Indu Mati Singh, 1993, "Workers' Participation in Management", in Ruddar Dutt (Ed.) *Workers' Participation And Workers' Ownership*, Delhi, Pragati Publications, pp. 208-215.

Singh, Mira and D.M. Pestonjee, 1990, "Job Involvement, Sense of Participation And Job Satisfaction: A Study In Banking Industry", *Indian Journal of Industrial Relations*, 26:2, pp. 159-165.

Singh, R.C, 1993, "The Scheme for Workers' Participation in Industry: A Review", in Ruddar Dutt (Ed.) *Workers' Participation And Workers' Ownership*, Delhi, Pragati Publications, pp. 320-326.

Singh, S, 1977, *Industrial Relations and Personnel Management*, Lucknow, Jyotsna Publications.

Singh, Sudama and Rabi Niwas Singh, 1993, "Workers' Participation in Management", in Ruddar Dutt (Ed.) *Workers' Participation And Workers' Ownership*, Delhi, Pragati Publications, pp. 299-305

Singhi, N.K, 1974, *Bureaucracy: Position and Persons*, New Delhi, Abinav Publications.

Sirianni, Carmen J, 1980, "Workers' Control in the Era of World War I: A Comparative Analysis of the European Experience", *Theory & Society*, 9:1, pp. 29-88.

Sockell, Donna, 1985, "Attitudes, Behaviour & Employee Ownership: Some Preliminary Data", *Industrial Relations*, 24:1, pp. 130-138.

Sorensen, Knut Holtan, 1985, "Technology and Industrial Democracy: An Inquiry into Some Theoretical Issues & Their Social Basis", *Organization Studies*, 6:2, pp. 139-160.

Srivastava, R.N, 1981, "Workers' Participation In Industry", *Lok Udyog*, 14:10, pp. 1-4.

Srivastava, S.P, 1990, "Workers' Participation and Industrial Democracy in India - Experiments and Experiences", in C. Lakshmanna et al. (Eds.) *Workers' Participation And Industrial Democracy: Global Perspective*, New Delhi, Ajanta Publications, pp. 227-246.

Srivastava, Surendrakumar, 1984, "Foreword", in *Vishnu Gopal's Industrial Democracy in India*, Allahabad, Chugh Publications, pp. ix-xi.

Srivastava, Suresh C, 1984, "Workers' Participation In Management", in R.S. Dwivedi (Ed.) *Manpower Management: An Integrated Approach To Personnel Management And Labour Relations*, New Delhi, Prentice Hall of India, pp. 265-300.

Stern, Robert N, 1988, "Participation by Representation: Workers on Boards of Directors in the United States and Abroad", *UM Work and Occupations*, 15:4, pp. 396-422.

Strauss, George, 1979, "Workers' Participation: Symposium Introduction", *Industrial Relations*, 18:3, pp. 247-261.

__________, 1963, "Some notes on power-equalization", in Harold, J. Levitt (Ed.) The *Social Science of Organizations*, Englewood Cliffs, Prentice-Hall, pp. 39-84.

__________, 1977, "Participative Management and Quality of Work Life", in Miller Richard B. (Ed.) *Participative Management: Quality of Work Life and Job Enrichment*, Park Ridge, Noyes Data Corporation, pp. 132-139.

Strauss, George and Gerald Silverman, 1977, "Making Participative Management Work", in Miller Richard B. (Ed.) *Participative Management Quality of Work Life and Job Enrichment*, Park Ridge, Noyes Data Corporation, pp. 140-153.

Strauss, George and E. Rosenstein, "Worker Participation: A Critical View", *Industrial Relations*, 9:2, pp. 197-214.

Styskal, Richard A, 1980, "Power and Commitment in Organizations: A Test of the Participation Thesis", *Social Forces*, 58:3, pp. 925-943.

Subbarao, A.V, 1990, "Industrial Relations Systems and the Needs of Three Asian Developing Countries - India, Srilanka, Singapore", in C. Lakshmanna et al. (Eds.) *Workers' Participation And Industrial Democracy: Global Perspective*, New Delhi, Ajanta Publications, pp. 99-117.

Subbarao, P. and N. Narayana, 1992, "Labour-Management Cooperation In Indian Railways", *Indian Journal of Industrial Relations*, 28:1, pp. 37-48.

Subramanian, K.N, 1967, *Labour Management Relations in India*, Bombay, Asia Publishing House.

Suri, G.K, 1973, "Participation And Productivity With Special Reference To The Scanlon Plan", in C.P. Thakur and K.C. Sethi (Eds.) *Industrial Democracy: Some Issues And Experiences*, New Delhi, Sri Ram Centre, pp. 205-225.

Szell, Gyorgy, 1990, "Participation, Workers' Control and Self - Management in a Global Perspective", in C. Lakshmanna et al. (Eds.) *Workers' Participation And Industrial Democracy - Global Perspective*, New Delhi, Ajanta Publications, pp. 3-12.

Talpule, Begaram, 1984, "An Approach to Workers' Participation in Management", in N. Krishnaswamy and S. Sampangiramaiah (Eds.) *Management Development Programme on Issues and Trends in Industrial Relations (Conference Proceedings)*, Bangalore, IIM, pp. 1-4.

Tanic, Zivan, 1969, *Workers' Participation in Management: Ideal and Reality in India*, New Delhi, Sri Ram Centre for Industrial Relations and Human Resources.

Tannenbaum, A.S, 1968, *Control in Organizations*, New York, McGraw Hill.

__________, 1975, "Hierarchy in Orgnizations: A Comparison of Hierarchy in Kibbutz and Other Socialistic and Capitalistic Enterprises", *The Kibbutz*, 2, pp. 47-62.

Tannenbaum, Robert and Fred Massarik, 1967, "Participation By Subordinates In The Managerial Decision Making Process", in S.G. Huneryager and I.L. Heckman (Eds.) *Human Relations In Management*, Bombay, D.B. Taraporevala Sons and Co. Ltd., pp. 592-605.

__________, 1970, "Sharing Decision-Making With Subordinates", in Dubin (Ed.) *Human Relations in Administration With Readings*, New Delhi, Prentice Hall of India, pp. 379-384.

Tannenbaum, Robert and W.H. Schmidt, 1958, "How to Choose a Leadership Pattern", *Harvard Business Review*, 36:2, pp. 95-101.

Tatur, Melanie, 1978, "Attempts toward Worker Participation in Administrative Functions in the Soviet Industrial Enterprise", *Ost-europa*, 28:4, pp. 318-337.

Tausky, Curt & F. Chelte Anthony, 1988, "Workers' Participation", *UM Work and Occupations*, 15:4, pp. 363-373.

Thakur, C.P, 1973, "Public Enterprise And Workers' Participation In Management", in C.P. Thakur and K.C. Sethi (Eds.) *Industrial Democracy: Some Issues And Experiences*, New Delhi, Sri Ram Centre, pp. 11-33.

Thakur, C.P. and K.C. Sethi, 1973, (Eds.) *Industrial Democracy:*

Some Issues And Experiences, New Delhi, Sri Ram Centre, pp. ix-x.

The Hindu, 1999(a), *Prosperity through industrialization.*

_________, 1999(b), IT: *Centre of gravity shifting towards Asia.*

Thimm, Alfred L, 1979, "Union Management "Codetermination" in Sweden", *The Journal of Social and Political Studies*, 4:2, pp. 147-173.

Thomason, George F, 1971, *Experiments in Participation*, London, Institute of Personnel Management , Oxford Circus.

_________, 1973, "Workers' Participation in Private Enterprise Organizations", in Campbell Balfour (Ed.) *Participation In Industry*, London, Croom Helm, pp. 138-179.

Toole, James O, 1973, *Work in America: Report on the Special Task Force to the Secretary of Health, Education and Welfare*, Cambridge, Mass, M.I.T. Press.

Treu, Tiziano and Serafino Negrelli, 1987, "Workers' Participation and Personnel Management Policies in Italy", *International Labour Review*, 126:1, pp. 81-94.

Trinczek, Rainer, 1989 , "Industrial Participation as Social Interaction: A Contribution to the Analysis of Industrial Relations within the Firm", *Zeitschrift fur Soziologie*, 18:6, pp. 444-456.

Tucker, James et al., 1989, "Employee Ownership and Perceptions of Work: The Effect of an Employee Stock Ownership Plan", *UM Work and Occupations*, 16:1, pp. 26-42.

Tyson, Shaun, 1987, *Personnel Management Made Simple*, London, Heinemann.

Vaid, K.N, 1968, *The New Workers*, Bombay, Asia Publishing House.

_________,1970, *Labour Welfare In India*, New Delhi, Sri Ram Centre for Industrial Relations.

Vaidya, S.A, 1974, "Productivity and Labour Participation in Management", in S.A. Sapre (Ed.) *Labour Participation In Management*, Bombay, Joint Management Council: Government Central Press, pp. 41-51.

Vakil, N.M, 1974, "Worker Participation in Management - A Practical Approach", in S.A. Sapre (Ed.) *Labour Participation*

In Management, Bombay, Joint Management Council: Government Central Press, pp. 11-19.

Varandhani, Garusharan, 1989, *Workers' Participation In Management - With Special Reference To India*, New Delhi, Deep & Deep Publications.

Vasudevan and M. Ghosh, 1985-86, *A Simple Study of Personnel Management*, New Delhi, New Heights.

Verma, Meera, 1993, "Participative Management Concept and Policy: An Indian Experiment", in Ruddar Dutt (Ed.) *Workers' Participation And Workers' Ownership*, Delhi, Pragati Publications, pp. 183-196.

Verma, M.K., 1972, "Workers' Participation In Management", in R.D. Agarwal (Ed.) *Dynamics of Labour Relations in India*, New Delhi, Tata McGraw Hill Publishing Company Ltd., pp. 192-199.

Verma, Pramod, 1991, "Workers' Participation or Union - Management Collaboration", *Vikalpa - The Journal For Decision Makers*, 16:4, pp. 64-65.

Vishnu Gopal, 1984, *Industrial Democracy in India*, Allahabad, Chugh Publications.

Vishwa Nath, 1992, *Workers' Participation In Management*, New Delhi, Mittal Publications.

Vroom, Victor H., 1960, *Some Personality Determinants of the Effects of Participation*, Englewood Cliffs, Prentice Hall.

Vroom, Victor H. And P. Yetton, 1973, *Leadership and Decision Making*, Pittsburgh, University of Pittsburgh Press.

Walker, K.F., 1977, "Toward the Participatory Enterprise: A European Trend", *Annals of the American Academy of Political and Social Science*, 431, pp. 1-11.

_________, 1973, "Workers' Participation In Management In Practice - An International Perspective", in C.P. Thakur and K.C. Sethi (Eds.) *Industrial Democracy: Some Issues And Experiences*, New Delhi, Sri Ram Centre, pp. 226-252.

Walker, K.E. & G. Bellecombe, 1967, "Workers' Participation In Management", *International Institute of Labour Studies*, Bulletin No. 2, pp. 64-125.

Wall, T.D. and J.A. Lischeron, 1977, *Worker Participation - A Critique of the Literature and Some Fresh Evidence,* Maidenhead, Berks, McGraw Hill.

Warrier, S.K., 1978, "Meaningful Participation in Management: A New Perspective, *Indian Journal of Industrial Relations,* 13, pp. 445-463.

Webb, S. and B. Webb, 1897, *Industrial Democracy,* London, Longman.

Westernholz, Ann, 1979, "Workers' Participation in Denmark", *Industrial Relations,* 18:3, pp. 376-380.

Westley, William A., 1979, "Problems and Solutions in the Quality of Working Life", *Human Relations,* 32:2, pp. 113-123.

Whyte, W.F., 1951, *Patterns of Industrial Peace,* New York, Harper.

Wilpert, Bernhard, 1984, "Participation in Organizations : Evidence from International Comparative Research", *International Social Science Journal,* 36: 2, pp. 355-366.

Wilpert, Bernhard and Kawalek Jurgen, 1988, "Participation and the Organization of Work", *Soziologische Revue,* 11:3, pp. 286-293.

Winster, Alain, 1974, "The Content of Work Tasks And Work Load", *Sociologie-du-Travial,* 16:4, pp. 339-357.

Winster, Geoffrey M., 1993, "Workers' Participation In Management", in Ruddar Dutt (Ed.) *Workers' Participation And Workers' Ownership,* Delhi, Pragati Publications, pp. 238-248.

Zeffane, Richard, 1990, "Socialism and Participative Management - A Comparative View of Systems in Algeria and Yugoslavia", in C. Lakshmanna et al. (Eds.) *Workers' Participation And Industrial Democracy: Global Perspectives,* New Delhi, Ajanta Publications, pp. 119-155.

Zivkovic, Miroslav, 1987, "Self - Management in Socialism and the One-Party System", *Socioloski Pregled,* 21:4, pp. 127-135.

Appendices

INTERVIEW SCHEDULES

APPENDIX - I

SCHEDULE FOR MANAGERIAL PERSONNEL

The Person

1. Name of the respondent:
____
2. Sex
( ) Male; ( ) Female
3. Age:________ years
4. Marital status
( ) Married; ( ) Unmarried;
( ) Widowed; ( ) Divorced;
( ) Other (Specify); __________
5. Number of children
Sons: __________
Daughters: __________
6. Wife
( ) Employed; ( ) Housewife;
( ) Unmarried.
7. Religion: ______________
8. Caste: ______________
( ) High; ( ) Intermediate; ( ) Low.
9. Educational level:______________

( ) High; ( ) Moderate;
( ) Low.

10. Type of education
( ) Technical;
( ) Non-technical;
( ) Other (Specify); ________

Organizational Context

1. Firm (Name): ____________
2. Sector
( ) Public; ( ) Private;
( ) Joint.
3. Type
( ) Manufacturing;
( ) Service; ( ) White-collar.
4. Year of establishment: ________
5. Size (No of employees): ______
( ) Small; ( ) Medium; ( ) Large
6. Technology
( ) Simple; ( ) Advanced;
( ) State-of-art (Highly advanced).
7. Licenced capacity: __________
8. Installed capacity: __________
9. Capacity utilization: _______%

Professional Background

1. Designation: ______________
2. Department: ______________
3. Division: ______________
4. Date of joining this firm: _______
5. Number of other firms worked for: ________________________

6. Total length of service: ________
7. First position held in this firm:

   ____

8. Professional training received
   1.
   2.
   3.
9. Special courses attended
   1.
   2.
   3.
10. Present salary: Rs.________ p.m.
11. Other perks and facilities
   1.
   2.
   3.

Workers' Participative Management (PM)- Management Perspective

1. Are you in favour of WPM? (Personal disposition)
   ( ) Yes; ( ) No; ( ) Don't know.
2. Give reasons for your opinion
   1.
   2.
   3.
3. If yes, (1) in what form?

   ____

   (2) at what level? ____________
4. Do you feel that PM is necessary?
   ( ) Yes; ( ) No.
   1. If yes, which two are the most efficient machineries of WPM?
   1.

2.

2. If no, give reasons.

1.

2.

3.

5. In which of the following areas do you prefer WPM?
   ( ) Working conditions;
   ( ) Wages, DA, bonus, etc;
   ( ) Recruitment;
   ( ) Promotion;
   ( ) Productivity;
   ( ) Training and skill development;
   ( ) Discharge, dismissals, lay-offs, etc.;
   ( ) Grievance handling;
   ( ) Welfare of workers;
   ( ) Sales and accounting;
   ( ) Development planning (Expansion);
   ( ) Regulation of technology.
6. What do you consider as an ideal degree of participation?
   ( ) Only management should have a final say;
   ( ) Only inform the workers about the above matters;
   ( ) Workers consensus to be taken;
   ( ) Workers views have to be accepted.
7. Do you feel that the intervention of Govt. in the implementation of PM is necessary?
   ( ) Yes, in advisory capacity;
   ( ) Yes, in statutory form;
   ( ) Yes, in a mediating role;
   ( ) Yes, other__________

   If no, give reasons.

   1.

   2.

8. Do you believe that WPM schemes could foster better industrial relations?

   ( ) Yes; ( ) Somewhat; ( ) No.

9. Do you think WPM would have positive implications for the organizational climate?

   ( ) Yes; ( ) To some extent;

   ( ) No.

10. Do you believe that WPM can actually boost productivity?

    ( ) Yes; ( ) Somewhat;

    ( ) No.

11. Do you support the view of "Workers' Directors"?

    ( ) Yes; ( ) No; ( ) Can't say.

12. Do you feel that more and more areas of management should come under the purview of WPM?

    ( ) Yes; ( ) No.

13. How would you describe the size of worker component in machineries of WPM?

    ( ) Too large; ( ) Just the right;

    ( ) Too small.

14. Which one of the following machineries does your management prefer for resolving conflicts?

    ( ) Collective Bargaining;

    ( ) Conciliation; ( ) Arbitration;

    ( ) Adjudication.

15. Does your management prefer Collective Bargaining and Productivity Bargaining to formal machineries of WPM?

    ( ) Yes; ( ) No;

    ( ) Can't say.

Participative Management - Management Experience

1. What are the machineries of WPM operating in your firm?

1.
2.
3.

2. Have you ever been a member of such a machinery?
   ( ) Yes; ( ) No.
3. How frequently these machineries are used/employed?
   ( ) Very frequently;
   ( ) Somewhat frequently;
   ( ) Seldom.
4. How do you rate the participation of workers in these machineries?
   ( ) Active;
   ( ) Somewhat active;
   ( ) Inactive.
5. How do you rate the participation of management representatives?
   ( ) Active;
   ( ) Somewhat active;
   ( ) Inactive.
6. How do you rate the response of workers to the schemes of WPM?
   ( ) Good;
   ( ) Somewhat good;
   ( ) Poor.
7. How do you rate the response of management to the schemes of PM?
   ( ) Good; ( ) Somewhat good;
   ( ) Poor.
8. Which one of the following issues figure most in WPM in your firm?
   ( ) Working conditions;
   ( ) Wages, bonus etc.;

( ) Welfare of workers;

( ) Productivity;

( ) Recruitment, retrenchment;

( ) Expansion of firm;

( ) Introduction of new technology;

( ) Grievance handling;

( ) Other (Specify); ____________

9. Do you feel that workers' participation did make any difference for the outcome?

( ) Yes, very much;

( ) Somewhat;

( ) Little.

10. How do you describe the participation of the workers' representatives?

( ) Active participants;

( ) Not so active;

( ) Passive listeners.

11. Do you think that workers' representatives are matured and informed well-enough to contribute to the process of management?

( ) Yes; ( ) Somewhat;

( ) No.

12. Do you think that the workers' representatives have the right aptitude and skills to make a positive contribution to the management of firm?

( ) Yes; ( ) No; ( ) Can't say.

13. In which area of management the WPM was more constructive and effective?

( ) Personnel and industrial relations;

( ) General administration;

( ) Production and quality control;

( ) Welfare;

( ) Rationalization.

14. Has WPM been more effective a machinery than the Collective Bargaining in promoting industrial peace in the firm?

    ( ) More effective; ( ) About the same; ( ) Less effective.

15. Which of the machineries are more effective in facilitating WPM? (In the order of effectiveness)

    1.

    2.

16. How many of the decisions taken in these machineries are actually implemented?

    ( ) Quite a few (Almost all);

    ( ) Some of them;

    ( ) Very few of them.

17. What are the main problems faced in the functioning of the machineries for WPM?

    ( ) Workers' apathy, workers' ignorance;

    ( ) Management apathy;

    ( ) Incompatibility of ideologies;

    ( ) Other (specify); ____________

18. At what level, the PM has been more effective?

    ( ) Shop-floor level;

    ( ) Department level;

    ( ) Division level;

    ( ) Board level;

    ( ) Other (Specify); ____________

19. Are workers basically inclined to participate and have a say in things that affect their working lives?

    ( ) Very much; ( ) Somewhat;

    ( ) Little.

20. Have unions been playing an important role in the machineries for PM?

    ( ) Yes; ( ) No;

    ( ) Can't say.

21. Have unions been a facilitating factors or constraining factors in the process of WPM?
    ( ) Facilitating factors;
    ( ) Constraining factors;
    ( ) Neither.
22. Has PM in any way changed the way your firm is administered?
    ( ) Yes, for better;
    ( ) Yes, for worse;
    ( ) No.

APPENDIX - II

SCHEDULE FOR TRADE UNION LEADERS

Personal Background

1. Name: ______________________
2. Age: _______ years
3. Sex:
   ( ) Male; ( ) Female
4. Religion: ____________
5. Caste: __________
   (H); (M); (L)
6. Sub-caste:____________
7. Educational level: _________
   (H); (M); (L)
8. Marital status: ___________
   (UM); (M); (D); (W); (S)
9. Number of children
   Male: _____ Female: _______ Total: _____
10. Type of family: _________
    (J); (N); (S)
11. Size of family: ___________
    (L); (M); (S)
12. Number of dependents:________
13. Number of earners in the family: ____________
14. Total family income Rs.
    __________p.m.
15. Place of birth: _________
    (R); (U)
16. Place of schooling: ________
    (R); (U)
17. Family occupation: __________

18. Father's occupation: ________
19. Mother's occupation: ________
20. Father's education: ________
21. Mother's education: ________
22. Migrant status
    ( ) Native; ( ) Migrant;
    ( ) Migrant from within the State;
    ( ) Migrant from outside the State.
23. Mother-tongue: ________

Professional Background

1. Are you employed?
   If yes, type of industry:
   ____
   (M); (S); (WC)
2. Size of industry: ________
   (L); (M); (S)
3. Sector: ________
   (PB); (PR)
4. Present designation: ________
   Department: ________
   Division: ________
5. Type of work
   ( ) Skilled; ( ) Semi-skilled;
   ( ) Unskilled; ( ) Clerical;
   ( ) Supervisory.
6. Length of holding present designation ________ years
7. First designation held:
   ____
8. Total length of service ______ years
   (L); (M); (S)

9. Number of firms worked-in so far
   ( ) Similar:______ Other: _____
   ( ) Total: ______ ( ) Not applicable
10. Vertical mobility experienced
    (H); (M); (L)
11. Salary/Wage: RS.________ p.m./p.w.
12. Type of training received: ______________________

Professional Life

1. Name of the union:

   ____

2. Date of establishment:

   ____

   Size: ___________ (Maj); (Min)
3. Affiliation: ______________
4. Recognition status: __________

   ____

5. Position held in the union:

   ____

6. Length of holding the position ________ years
7. What other positions have you held in the union in the past?
   1.
   2.
   3.
8. Total length of union membership _________ years
9. Participation in union affairs
   ( ) Very Active;
   ( ) Active;
   ( ) Not so active.
10. Participation in union elections
    ( ) Very Active;

( ) Active;

( ) Not so active.

11. Competition in union elections

( ) Very close; ( ) Close;

( ) Somewhat close.

12. Responsiveness of union to membership needs

( ) High;

( ) Moderate;

( ) Low.

13. Leadership turnover

( ) High;

( ) Moderate;

( ) Low.

14. Accessibility of union leadership

( ) High;

( ) Moderate;

( ) Low.

15. Union militancy

( ) High;

( ) Moderate;

( ) Low.

16. Union management relations

( ) Cordial;

( ) Hostile;

( ) Neither.

17. Are you member of a political party

( ) Yes; ( ) No.

If yes,

Name of the political party:

____

18. Highest position held in the political party

( ) Member;

( ) Organizer;

( ) Executive body member;

( ) Officer bearer (specify).

( ) Not applicable

19. Length of holding such office ________________ years
20. Total length of party membership:________
21. Influence of political party on the functioning of union

    ( ) Very much; ( ) Somewhat;

    ( ) Little.
22. Do you agree with party influence on union?

    ( ) Strongly agree; ( ) Agree;

    ( ) Disagree.
23. Has political involvement in any way helped the union in bargaining with the management?

    ( ) Considerably; ( ) Somewhat;

    ( ) No.
24. Does out-side leadership enhance bargaining efficiency of the union?

    ( ) Considerably; ( ) Somewhat;

    ( ) No.
25. Are unions with outside leadership better managed?

    ( ) Yes; ( ) Somewhat;

    ( ) No.

Professional Orientations

1. On the whole, are you satisfied with your job?

   ( ) Yes;

   ( ) Somewhat;

   ( ) No.
2. Would you like to change the job if you get an opportunity?

   ( ) Yes; ( ) Can't say;

   ( ) No.

3. If you could go back to the age of 16 and live your life once again, would you still prefer the job you are in now?

   ( ) Yes;

   ( ) Don't know;

   ( ) No.

4. Would you suggest the job you are in to your son/brother/kin?

   ( ) Yes;

   ( ) Don't know;

   ( ) No.

5. If you had more free time, would you prefer to spend it on the job or with family?

   ( ) On Job;

   ( ) With family;

   ( ) Don't know.

6. Have you ever thought of quitting your present firm?

   ( ) Many times;

   ( ) Sometimes;

   ( ) Never.

7. Given an opportunity do you like your son/brother and kin to join your firm?

   ( ) Yes;

   ( ) Don't know;

   ( ) No.

Workers' Participative Management -Union Perspective

1. Do you think that workers should have a say in the management of the firm?

   ( ) Yes; ( ) To some extent;

   ( ) No.

   If yes, in what matters?

   1.

2.

3.

If no, give reasons.

1.

2.

3.

2. What according to you is the ideal form of participation?

( ) Direct participation;

( ) Through union;

( ) Through elected representatives;

( ) Other (Specify); ________

3. Do you think that the managements are in favour of PM?

( ) Very much;

( ) Somewhat;

( ) No.

4. Do you think that the workers have the requisite aptitude and skills for PM?

( ) Yes;

( ) Can't say;

( ) No.

5. Is there a need to train the workers for participation in management?

( ) Yes;

( ) Don't know;

( ) No.

6. At what level do you think the workers should participate in the management?

( ) Shop-floor;

( ) Department level;

( ) Division level;

( ) At the Board Room.

7. Which are the most efficient machineries of WPM? (Mention in the order of merit)
   1.
   2.
   3.
8. Which of the following areas do you prefer for PM?
   ( ) Working conditions;
   ( ) Wages, DA, bonus, etc.;
   ( ) Recruitment;
   ( ) Promotion;
   ( ) Productivity;
   ( ) Training and skill development;
   ( ) Grievance handling;
   ( ) Welfare of workers;
   ( ) Sales and accounting;
   ( ) Development planning;
   ( ) Regulation of technology;
   ( ) Other (Specify); ____________
9. What do you consider as an ideal degree of WPM?
   ( ) Only management should have a final say;
   ( ) Only inform the workers about the above matters;
   ( ) Workers' views may be obtained;
   ( ) Workers' consensus be taken;
   ( ) Workers' views have to be accepted.
10. Do you feel that Govt. intervention in PM is necessary?
    ( ) Yes, in advisory capacity;
    ( ) Yes, in regulatory/statutory capacity;
    ( ) Yes, in a mediating role;
    ( ) Other (Specify) ________;
    ( ) No.
    If no, give reasons.

1.

2.

3.

11. Do you believe that WPM could foster better industrial relations?

    ( ) Yes; ( ) To some extent;

    ( ) No.

12. Do you think that WPM would have positive implications for organizational climate?

    ( ) Yes; ( ) To some extent;

    ( ) No.

13. Do you think that PM can boost productivity?

    ( ) Yes; ( ) To some extent;

    ( ) No.

14. Do you feel that more areas of management should come under the purview of WPM?

    ( ) Yes;

    ( ) No;

    ( ) Present scope is good enough.

15. How would you describe the size of worker component in the machineries of WPM?

    ( ) Too large;

    ( ) Just the right;

    ( ) Too small.

Participative Management - Union Experience

1. How frequently the machineries of PM are employed/ used?

   ( ) Very frequently;

   ( ) Some what frequently;

   ( ) Seldom.

2. How do you describe the participation of management representatives in these machinereis?

( ) Active;

( ) Somewhat active;

( ) Inactive.

3. How do you describe the response of workers to the schemes of PM?

( ) Good;

( ) Somewhat good;

( ) Poor.

4. What are the issues that figure most in the PM?

( ) Working conditions;

( ) Wages, bonus, etc.;

( ) Welfare of workers;

( ) Productivity;

( ) Recruitment, retrenchment;

( ) Expansion of firm;

( ) Introduction of new technology;

( ) Grievance handling;

( ) Any other (Specify);

5. Do you feel that workers' participation did make any difference for the outcome?

( ) Yes, very much;

( ) Somewhat;

( ) Little.

6. Has participation of union leaders improved the outcome?

( ) Yes, ( ) No;

( ) Can't say.

7. Are the workers' representatives mature and informed well enough to contribute to a positive outcome?

( ) Yes; ( ) Somewhat;

( ) No.

8. Do union leaders have the right aptitude and skills to make a positive contribution to WPM?
   ( ) Yes; ( ) To some extent;
   ( ) No.
9. Do the workers' representatives suffer from inferiority complex and fear while participating in the machineries of WPM?
   ( ) Yes; ( ) To some extent;
   ( ) No.
10. In which area of management the WPM was more constructive and effective?
    ( ) Personnel and industrial relations;
    ( ) General administration;
    ( ) Production and quality control;
    ( ) Welfare;
    ( ) Rationalization and development.
11. Has WPM been a more effective machinery than Collective Bargaining in promoting industrial peace?
    ( ) More effective;
    ( ) About the same;
    ( ) Less effective.
12. How many of the decisions taken in the machineries of WPM were actually implemented?
    ( ) Quite a few (almost all);
    ( ) some of them;
    ( ) Very few of them.
13. What are the main problems faced in the functioning of the machineries of PM?
    ( ) Workers' apathy, workers' ignorance;
    ( ) Management apathy;
    ( ) Incompatibility of ideologies;
    ( ) Other (Specify);

    ____

14. Has management taken any steps to improve WPM?
( ) Yes; ( ) No; ( ) Don't know.
If yes, specify ___________
1.
2.
If no, give reasons.
1.
2.

15. At what level, the WPM has been more effective?
( ) Shop-floor level;
( ) Department level;
( ) Division level;
( ) Board level;
( ) Other (Specify); ___________

16. Are the workers basically inclined to participate and have a say in things that affect their working lives?
( ) Very much; ( ) Somewhat;
( ) Little.

17. Have unions been playing an important role in the machineries of WPM?
( ) Yes; ( ) No;
( ) Don't know.

18. Have unions been a facilitating factors or constraining factors in the process of PM?
( ) Facilitating factors;
( ) Constraining factors;
( ) Neither.

19. Has WPM in any way changed the way the firm is administered?
( ) Yes for better;
( ) Yes for worse;
( ) No.

20. Do the workers' representatives really represent the workers' needs and aspirations in WPM?
( ) Totally; ( ) To some extent;
( ) Seldom.
21. Do the workers' representatives misuse/take undue advantage of being in the machineries of WPM?
( ) Quite often; ( ) Sometimes;
( ) Never.

APPENDIX - III

SCHEDULE FOR WORKERS

Personal Background

1. Name: ____________________
2. Age: _______ years
3. Sex: ( ) Male; ( ) Female
4. Religion: ___________
5. Caste: (H); (M); (L)________
6. Sub-caste:___________
7. Educational level: _________
   (H); (M); (L)
8. Marital status: ___________
   (UM); (M); (D); (W); (S)
9. Number of children
   Male: _____ Female: ______
   Total: _____
10. Type of family: _________
    (J); (N); (S)
11. Size of family: __________
    (L); (M); (S)
12. Number of dependents:________
13. Number of earners in the family: __________________
14. Total family income: Rs.
    ___________p.m.
15. Place of birth: _________(R); (U)
16. Place of schooling: _____(R); (U)
17. Educational level of the family
    (H); (M); (L)
18. Family occupation: _________
19. Father's occupation: _________
20. Mother's occupation: _________

21. Father's education: ________
22. Mother's education: ________
23. Mother-tongue: ________

Professional Background

1. Type of industry: ________
   (M); (S); (WC)
2. Size of industry: ________
   (L); (M); (S)
3. Sector: ________
   (PB); (PR)
4. Present designation: ________
   Department: ________
   Division: ________
5. Type of work
   ( ) Skilled; ( ) Semi-skilled;
   ( ) Unskilled; ( ) Clerical;
   ( ) Supervisory.
6. Length of holding present designation ________ years
7. First designation held: ________
8. Total length of service ______ years
   (L); (M); (S)
9. Number of firms worked-in so far
   Similar:________Other:______ Total:______
   ( ) Not applicable
10. Vertical mobility experienced
    (H); (M); (L)
11. Salary/Wage: Rs.________ p.m./p.w.
12. Type of training received:
    ____

Professional Life

1. Membership of union
   ( ) Yes; ( ) No;
   ( ) No union.
   If yes,
   1. Name: ____________
   2. Date of establishment:
      ____
   3. Size: ____________
   4. (Maj); (Min): ____________
   5. Affiliation: ____________
   6. Political allegiance: ________
      (R); (M); (L)
   7. Recognition status: ________
2. Position held in the union
   ( ) Member;
   ( ) Executive member;
   ( ) Office bearer;
   ( ) Not applicable.
3. Length of union membership ____________ years
4. Participation in union affairs
   ( ) Active; ( ) Not so active;
   ( ) Not at all active.
5. Participation in union elections
   ( ) Active; ( ) Not so active;
   ( ) Not active; ( ) N.A.
6. Union responsiveness to workers' needs/opinion
   ( ) High; ( ) Moderate;
   ( ) Low.
7. Union leadership
   ( ) Responsive;

( ) Not all that responsive;

( ) Not at all responsive.

8. Union-management relations

   ( ) Cordial; ( ) Hostile;

   ( ) Neither.

9. Scope for professional growth in the firm

   ( ) High; ( ) Moderate;

   ( ) Low.

Professional Orientations

1. On the whole, are you satisfied with your job?

   ( ) Yes; ( ) Somewhat;

   ( ) No.

2. Would you like to change the job if you get an opportunity?

   ( ) Yes; ( ) Can't say; ( ) No.

3. If you could go back to the age of 16 and live your life once again, would you still prefer the job you are in now ?

   ( ) Yes; ( ) Don't know;

   ( ) No.

4. Would you suggest the job you are in to your son/brother/kin?

   ( ) Yes; ( ) Don't know;

   ( ) No.

5. If you had more free time, would you prefer to spend it on the job or with family?

   ( ) On job; ( ) With family;

   ( ) Don't know.

6. Given an opportunity do you like your son/brother and kin to join your firm?

   ( ) Yes; ( ) Don't know;

   ( ) No.

Participative Management (PM) -Workers' Perspective

1. Do you think that workers should have a say in the management of the firm?
   ( ) Yes; ( ) To some extent;
   ( ) No.
   If yes, in what matters?
   1.
   2.
   If no, give reasons.
   1.
   2.
2. What according to you is the ideal form of participation?
   ( ) Direct participation;
   ( ) Through union;
   ( ) Through elected representatives;
   ( ) Other (Specify); ____________
3. Do you think that the management is in favour of WPM?
   ( ) Very much; ( ) Somewhat;
   ( ) No.
4. Do you think that the workers have the requisite aptitude and skills for PM?
   ( ) Yes; ( ) Can't say; ( ) No.
5. As the things stand in your firm, do you feel that there is a need for WPM?
   ( ) Very much; ( ) Little/No.
   ( ) To some extent;
   If yes, at what level do you think the workers should participate in the management?
   ( ) Shop-floor;
   ( ) Department level;
   ( ) Division level;
   ( ) At the Board Room level.

6. Which are the most efficient machineries of WPM?
   1.
   2.
   3.
   4.
7. Which of the following areas do your prefer for workers' participation in management?
   ( ) Working conditions;
   ( ) Wages, DA, bonus, etc;
   ( ) Recruitment;
   ( ) Promotion;
   ( ) Productivity;
   ( ) Training and skill development;
   ( ) Grievance handling;
   ( ) Welfare of workers;
   ( ) Sales and accounting;
   ( ) Development planning;
   ( ) Regulation of technology;
   ( ) Other (Specify); ___________
8. What do you consider as an ideal degree of WPM?
   ( ) Only management should have a final say;
   ( ) Only inform the workers about the above matters;
   ( ) Workers views may be obtained;
   ( ) Workers consensus to be taken;
   ( ) Workers views have to be accepted.
9. Do you feel that Government intervention in PM is necessary?
   ( ) Yes, in advisory capacity;
   ( ) Yes, in regulatory/statutory capacity;
   ( ) Yes, in a mediating role;
   ( ) Other (Specify); ___________
   ( ) No.

If no, give reasons.

1.

2.

10. Do you believe that WPM could foster better industrial relations?

( ) Yes; ( ) To some extent;

( ) No.

11. Do you think that PM would have positive implications for organizational climate?

( ) Yes; ( ) To some extent;

( ) No.

12. Do you think that PM can boost productivity?

( ) Yes; ( ) To some extent;

( ) No.

13. Do you feel that more areas of management should come under the purview of WPM?

( ) Yes; ( ) No;

( ) Present scope is good enough.

14. Do you prefer Collective Bargaining and Productivity Bargaining to formal machineries of WPM?

( ) Yes; ( ) No;

( ) Can't say.

Workers' Participative Management -Workers' Experience

1. Are you aware of any machineries of WPM operating in your firm?

( ) Yes; ( ) No.

If yes, for how many years?

____________________ years.

2. How do you rate the participation of workers in these machineries?

( ) Active; ( ) Somewhat active;

( ) Inactive.

3. How do you rate the participation of management representatives in these machineries?

   ( ) Active; ( ) Somewhat active;

   ( ) Inactive.

4. How do you rate the managements' response to the schemes of WPM?

   ( ) Good; ( ) Somewhat good;

   ( ) Poor.

5. What are the issues that figure most in the PM in your unit?

   ( ) Working conditions;

   ( ) Wages, bonus, etc.;

   ( ) Welfare of workers;

   ( ) Productivity;

   ( ) Recruitment-retrenchment;

   ( ) Expansion of firm;

   ( ) Introduction of new technology;

   ( ) Grievance handling;

   ( ) Any other (Specify);

   ____

6. Has participation of workers' representatives improved the outcome?

   ( ) Yes; ( ) No; ( ) Can't say.

7. Are the workers' representatives mature and informed well enough to contribute to a positive outcome?

   ( ) Yes;

   ( ) Somewhat;

   ( ) No.

8. Do the workers' representatives raise relevant issues in the machineries of WPM?

   ( ) Yes;

   ( ) No;

   ( ) Don't know.

9. Do the workers' representatives suffer from inferiority complex and fear while participating in the machineries of WPM?

   ( ) Yes;

   ( ) To some Extent;

   ( ) No.

10. In which area of management the WPM was more constructive and effective?

    ( ) Personnel and industrial relations;

    ( ) General administration;

    ( ) Production and quality control;

    ( ) Welfare;

    ( ) Research and development.

11. Has WPM been a more effective machinery than Collective Bargaining in promoting industrial peace?

    ( ) More effective;

    ( ) About the same;

    ( ) Less effective.

12. Which one of the machineries is more effective in facilitating WPM? (In order of effectiveness)

    1.

    2.

    3.

    4.

13. How many of the decisions taken in the machinereis of WPM were actually implemented?

    ( ) Quite a few (almost all);

    ( ) Some of them; ( ) Very few of them

14. What are the main problems faced in the functioning of the machineries of WPM?

    ( ) Workers' apathy, workers' ignorance;

    ( ) Management apathy;

( ) Incompatibility of ideologies;
( ) Other (Specify); __________

15. At what level, the WPM has been more effective?
( ) Shop floor level;
( ) Department level;
( ) Division level;
( ) Board level;
( ) Other (Specify); ________

16. Are the workers basically inclined to participate and have a say in things that affect their working lives?
( ) Very much; ( ) Somewhat;
( ) Little.

17. Have unions been playing an important role in the machineries of WPM?
( ) Yes; ( ) No;
( ) Don't know.

18. Have unions been a facilitating factors or constraining factors in the process of PM?
( ) Facilitating factors;
( ) Constraining factors;
( ) Neither.

19. Has WPM in any way changed the way your firm is administered?
( ) Yes, for better;
( ) Yes, for worse;
( ) No.

20. Do the workers' representatives really represent the workers' needs and aspirations in WPM?
( ) Totally;
( ) To some extent;
( ) Seldom.

21. Do the workers' representatives misuse/take undue advantage of being in the machineries of PM?

    ( ) Quite often;

    ( ) Sometimes;

    ( ) Never

APPENDIX - IV

INFORMATION SCHEDULE

1. Type of organization
   ( ) Manufacturing;
   ( ) Service;
   ( ) White collar.
2. Sector
   ( ) Public;
   ( ) Private;
   ( ) Joint.
3. Size of organization
   ( ) Less than 500 (Small);
   ( ) 500-2000 (Medium);
   ( ) More than 2000 (Large).
4. Date of establishment
   ( ) Before 1960;
   ( ) Between 1960 to 1980;
   ( ) After 1980.
5. Skill composition
   ( ) Unskilled: __________%;
   ( ) Semi-skilled: _________ %;
   ( ) Skilled: __________ %.
6. Workforce composition
   Operatives: _____________
   Supervisory: ____________
   Clerical: ________________
   Managerial: ____________.
   Total investment Rs.__________
7. Type of technology employed
   ( ) Indigenous; ( ) Improved;
   ( ) Imported (State-of-art).

8. Installed capacity

   ______________ Units per day

   ______________ Not applicable

9. Capacity utilization: _________ %

   ( ) Less than 75%;

   ( ) 75% to 90%;

   ( ) More than 90%.

10. Operating status

    ( ) Earning profit (H.M.L.);

    ( ) Making it even;

    ( ) Incurring loss (H.M.L.).

11. Number of unions operating: ____

    Size: _______________

    Affili: _______________

    Maj/Min: _______________

    Rec/Non-R: _______________

    Remark: _______________

12. Percentage of union membership among the workforce

    ________%

    ( ) Less than 50% (Low);

    ( ) 50% to 75% (Moderate);

    ( ) More than 75% (High).

13. Organizational structure

    Number of divisions: ______

    Number of departments: ______

14. Degree of centralization

    ( ) High;

    ( ) Moderate;

    ( ) Low.

15. Degree of formalization

    ( ) High;

    ( ) Moderate; ( ) Low.

16. Degree of bureaucratization
    ( ) High;
    ( ) Moderate;
    ( ) Low.
17. Degree of specialization
    ( ) High;
    ( ) Moderate;
    ( ) Low.
18. Degree of delegation of authority
    ( ) High;
    ( ) Moderate;
    ( ) Low.
19. Communication process
    ( ) Formal;
    ( ) Informal;
    ( ) Mixed.

Climate of Industrial Relations

1. Number of strikes/lockouts during the last five years
   Duration of strike: ______
   Lockout: ______
   Mandays lost during strike: ______
   Lockout: ______
2. Number of disputes during the last five years: ______
3. Number of unresolved disputes as of now: ______
4. Union-management relations
   ( ) Cordial; ( ) Normal;
   ( ) Hostile.
5. Most frequently resorted method of resolving industrial disputes
   ( ) Collective Bargaining;
   ( ) Conciliation;

( ) Arbitration;
( ) Adjudication.

6. Most effective method of resolving industrial disputes
( ) Collective Bargaining;
( ) Conciliation;
( ) Arbitration;
( ) Adjudication.

7. Type of strike
( ) Peaceful;
( ) Hostile;
( ) Not applicable.

8. Maximum duration of strike: ____
( ) Less than 15 days (Short);
( ) 15 days to a month (Moderate);
( ) More than a month (Long).

9. Main cause of strike
( ) Wages and bonus;
( ) Working conditions;
( ) Recognition of union;
( ) Institutional.

10. Number of retrenchments during the last five years: ______
Main reason for retrenchment: _____
Case of violence during the last five years
On workers: __________
On management: _________

Organizational Climate

1. Overall job satisfaction
( ) High;
( ) Moderate;
( ) Low.

2. Overall commitment
   ( ) High;
   ( ) Moderate;
   ( ) Low.
3. Overall morale
   ( ) High;
   ( ) Moderate;
   ( ) Low.
4. The responsiveness of superiors
   ( ) High;
   ( ) Moderate;
   ( ) Low.

Organizational Function

1. Recruitment
   ( ) Rational;
   ( ) Not so rational.
2. Promotion
   ( ) Rational;
   ( ) Not so rational.
3. Training
   ( ) Effective;
   ( ) Not so effective.
4. Sales
   ( ) Exceeding targets;
   ( ) Just reaching targets;
   ( ) Short of targets.
5. Research and development
   ( ) Efficient;
   ( ) Not so efficient;
   ( ) Not existing.
6. Source of recruitment

( ) Employment exchange;
( ) Contractors;
( ) Advertisement;
( ) Campus recruitment.

7. Bases for promotion
   ( ) Seniority;
   ( ) Merit;
   ( ) Seniority-cum-merit;
   ( ) None.

Workers' Participative Management (PM)

1. Nature of workers' participation in management
   ( ) Through formal machineries;
   ( ) Informal (Informal consultation at various levels);
   ( ) Both.
2. Machineries of WPM in operation
   ( ) Joint Management Councils;
   ( ) Shop-floor Councils;
   ( ) Works Councils;
   ( ) Production Committee;
   ( ) Safety Committee;
   ( ) Any other (Specify);
   ____
3. Composition of JMCs
   ( ) Management: ________
   ( ) Union: ________
   ( ) Supervisors: ________
   ( ) Workers: ________
   ( ) Total: ________
4. Frequency of JMC meetings once in ________ months.
5. Date of establishment:
   ____

6. Management areas dealt with by the JMCs
   ( ) Recruitment;
   ( ) Production;
   ( ) Training;
   ( ) Working conditions;
   ( ) Rewards;
   ( ) Promotions;
   ( ) Discipline;
   ( ) Welfare;
   ( ) Sales;
   ( ) Finance matters;
   ( ) Other (Specify); ___________
7. Extent of participation by workers' representatives
   ( ) High;
   ( ) Moderate;
   ( ) Low.
8. Nature of workers' participation in JMCs
   ( ) Active;
   ( ) Somewhat active;
   ( ) Not active.
9. Workers' say in JMCs
   ( ) Much;
   ( ) Somewhat;
   ( ) Less.

Shop-Floor Councils

1. Composition
   Workers No: ______
   Supervisors No: ________
   Management representatives No: ___________
   Total: __________
2. Frequency of meeting once in __________
   As and when required

3. Major concerns
   ( ) Working conditions;
   ( ) Rewards; ( ) Discipline;
   ( ) Production; ( ) Grievances.
4. Effectiveness
   ( ) High;
   ( ) Moderate;
   ( ) Low.
5. Participation of workers' representatives
   ( ) Active;
   ( ) Somewhat active;
   ( ) Not active.

Other machinereis of WPM operating in the firm, their composition and functioning:

Sl. No.	*Machinery*	*Composition*	*Frequency of meeting (H.M.L)*	*Areas of participation*	*Extent of participation*	*Functioning since*
1.						
2.						
3.						
4.						
5.						

NOTES:

Index

❑❑❑